Rituals of Mediation

Rituals of Mediation

International Politics and Social Meaning

François Debrix and Cynthia Weber, Editors

University of Minnesota Press

Minneapolis

London

Copyright 2003 by the Regents of the University of Minnesota

All rights reserved. No part of this publication may be reproduced, stored in
a retrieval system, or transmitted, in any form or by any means, electronic,
mechanical, photocopying, recording, or otherwise, without the prior written
permission of the publisher.

Published by the University of Minnesota Press
111 Third Avenue South, Suite 290
Minneapolis, MN 55401-2520
http://www.upress.umn.edu

Library of Congress Cataloging-in-Publication Data

Rituals of mediation : international politics and social meaning /
François Debrix and Cynthia Weber, Editors.
    p.   cm.
  Includes bibliographical references and index.
    ISBN 0-8166-4074-2 (HC : alk. paper) — ISBN 0-8166-4075-0 (PB : alk.
paper)
    1. Intercultural communication.   2. International relations and
culture. 3. Cultural relations. I. Debrix, François. II. Weber,
Cynthia.
  HM1211 .R57 2003
  303.48'2—dc21   2003001868

Printed in the United States of America on acid-free paper

The University of Minnesota is an equal-opportunity educator and employer.

12 11 10 09 08 07 06 05 04 03   10 9 8 7 6 5 4 3 2 1

Contents

Preface   vii
François Debrix and Cynthia Weber

Acknowledgments   xix

Introduction: Rituals of Mediation   xxi
François Debrix

PART I
Sites of Mediation

ONE
Site Specific: Medi(t)ations at the Airport   3
Debbie Lisle

TWO
Spatializing International Activism:
Genetically Modified Foods on the Internet   30
Jayne Rodgers

THREE
Postcards from Aztlán   49
Patricia L. Price

PART II
Sights of Mediation

FOUR
Salgado and the Sahel:
Documentary Photography and the Imaging of Famine   69
David Campbell

FIVE
Sensationally Mediated Moralities: Innocence, Purity, and Danger   97
Moya Lloyd and Marysia Zalewski

SIX
Site Improvements:
Discovering Direct-Mail Retail as "B2C" Industrial Democracy   115
Timothy W. Luke

PART III
Mediation, Cultural Governance, and the Political

SEVEN
Culture, Governance, and Global Biopolitics   135
Michael Dillon

EIGHT
Spinning the World: Spin Doctors, Mediation, and Foreign Policy   154
Robin Brown

Epilogue: Romantic Mediations of September 11   173
Cynthia Weber

Contributors   189

Index   191

Preface

François Debrix and Cynthia Weber

The joint configuration of two amorphous concepts, the cultural and the international, in popular habits, social practices, and politics increasingly demands theoretical and practical attention. Cultural analysts have long known that making sense of everyday culture requires an appreciation not only for high politics but also for everyday "internationals." And international studies theorists and practitioners more and more often recognize how banal, mechanical, and partial their visions of what counts as international appear without an appreciation for everyday cultural sites and sights.

Making sense of cultural internationals or international culturals requires a close examination of the rich and varied relationship between these two pluralized and pluralizing terms. To capture this relationship and maintain its pluralizing quality, it is useful to introduce another term: mediation. Although both cultural studies and international relations offer numerous definitions of mediation, our use of the term comes from neither discipline. We use mediation to refer to a site of representation, transformation, and pluralization where cultural and international rituals are performed. These rituals, in turn, perform what are taken to be culturals and internationals. Understood as a series of rituals that produce culturals and internationals, mediation allows us to engage cultural and international practices—transnational cultural interactions—without requiring us to adopt uniform definitions or methodological approaches.

This volume gathers together the work of scholars from many different disciplinary locations and interdisciplinary locutions—political theory, women's studies, communication studies, cultural geography, international relations, and cultural studies. Whether analyzing traditional or nontraditional topics, each essay adopts a cross-disciplinary perspective that foregrounds the role of mediation in international/cultural relations in order to engage two specific research questions: (1) How might we make theoretical and practical sense of transnational cultural interactions? (2) How might we make theoretical and practical sense of the ways sites and sights of mediation—as well as the discourses that construct them—represent, transform, and remediate internationals?

The volume begins with an introduction by François Debrix that serves as a conceptual and critical prologue for the book. Debrix clarifies the meaning of the term *mediation* as it is used in the volume. Mediation, he suggests, is a method that makes social meanings possible. As an instrument of meaning, mediation can take place across various social contexts and cultural practices. Debrix offers three possible social uses of mediation, which he renames "rituals of mediation." The method of mediation can take place as a ritual of representation, a ritual of transformation, or a ritual of pluralization. By and large, the transnational cultural relations explored in this volume are represented, transformed, or pluralized by these different rituals. All three ritualistic modalities of mediation are concerned with the production of social meaning. But all three rituals operate on the basis of different theoretical and philosophical beliefs and, consequently, the meanings they produce are at variance.

Rituals of representation assume that the operation of mediation is neutral and value-free. The proponents of such a usage argue that mediation's sole objective is to transfer or confer meaning by relating two domains of experience, which, at the same time, must be kept separate. To fulfill this operation of passage of meaning, mediation is presented as a site that transmits but never alters. According to this method of mediation, mediators are neutral agents of representation. By contrast, rituals of transformation affirm that the method of mediation takes an important part in altering social meaning. Mediation is not a neutral operation that transfers and leaves unchanged the two subject and object positions. Rather, mediation is a rite that enables social change. In rituals of transformation, the human subject becomes a creative mediator who uses mediation to make the world to his or her own image. Even when critics of this affirmation of the modern subject voice their discomfort about such a practice, they do not relinquish this ritual of mediation altogether. Instead, they claim that better social conditions, different cultural realities, or new political subjectivities can be discovered through a better use of mediation as a ritual of transformation. Many critical enterprises today, including some found in this volume, remain closely associated with this use of mediation.

Finally, Debrix suggests that a third ritual of mediation can be put to use too. Better adapted to postmodern times and often mobilized in the following chapters, this third ritual still intends to produce social meanings. But the meanings it produces are achieved by refusing to adopt the previous two rituals and challenging them both. Unlike representation and transformation, rituals of pluralization consist of deploying novel uses, or pointing to existing uses, of mediated forms and objects that leave open as many social, cultural, and political possibilities as possible. Far from closing signification, this kind of mediation encourages further debate and discussion. Debrix turns to the work of Polish artist Krzysztof Wodiczko, which reveals the pluralizing potential of mediation. At the same time, Wodiczko's artwork is an engagement with mediation that critically illustrates why other rituals of a representational or transformative kind negate plural cultural practices. This last critique is an important point that the subsequent chapters recognize as well by showing that contemporary transnational cultural interactions often fall prey to all sorts of closures of meaning.

After this introduction, the volume is divided into three main sections. Part I, "Sites of Mediation," is composed of three chapters that both locate and dislocate practices of mediation in the international context. Far from taking for granted a vision of the international that would be anchored to the political relations between sovereign states (and their practices), the chapters in this section displace the international by transposing it to cultural sites that are at once common (to many cultural practices across the globe) and uncanny (to traditional international relations literatures and beliefs). Among such sites are the airport (Lisle), the Internet (Rodgers), and imaginary borders (Price).

Debbie Lisle introduces the notion of "mediated power." Contesting the idea that power is a known quantity, something to be possessed and utilized, mediated power is instead fluid and exchanged. Practices and effects of mediated power are meant to be circulated, transformed, and rearticulated. Lisle reveals how the airport is a space where new effects and practices of mediated power take place. Mediated power, she suggests, allows us to view and experience the airport as a postmodern site of flux and movement rather than as a modern domain of control, security, and sovereignty. At the same time, though, approaching the airport from the perspective of its mediated practices of power challenges postmodern approaches that emphasize the empty yet excessive architectural formalism of this space. Even within supermodern spaces marked by an overload of signification (such as the airport), power is exchanged and hegemonic formations sometimes coalesce. Thus, this ambiguous mediation of the airport (at once modern and postmodern, regulated and free-flowing, securitizing and destabilizing) is a different modality of power. In the mediation of the airport, power is evidenced in the way it adapts to the changes from the modern to the postmodern, the regulated to the fluid, and vice versa. This constant transformation of power, its inherent duplicity, makes the airport a revealing site of mediation. As Lisle indicates, it is a site where we can witness the passage from sovereign power to mediated power.

Jayne Rodgers studies yet another site of mediation where classical representations of (modern) culture and politics are destabilized. In her chapter, the space of mediation is occupied by the Internet. In her view, the Internet has transformative potentials to the extent that it internationalizes our ways of thinking, acting, and experiencing social and political realities. Communications on the Internet modify traditional conceptual maps of the nation and culture. Henri Lefebvre's problematization of modern spaces is introduced by Rodgers to give Internet communications a more appropriate mapping. In these new communicative spaces, transnational and transcultural dynamics are propagated to challenge previous modes of cultural identification and political representation. Rodgers identifies one specific instance of mediating transformation of culture and politics by means of the Internet. She argues that the distribution of foods containing genetically modified organisms (GMOs) into the global market was mostly opposed and resisted through a new activist discourse that found its (transnational, transcultural) support on the Internet. Although the Internet also facilitated the diffusion of GMO issues and products, in return, anti-GMO activist discourses marked the significance of Internet technologies to achieve (global) political transformations (here, in the economy and culture of food production/consumption). The Internet, she concludes, is thus a powerful transformative site of mediation that is capable, both conceptually and practically, of transcending most dichotomies on which politics and culture have traditionally relied.

In chapter 3, Patricia Price pushes the dislocation of traditional visions of the international further by adopting a poststructural and performative approach to the analysis of the border as a site of mediation. Intent on offering a pluralized view of the border as mediation, Price takes us to imaginary territories and landscapes. Her chapter introduces the mythical notion of Aztlán, an imagined homeland with no traditionally recognizable geographical marking that is often used as a symbol of Chicano nationalism in the U.S. Southwest. Not visible on any maps, Aztlán is a space that is not one. Yet, it is a territory that evokes strong emotional and nationalist ties. Aztlán is a space of national affirmation that physically does not exist because it has no borders. Instead, its borderlessness counters the so-called image of the impenetrable U.S.–Mexico political border. For many, Aztlán *is* the border, that which delineates a territory more meaningful than Mexico or the United States as nation-states. Unlike the apparent rigidity of the wall that separates Mexico and the United States, Aztlán is a bordering mediation that is spaceless and shapeless. In Aztlán, the mediation of the border is displaced to other signs, symbols, and icons. One such sign is the image of the Virgin of Guadalupe, omnipresent in the Chicano cultural imaginary. Another is the quite material presence of the border between the United States and Mexico, which is often defaced and refaced, and sometimes becomes the object of murals or cultural shrines by people on both sides. Even this physical demarcation—the very mark of the international in the U.S. Southwest—is not necessarily perceived as a two-dimensional space (North/South, in/out, us/them). Instead, Price intimates, this border is often recaptured to then be resituated in the cultural imaginary of Aztlán. The border—a line meant to mediate between two different nation-states (both to connect and to keep separate)—is multidimensional too. As it divides, it also enables imaginary cultural constructs and identifications. The border is not just a line of separation. It is also a full site of mediation (as opposed to the empty space of representational mediation perhaps) replete with multiple characters and visions (circulating virgins, border stalkers, immigrants, security forces). Price chooses to call these (re)figurations of the borderland imaginary "postcards." Her postcards from the border and Aztlán are haunting disseminations of an international that has been pluralized.

The three sites explored in Part I (the airport, the Internet, the border) do not just displace what we traditionally take to be the international. In many ways, they also re-create the international as a succession of different transnational cultural interactions made possible by, or instead achieved through, a rejection of specific techniques and rituals of mediation (for example, transiting through airports, mobilizing political activism in digital space, or crossing borders).

Part II, "Sights of Mediation," consists of three chapters that, at first glance, appear to introduce the international through the filtering lens of mediated techniques of representation (photography, art exhibits, and retail catalogs). But these chapters do not simply try to figure out how international relations are represented or even transformed by art forms, visual media, or consumer objects. Rather, they turn the space of international relations on its head by revealing that there are as many internationals as there are cultural (often visual) re-mediations of contemporary transnational interactions.

In chapter 4, David Campbell is interested in the mediation of photographic displays. Turning to Sebastião Salgado's documentary photography, Campbell argues that photography is a potentially powerful representation of multiple realities of international politics. Detailing Salgado's evocative pictures of the inhabitants of the African Sahel (and the "uncertain grace" they exude), Campbell's chapter is a reflection on the way lives in the modern world are bound and shaped, constrained and constituted, by a complex of manifold social forces. Salgado's photography of the Sahel and its people is a peculiar vision. This sight that mediates (for the viewer and the photographer in particular) a certain vision of the "other" is not simply to be understood as an aesthetic allegory. While this mediating sight provides us with a conceptual instrument for grasping our "being-in-the-world," it also puts us into contact with other realities. One of these other realities of the international domain is the image of disasters and the photographic registration of famine victims. Salgado's photographic mediations capture such images but, more important, force us to reconsider whether such an aestheticization of the dramas of international life is at all avoidable. Here, Salgado's photographic style, his approach to the subject (to the "other"), is crucial. Salgado does not use his aesthetic medium to produce yet another representation of the colonial or inferior "other" through which the power and dominant ideology of the Westerner are reinforced (what

Campbell calls "colonial economies of representation"). Rather, Salgado's aesthetic approach to photography restores to the "other" dignity, identity, and power. It is an ethical engagement with mediation that grants the photographic subjects a part (and a place) in the political negotiations and debates of the international.

Moya Lloyd and Marysia Zalewski's sight of mediation is a traveling art exhibit. Their chapter offers a critical gender reading of the *Sensation* exhibit, an art show that raised eyebrows and disturbed sensibilities with its array of shocking images. Intended to showcase the works of "young British artists," this traveling exhibit was first seen in London and then moved across the Atlantic to New York. The *Sensation* show gives Lloyd and Zalewski the opportunity to interrogate some of the ways in which the international is articulated, displayed, and transported through culturally and politically mediated interpretations. Lloyd and Zalewski concentrate their analysis on two works that were found particularly shocking. One is Chris Ofili's painting of the Virgin Mary covered with elephant dung along with photos of genitalia. This painting caused the most outrage when the exhibit came to New York's Brooklyn Art Museum. New York City Mayor Rudolph Giuliani attacked the show and threatened to withdraw funding to the museum. The other artwork Lloyd and Zalewski focus on is Marcus Harvey's painting of Myra Hindley—a child killer forever associated in British culture with the "Moors Murders"—which was the object of much controversy when it was first displayed in London because Hindley's portrait is composed of thousands of child-sized handprints. Lloyd and Zalewski ask why these artistic sights, in different cross-cultural contexts, caused so much outrage. What social and cultural responses do these displays mediate? Their answer suggests that the response of shock, repulsion, and outrage that these two paintings received is indicative of the way cultural constructs in the international "normalize" the role and place of woman. What was found to be particularly disturbing by audiences about both artworks is that certain (gendered) meanings of woman were being used, circulated, and played with in these paintings. In a sense, both Ofili's and Harvey's works problematized the meaning of woman in cross-cultural contexts, and this is precisely what was found to be unacceptable. The fact that, as Lloyd and Zalewski mention, Mary and Myra could be one and the same figure and person (they both are "woman"), and not only because their names are anagrams, further explained the discomfort provoked by these mediated sights. Lloyd and Zalewski conclude that the sign of the inter-national—similar to the sign of "woman" that the international often helps to normalize—is often secured through what they term "the vio-lence of abjection." The violence of abjection makes use of certain medi-ated sights (such as the *Sensation* exhibit) in order to foreclose cultural meanings, political possibilities, and gender representations.

Chapter 6, "Site Improvements: Discovering Direct-Mail Retail as 'B2C' Industrial Democracy" by Timothy Luke, offers a different view of the relationship between mediation and abjection. According to Luke, it is not only the case that certain sights of mediation are being contained and abjected but, in contrast, that mediated sights can be the instru-ment of containment and abjection. Direct-mail retail catalogs, from *Pottery Barn* to *Levenger, L. L. Bean's* to *The Sharper Image,* re-mediate the relationship between the body (and its quest for perfection) and consumer goods. Through retail catalogs, an entire panoply of the self in search of perfectibility is reinvented. But this individualized perfectibil-ity can only be achieved through possession of the attributes and lifestyles championed by these consumer propaganda literatures. Additionally, the places where those lifestyles are to take place must be perfected as well. In short, it is only through the object that the subject can fulfill his or her desires and needs. The mediation of the object and the ideology of perfectibility that this mediation advances reconfigure the notion of social control and bring it down to the level of the micromanagement of what Luke calls "people's everyday life-worlds." In this re-mediated social environment where the mediation of objects (their appearance in a certain place) redefines what counts as meaningful, democracy, both domestically and globally, is redefined by the motto that "better things will bring better living" and ethical development transnationally becomes synonymous with "getting the goods."

Through the re-mediations of contemporary transnational interac-tions examined in this section, traditional practices and processes of international relations thinking such as the relationship between self and other (Campbell), the construction of national/international cultures through discourses of gender, normalization, and abjection (Lloyd and Zalewski), and the globalization of capital, democracy, and ethics through direct mail retail and consumer objects (Luke) are problematized. By problematizing established international relations practices, these sights of mediation pluralize the international and encourage the production of multiple transnational cultural meanings.

Part III, "Mediation, Cultural Governance, and the Political," brings mediation and the international back into the domain of the overtly political. The essays in this section remind us that the production of social meaning, transnationally and culturally, is always a political question. At stake in rituals of mediation is the location of a certain vision of the international as a model of production of social meaning. Producing and maintaining social meaning determines cultural practices. As Michael Dillon's essay indicates, constructing an international and a domestic as sites of production of social meaning and cultural practices is a (bio)political operation as well. Contrary to traditional beliefs and uses in international relations, this production of meaning through cultural practices is biopolitical rather than geopolitical precisely because its goal is to achieve control over life. As an ideological and political enterprise that seeks to control life by determining what counts as meaningful normal social behavior and cultural value, global governance of necessity taps into the cultural domain transnationally to better regulate it. Through the propagation of selected social and cultural meanings that mostly replay modernization and Westernization themes and often wish to anonymously spread through the use of commonsensical but vague notions such as globalization or the global, specific regimes of cultural governance as biopower are established where plural cultural possibilities once stood. To once again stand, these plural cultural possibilities need to resist the representational rituals of mediation that circulate these cultural modernization/globalization schemes. Today, the ideological locales that perform such rituals of mediation (as representation) of meaning are international institutions such as the World Trade Organization, the International Monetary Fund, and many others. Resistance, then, must be directed against these sites of mediation, which pass for neutral and yet maintain the regimes of biopower and cultural governance.

Yet, such a resistance to controlled mediations of (bio)power and cultural governance is difficult to deploy. As Robin Brown's essay shows, spaces and sites of mediation in the international are rarely left open and willing to accommodate plural meanings. Not only do such sites of international mediation enable regimes of biopower, but they are also sometimes put to the service of more traditional geopolitical interests. Brown's study of "media spin-doctoring" reveals that traditional foreign-policy making is unwilling to abandon the denomination of the international to some of the plural transnational cultural interactions and domains of political activity described in the previous chapters. In fact, the very task of spin-doctoring on the part of governmental leaders and policy makers (and their press secretaries) suggests that the struggle over mediation (who uses it to do what?) is far from being lost by conventional geopoliticians. In a sense, spin-doctoring is a postmodern technique of mediation reappropriated by modern policy makers and traditionalist guardians of the international. By using spin-doctoring as a method of mediation, these more conventional mediators hope to produce a "cultural spin" that will restore international relations to its classical regime of political representation and power.

In the Epilogue, Cynthia Weber provides a sense of closure to the volume (by returning to the concept of mediation) and at the same time opens it up to further discussion and debate. Weber tells a final story (at least for this volume) about mediation and the international by taking us back to the idea of "romantic mediation" first used by Debrix in the Introduction. Trying to make sense of the post-September 11 cultural and political mediations of the international, Weber analyzes how, in the immediate aftermath of the terrorist "attacks on America," the United States' new "war against terror" was the subject of cinematic, material, and rhetorical romantic mediations through idealized remembrances of Pearl Harbor. Pearl Harbor's romantic gesture is to provide the United States with a sense of historic destiny, moral duty, and heroic agency that transposes its "war against terror" into a triumphalist narrative about its inevitable and justifiable victory in war. Taking up Debrix's observation that romantic mediations not only transform subjects and their worlds for the better but also produce alienation and subjection, Weber travels from "acceptable" American romantic mediations of September 11 at Pearl Harbor to "unacceptable" American counterromantic mediations of September 11 at Palm Harbor. Palm Harbor was the home of fifteen-year-old Charles Bishop, the boy who flew a light aircraft into the forty-two-story Bank of America building in downtown Tampa in January 2002 and left a suicide note expressing his sympathy for Osama bin Laden and the September 11 hijackers. In identifying with and imitating the act of the

September 11 hijackers in New York City, Bishop's Palm Harbor mediations of September 11 create a rupture in the Pearl Harbor narrative. They replace heroism with antiheroism, moral certainty with moral ambiguity, progressive time with repetitive time, and a belief in the ability to secure the homeland and the self with troubling questions about how the circulation of youth violence in the United States—such as Bishop's and that of school shooters—renders the homeland and the country's idea of itself insecure. The Epilogue suggests that, in the aftermath of September 11, rituals of mediation (what counts as social meaning and how is social meaning achieved?) are more than ever sites and sights of political appropriation and contestation where new domestic and international cultural domains (the homeland versus transnational terror) are being produced.

Acknowledgments

Rituals of Mediation is the inaugural project of the Centre for International Studies at the University of Leeds. The Centre hosted a spring 2000 seminar series on the topic funded by the Institute for Politics and International Studies (POLIS) at the University of Leeds. Papers from the original seminar series plus additional papers were presented at the cultural studies conference organized by Stefan Herbrechter at Trinity-All Saints College in Leeds in April 2000. Several chapters in this volume were also presented at the spring 2001 Research Symposium of the Department of International Relations at Florida International University and at the International Studies Association Annual Meeting in Chicago in March 2001. We would like to thank the centers and institutions that sponsored and hosted these events.

The project as a whole benefited greatly from the comments and suggestions provided by all of its contributors and a number of additional scholars, including Clair Apodaca, Charlie Dannreuther, James Der Derian, Hugh Dyer, Jenny Edkins, Stefan Herbrechter, Nick Onuf, and Jason Ralph. Three anonymous reviewers for the University of Minnesota Press also offered very useful advice that strengthened the manuscript. We also wish to thank Audrey Church for the editorial work she provided. As usual, our gratitude goes to our editor, Carrie Mullen, whose dedication and support made this volume possible.

INTRODUCTION

Rituals of Mediation

François Debrix

The Method(s) of Mediation

Outside of a specified social context, the term *mediation* can mean a lot of things. Traditionally found in theological scriptures, philosophical essays, and diplomatic treatises, mediation is now frequently employed in biology, geometry, photography, film theory, medicine, and spiritualism. Despite the wide application of the term, mediation generally denotes a few core ideas and concepts. Most commonly, mediation refers to the ability to occupy a *middle point* between two distant or opposite poles. To mediate is basically to provide a point of contact, an intersection, a place of communication or dialogue between two different positions.[1]

In international relations, mediation has generally been taken to signify a set of operations that involve the intervention of a neutral party in between two opposing or conflicting actors. The operation of mediation is traditionally intended to bring or maintain peace between antagonistic political units (mostly states).[2] Sometimes, in the course of the mediation, the neutral party may create and offer his or her own solutions in order to facilitate communication between both opponents.[3] Most of the time, however, the neutral agent simply "transmits and interprets the proposals of the principal parties."[4] To do so, the mediator must have been found "acceptable to both parties."[5] The understanding of mediation found in classical international diplomatic and legal literatures is not universal or even unique. Yet, it is often a privileged interpretation. Mobilizing the term *mediation* in an international relations context generally implies that issues such as peace settlement, conflict negotiation, peacekeeping, or diplomatic protocol are being addressed. Put differently, the discipline of international relations has found a way of objectifying the term *mediation* so that one kind of meaning is prioritized and, consequently, one type of social activity (generally, peaceful, neutral interposition) is enabled. What international relations scholars fail to recognize is that there is nothing objective about the meaning that they ascribe to mediation and that, instead, the meaning of the term is the result of a social context within which the term is given significance.

For the purposes of this volume, it could be tempting to simply apply the traditional meaning of mediation enshrined in international relations literatures because, after all, this text is also about international affairs. But this meaning of mediation is not sufficient for, or even accurate to, the type of international relations explored in this volume. Mediation in international relations is generally granted signification because it refers to specific procedures that find their place in a social context defined as a series of interactions between subjects across territorially recognized units of meaning (nation-states, political blocs and alliances, structures and levels, hegemons and dyads, etc.). By contrast, to the extent that international relations is represented in this volume, it is as a broad domain of transnational cultural interactions where classical units of meaning on which the discipline of international relations was built are being challenged. It is also far from obvious that the transnational cultural interactions this volume examines form one clearly identifiable social context from which one single meaning of mediation can be derived. Instead of a common social context shared by all contributors to this volume, many social practices are highlighted that give us multiple visions of what international relations might mean today. The social and cultural practices explored in this volume do not allow one to reconstitute a field of international relations but, rather, give us insights into the many internationals that emerge as the result of various transnational cultural interactions.

As I suggested, speaking of mediation without a prior social context can be an arduous task. At the same time, though, assuming one social context of mediation that may be commanding enough to encompass the transnational cultural interactions examined in this volume would not be helpful either. To bypass this difficulty, I want to suggest that mediation may be analyzed not in a specific context (which might not be generalizable to others), or in all sorts of social contexts, for that matter (which would make for a superficial analysis), but rather as a method. As the following essays make clear, mediation is a method that makes possible social meanings, many social meanings. As an instrument of meaning, a tool of signification, mediation can be seen to take place across social practices and in different social contexts. Differences of interpretation as to the way mediation is supposed to operate can be found in different social contexts. But all social contexts have recourse to a form of mediation as a methodology through which meaning is given to specific social practices. As an instrument of meaning, mediation's task is typically to achieve desirable relations between subject and object positions (as postulated by the social system within which the method of mediation operates). Mediation can establish desirable relations by connecting or distancing. As a connecting or distancing technique of meaning, mediation also contributes to the arrangement of beliefs, norms, institutions, and identities in any given society. Mediation maintains the social meanings and relations that are established between subjects and objects in different social contexts.

Treating mediation as a methodology is not novel. Scholars who have emphasized the impact of ritualistic actions and events in the formation of social and cultural systems have indirectly provided us with an understanding of mediation as a method of social signification. Sociologists and anthropologists of *ritual practices* have noted that rites of mediation performed by mediating agents (humans, animals, natural elements, meteorological phenomena, manufactured objects, institutions) contribute to the production and reproduction of meaning in society.[6] These mediating agents and their rites guarantee the passage from the old to the new, the past to the future, the primitive to the enlightened, the submissive to the dominant. Rites of passage guarantee that social hierarchies are preserved or that new ones are created.[7] Social mediations are empowering rituals that give societies leaders and followers, rulers and ruled, states and citizens. Additionally, rituals of mediation create political hierarchies and cultural differences that support the deployment of ideological beliefs.

The method of mediation can give rise to multiple social rituals, including the rituals that may be found to be part of the transnational cultural interactions explored in this volume. The sociocultural practice of international relations today, as a series of different internationals, is brought about through processes of mediation. Although I suggest that mediation can be taken as a method that guarantees the inscription of social/cultural meaning, I do not believe that all forms of mediation necessarily produce the same kind of meaning. Put differently, not all rituals of mediation enable the same rites of passage. Studies that place the emphasis on the social aspects of mediation have a tendency to interpret mediating rituals as methods of social *communication* or techniques of cultural and political *representation* that assume that the methodology (mediation) is neutral or value-free. Mediation and the mediator, it is argued, perform their task of transferring or conferring meaning. Mediating rituals allegedly do not create meaning. They merely transport signification from one social domain to another without affecting it along the way. Such studies do not take the notion of mediation as a methodology very far. They also remain stuck in a positivist understanding of the way social meaning takes place as they affirm the neutrality of the method of analysis. Additionally, these studies demonstrate a limited understanding of the notion of rite and ritual.

More critical sociologists and anthropologists have shown that rites of passage do not always take place as planned. Their effects sometimes leave much to be socially and structurally desired. Some scholars have even suggested that rituals of mediation are capable of unleashing a surplus of meaning that does violence to the communicative and representational processes these methods are supposed to achieve. Georges Bataille's interpretation of sacrificial rites and his notion of the "accursed share" of capital reveal that mediation can yield representational excess and even offer a moment of release from the logic of communication.[8] While recognizing that rituals of mediation often have a stabilizing function and guarantee the communicative and representational effects they are supposed to establish, one needs to also accept that such rituals are not always easily contained inside the neutral space where they are confined. Critical social anthropologists Felicia Hughes-Freeland and Mary Crain suggest that classical methodologies can be turned into critical tools. As a methodological tool, a ritual of mediation can be deviated from the original function it was designed to occupy within one specific social system. Mediation can be recycled and put to use for more critical work. As Hughes-Freeland and Crain put it, a ritual can become a "contested space for social action and identity politics—an arena for resistance, negotiation and affirmation."[9]

This second understanding of mediation still purports to use mediation as a method through which social meanings are constructed. But it also suggests that methods of meaning can be diverted from their original path, thus giving rise to differentiated social practices. This second use of the method of mediation has been found attractive by many (but perhaps less so in international relations). With the explosion of all sorts of cultural media over the past two centuries, many have claimed that mediation not only serves to transfer meaning by connecting or distancing subject and object positions, but that it can also construct and transform social reality. Taking into account the transformative power of some media, more critical cultural and social analysts have noted a conceptual shift: "Instead of a ritual process which moves from one moment to another in time and space [representation], ritualised performative practices [of mediation] embody creativity and constraint to be thought of as simultaneous, co-present, and co-dependent, and embodied in different forms of participation."[10] The idea of using the notion of mediation for transformative purposes may have developed with the arrival of new modalities of transmission of meaning between subjects and objects (photography, telephone, radio, television, film, etc.). But the advent of mediation as *transformation* also coincides with the emergence of a modernist cultural avant-garde (from romantics to surrealists), which has revolutionized the meaning of aesthetics over the past two centuries. Approaches to mediation as a method of transformation of meaning have the merit of challenging the taken-for-granted dualisms between subjects and objects perpetuated by theories of representation and communication. Understood as "contested spaces" for action and identity in society, rituals of mediation do not simply connect or differentiate. Instead, these rituals initiate novel forms of thought, announce the emergence of different aesthetic sensitivities, usher in new creative possibilities, and make visible radical political choices.

The aim of this introductory essay is not to substitute a more innovative version of mediation for a previous, more dominant one. The point is rather to show the types of uses mediation as a method can be put to. Although adopting the understanding that mediation is a method of transformation of social meaning can be appealing to many critical enterprises, proponents of this usage also frequently seek to impose new subjectivities where prior systems of representation and communication once stood. On behalf of so-called emancipating ideologies, transformative mediations often end up privileging a dominant subject position. At times, this dominant subject has gone under the name of Modern Man (and both terms have sometimes escaped problematization).

A third ritual of mediation, a third interpretation of the method of mediation different from representation and transformation, can be put to use too. Better adapted to postmodern times that have seen a proliferation of transnational cultural interactions, this method of mediation is often employed in the following essays even when their purpose is sometimes to identify the social meanings achieved by more representational or transformative methods. According to this usage, neither one of the previous two methods of mediation may be privileged. In fact, both rituals of representation and transformation can be and should be problematized. But the problematization of representational and transformative rituals is only one part of what this method of mediation does. This third ritual of mediation resists the temptation of closing up cultural interpretation and of imposing a certain, privileged meaning that is often the outcome of the previous two rituals. Instead, this other use of mediation encourages a plurality of cultural meanings and enables the deployment of multiple political possibilities.

International projection artist Krzysztof Wodiczko is an emblematic figure of this third approach to mediation. Wodiczko makes mediation the main methodology of his artistic work. But his visual projections and installations are examples of a different way of creating social meaning. In his artistic projects, he refuses to give precedence to any single use of mediation. Instead, he offers the possibility that different uses of mediation may take place all at once. People may see his mediations as vehicles for all sorts of meanings. The mediations do not come equipped with a predetermined signification either. Rather, they unleash a whole range of signification possibilities that the observer (of Wodiczko's art) can choose to appropriate or not. I suggest that Wodiczko's choice of mediation provides a useful allegorical presentation of the type of methods of mediation adopted in this volume. Wodiczko's art projects stand as examples of mediating rituals that do not represent or transform but, more humbly perhaps, enable debate and discussion. This kind of ritual of mediation does not provide a closure of meaning but, instead, resists the temptation to foreclose narrative and cultural possibilities. I call this third use of mediation a ritual of *pluralization*. Its objective is not to convey meaning or even assign a different signification by dislodging a previous belief system. Rather, the point of this method of mediation is to leave open as many social and cultural meanings as possible.

In what follows, I detail these three methods of mediation, which I rename *rituals of representation, rituals of transformation,* and *rituals of pluralization.* I explain the type of social and cultural practices that they enable and examine the theoretical contexts within which such methods appear to be justified.

Rituals of Representation

Mediation is often affirmed as the process through which a "transcendent Deity is enabled to produce effects in the world without being himself the immediate agent of these effects."[11] This definition is first provided by Judeo-Christian scriptures and theology. The mediator—he who occupies the site of mediation—is a "go-between" who enables the passage of human subjects from one plane of existence (the physical world) to the next (the metaphysical world). In this model, Jesus Christ generally functions as the prototypical figure of mediation. In Christian literatures, Jesus is described as both a revealing mediator who speaks God's words and a redeeming agent who comes to this world to atone for all human beings' sins. The rite of passage that Jesus performs is a fundamental connection, a point of reconciliation between God and his people. As a mediator, Jesus has access to both worlds. He exhibits both metaphysical (God's son) and physical (his human crucifixion, his suffering in the flesh) traits.[12]

Through the figure of Jesus Christ, the method of mediation and the way it serves to convey meaning are anchored in a peculiar spatial imaginary. Mediation is presented as a unique space within which necessary rites are performed. It is an ambivalent space (neither here nor there) that can only facilitate one type of ritual: a reciprocal exchange between God's words and the believers' faith through which meaning is achieved. In this self-contained space where only this kind of exchange takes place, the mediator's actions are limited to what his duty commands him to do. The mediator's duty is to keep the gate closed most of the time, and open only when the moment of exchange has arrived. As gatekeeper and enabler, the mediator's rite of passage defines a specific right of passage. This ritual of mediation that creates rights is what can be called *representation*.

Representation is a double process, a back-and-forth kind of exchange. First, in strictly communicative terms, the mediator *represents* God to humans on Earth. While God is thus presented with a human face (hence, not a direct presentation but a re-presentation of God), God is also buffered by the mediator. According to this belief system, in order to justify the desire to gain access to the "otherworldly," the metaphysical domain must remain separate from the physical world. Thus, Jesus' mediation also protects God's kingdom from the perversions, evils, and temptations often found in the physical world. In return, the figure of Jesus *represents* the right of access of men to God's realm. Bearing as his cross the weight of all human sins, Jesus comes to Earth to show the way, reveal how the rights to God's kingdom can be obtained. Jesus' mediating task, then, is also to give God's chosen few specific rights that will guarantee their re-presentation (a second presentation of their selves now freed from physical frailties) in the afterlife. Come judgment day, those who possess these rights will be differentiated from those who never made amends for their sins and cannot hope to be redeemed. Only those who have been granted these rights will pass on.

The technique of mediation as a way of inscribing meaning in the world is "the central idea in the Christian doctrines of atonement and redemption."[13] It is also crucial to the notion of representation through which most of Western philosophy understands the relationship between the human self and the world. Two important results are achieved by the use of mediation as a ritual of representation. First, a fundamental binary opposition between a supreme realm of being governed by universal laws and insufficient, incomplete, and often needy human subjects drifting about in the physical world is created.[14] The "go-between" rite of mediation anchors a pervasive dichotomous understanding of the world that presents itself as a set of essential oppositions (man/God, passion/reason, object/subject, evil/good, false/true). As a result of this construct, representation becomes what ill-construed subjects in need of answers (about themselves, their meaning, the world) long to achieve. They crave representation (to be presented again and differently from what they physically are left to be) as, for example, God's people, rational human beings, enlightened selves, voting subjects, or nationals of a state. By seeking representation through multiple premodern and modern rites that follow the model of the Judeo-Christian ritual of passage, these subjects of mediation assume that meaning will be given to their existence by adopting daily prescriptions (morals, rules, laws) that they believe are endowed with the power and will of the metaphysical world. It is toward these prescriptive and normative doctrines that the subjects of mediation craving representation turn when the material world presents them with questions and obstacles. The basic dichotomy established by this ritual of mediation calls for metaphysical solutions to material problems. These solutions can be discovered only by reaching beyond the subject and his or her physical capacities.

The modern Cartesian turn toward a thinking subject is another typical example of this practice of mediation. It assumes that human senses must be doubted and rejected before the subject can finally reach the ability to think for himself (the cogito).[15] Descartes's "I think, therefore I am" dictum signifies not so much the self-mastery of the thinking subject, but rather the quest for something greater and more meaningful than the subject's many experiences with his or her world. Only when the physical world has been processed by the laws of reason can it be trusted and accepted. Descartes brings the supernatural and the universal down into the human mind. But the basic dichotomy between two levels of experience and the need for a representation of the first into the second are maintained.

The second major consequence of this ritual of mediation is the assumption that representation can only take place if the work of mediation (the ritual performed by the mediator) remains constant and unchanged. Neither of this world nor of the other, the mediator must occupy a "neither man's nor God's land" where characteristics from both worlds nonetheless come in contact. For meaning to be passed on and representation to be realized, both worlds must remain separate and distinguishable. The space of mediation buffers both worlds. Although the mediator's space buffers, it cannot be completely hermetic either. In the technique of mediation invented in Judeo-Christian scriptures, the mediator filters what must be exchanged, passes it on to the proper domain, and closes the gate behind so that no superfluous contact is made possible and the fundamental difference between both worlds is preserved. But for this representation to succeed, the space of mediation must remain neutral. The ritual of mediation is a rite of passage that transmits but never alters.[16] This neutral rite and site guarantees that representation takes place without any transformation of meaning along the way. For representation to succeed and meaning to be inscribed, the mediator must remain confined to this space. Thus, the agency of the mediator is reduced to this ability to pass on meaning when requested. But the mediator possesses no will of his, her, or its own, no capacity to will change or even to act upon it. In this kind of passing site, rites and rights of passage take place without taking too much space. The mediation contributes to the transmission of meaning but makes no difference. In passing sites of mediation, mediators transport, transcribe, and translate. They carry out their task without modifying the system. Simply, they are neutral agents of representation.

Rituals of Transformation

Much of romanticism's intent consisted of restoring the link between nature and the human self, which, romantics believed, modern rationalism (following Descartes) had repudiated. Insisting that truth about the human experience can be found "neither by way of the deductions of reason nor through the inquiries of science but rather through pure inspiration, aided by individual genius," romantics claimed a unity between the human spirit and the world.[17] Instead of emphasizing a dual structure of meaning in modernity, romantics approached modernity as a vast field of unmediated experiences inside which the individual self was free to express his or her emotions and develop his or her creative capacities.

The romantic turn has revolutionary consequences for the practice of mediation. With romanticism, the former dichotomies between mind and matter, reason and passion disappear. Rituals of representation become pointless to the romantic mind. This does not mean, however, that the method of mediation is abandoned. On the contrary, the romantic movement is filled with brand-new mediating rituals. Newly created or rediscovered aesthetic techniques and art forms offer multiple new media through which the self can express his or her relation to the world. With the advent of romanticism and the gradual dissipation of the rationalist regime of representation, rituals of mediation are put to different uses. Mediation now becomes a method of self-expression, a practice of *transformation* of the world.

Creative sensibilities take over the concept of mediation. Mediation is a technique reserved to the self who takes a pause to contemplate the world, reflects on his or her place in accordance with nature, and then finds the proper aesthetic medium that can best express the grandeur of the entire edifice (world and man as one).[18] In this social belief system, the human subject becomes the mediator. And the mediator is asked to take control of his or her existence and to bear witness of this new Enlightenment through his or her creations. From Goethe's prose to Schopenhauer's philosophy, it is up to the mediator as aesthete to transform the old rationalistic world and to reveal the beauty of the communion between humans and nature. Although such a beauty finds different poetic expressions in the romantic movement, it is often simply allegorized as Modern Times.

Whereas mediating rituals were once mobilized to guarantee the necessary passage of meaning from one domain of experience to another, mediation is now deployed to transform, affirm, and glorify. It may be argued that this new use of mediation does not completely reject the idea of representation. After all, it is Modern Man (with capitals to denote his intended mastery) that is being reified through romantic aesthetic constructions. Still, the presentation of Modern Man is no longer achieved through a transfer of meaning and essence from one domain of experience to another. The representation of Modern Man is no longer guaranteed by a relationship maintained (by the mediator) between a dominant subject and its dominated objects of faith, protection, or power. At best, it can be said that romantic (re)presentations *present* a different reality. It is, I believe, more accurate to label these transformative rituals re-creative or re-imaginative rather than representational. These mediations are deployed to (re)invent the human self and his or her relation to the world. Through romantic mediations, the modern self is defined in new ways that eschew the dual categories of meaning that once imposed the domination of reason or God in prior (modern and premodern) systems of representation.

This is not to say that rituals of transformation like those championed by romantics do not create their own subjectivities. Clearly, they do, and intentionally so. As a direct outcome of romantic mediation, Modern Man becomes the main (often heroic) source of meaning in society. Romantic mediations transform previous social systems in order to establish Modern Man as the newly dominant subject of (modern) history. Mediation as a method of transformation produces social meanings that enable the institutionalization of certain relations of power, domination, and exploitation. These new relations of power, domination, and exploitation (similar to prior hierarchies under systems of representation) often rely on subject/object dichotomies too.

Rituals of transformation reproduce dichotomies that may no longer be of a representational kind (between mind and matter, God and human beings) but are nonetheless just as pervasive. They are all the more pervasive in that they are part and parcel of one single domain of experience, the material world, that all human beings partake of. Social dualisms are no longer buffered by the belief in an essential difference between a physical and a metaphysical world. Instead, romantic mediations affirm dichotomies that take place between human subjects in daily social interactions. Modern Man is equipped with qualities that not all of his fellow beings possess. Some selves are more heroic and meaningful (to modernity) than others. Put differently, one man's self-affirmation is often another man's alienation. A difference is thus instituted between human subjects on the basis of one's use of mediation. Some men are able to find the means to transform their world while others have to follow suit. Mediation is the method that perpetuates such differences as those with the ability to transform society become those who inscribe processes through which meaningful life (in this world) can be attained. As some critics of the romantic mind have noted, as much as mediation transforms (and creates subjectivity), it also alienates (and produces subjection).

Toward the middle of the nineteenth century, a critical reappraisal of the value of the method of mediation is performed by several thinkers. These thinkers do not necessarily reject the romantic ideal of transformation. But they wish to point to the social inequalities that the practice of romantic mediation sometimes creates. Baudelaire is an important figure in this shift within romanticism. An early proponent of the romantic hero, his poetry suddenly changes to shed some light on the dark side of Modern Man's world. In the shadows of modernity's progress, many human beings cannot hope to rise to the level of the new romantic hero. For the poor and marginalized in particular, modern life is about hard labor in the cities, not about bucolic celebrations of man and nature. Being part of modernity's splendor is a social privilege that is not shared by all men. To obtain this privilege, it is not enough to extol the virtues of modernity as if everyone had an equal chance to partake of it. Rather, this privilege relies on membership in certain social-economic classes. Some classes are more likely to benefit from the vision of Modern(ized) Man while others are left to produce the conditions necessary for the privileged class to sustain its romantic way of life. Thus, a basic dichotomy between human subjects based on their membership in social classes also becomes the defining characteristic of this (new) modernity. As Marx and others, such as Baudelaire, started to suggest, the modern subject of romanticism who affirms himself or herself through new techniques of mediation is first and foremost a bourgeois subject.

Coming to this realization, Baudelaire sets out to rectify romantic mediations. Still, he does not abandon the transformative potential of artistic mediation. He continues to work with poetry as a medium of transformation. But poetry, he believes, has to be fully transformative. The transformative work of poetry cannot result in the affirmation of one type of human subject and privileged social class. Transformative mediations must prolong the critical work. The critical work of romantic mediation cannot end as long as a large part of modernity remains in the shadows. Baudelaire performs such a transformed version of Modern Man in his *Paris Spleen* collection of prose poems.[19] In this work, Baudelaire's poetry unleashes a detailed description of what Marshall Berman has called "primal scenes." The Baudelairean primal scene is a poetic narrative that depicts a mundane reality, encountered by the *flâneur* (the wandering romantic observer) in his daily walks through the city (the *flâneur* is mostly a masculine subject). The objective of the primal scene is to reveal "some of the deepest ironies and contradictions of modern city life."[20] Through the primal scene, romantic modernity's contradictions are displayed. It is shown that "[t]he setting that makes all urban humanity a great extended 'family of eyes' also brings forth the discarded stepchildren of that family."[21] In the midst of modernity's new inventions and constructions (the wide boulevards, the first mechanized factories, gas lampposts, etc.), scenes of another modernity are made visible through Baudelaire's prose. Piles of rubble, children begging for food and money, violence and alcoholism among the lower classes become daily sights as well. Baudelaire's poetry is no longer lyrical like traditional romantic poetry.[22] It becomes socially realistic and vivid. As a social mediator, the poet can no longer drone on about the beauty of the soul or the grandeur of nature. These are simply abusive and distorting images of the actual reality of the modern world. The mediating poet needs to imprint a different image, one that cannot easily go away. The "eyes of the poor"[23] must remain a pregnant and uncomfortable image, even when expressed through poetry.

Baudelaire's primal scenes are not glamorous rituals of transformation. But they are a necessary vector of change. They accuse more than they laud Modern Man's world. They make use of blatant contrasts in the hope that these might trigger some social reforms. After all, the scenes portrayed by Baudelaire are those that the romantic bourgeois can see too and that should unsettle his modern comfort. At every street corner, Modern Man is faced with the erupting sight of the city's underbelly. To be effective, Baudelaire intimates, the method of mediation must make use of irony and contrast. The romantic subject must be shocked and made to feel torn inside. Instead of ignoring the differences that modernity creates and on which bourgeois man thrives, mediation has a duty to be socially aware by pointing to the existing social divisions. Mediation has a social role to play. It can become a political tool that effectively demonstrates the exploitation of some part of modernity caused by Modern Man himself. Rituals of mediation must be constantly deployed so that social and political transformations can fully take place. The method of mediation cannot be laid to rest until the dominant and discriminating subjectivities have finally been erased. In this (post)romantic context, mediators are actively engaged agents of transformation.

Rituals of Pluralization

Polish-born performance artist Krzystof Wodiczko is perhaps one of the best-known contemporary proponents of the inclusion of art in the public domain. Presenting his work as a series of ephemeral interventions, Wodiczko is most famous for his outdoor projections. Refusing to be constrained by the architectural structuralism of the art gallery, he has taken his creativity to public spaces all over the world. Generally, his technique consists of beaming images borrowed from all sorts of contexts (newspaper clippings, body parts, weaponry photos from military reviews, etc.) onto city buildings.[24] In one of his early public interven-

tions in Halifax, Nova Scotia, Wodiczko projected "male hands extending from suit sleeves onto the flat sides" of corporate buildings.[25] In another projection in Dayton, Ohio, a few years later, Wodiczko covered
the facade of a public theater with statues of soldiers and downward-
pointing missiles to decry the "escalation of the arms race in the first
years of Reagan's presidency."[26]

Despite the fact that Wodiczko's early artistic projections seem to
"underscore the role of architecture as a vehicle of authority,"[27] most of
his subsequent interventions convey more complex and plural significations. Some of his works appear to highlight the social oppression of
certain groups at the hands of more privileged and hegemonic classes.
One of these socially engaged projects is his *Homeless Projection: A Pro-
posal for the City of New York,* which was first presented at 49th Parallel
in the Center for Contemporary Canadian Art in New York in 1986.[28] In
this *Homeless Projection,* Wodiczko offered a different view of New York
City. While the city's public spaces were being taken over by corporate
advertising and urban planning whose "municipal art" sought to restore the majesty of New York's monuments (clean is good for business),
Wodiczko visually interfered with these political schemes. He proposed
to *transform* New York's public places, but in quite a different fashion.
Wodiczko chose to superimpose on some of the city's monuments and
statues a projection of images that did not exalt the so-called grandeur
of New York's eternal values (individual freedom, spirit of enterprise,
multiculturalism, etc.). Instead, his slide shows made to cover (not de-
face, but reface) these famous monuments displayed all sorts of attributes and belongings generally believed to pertain to New York City's
homeless population. Bandages, crutches, brown bags, leftover food
were visually pasted over these monumental sites. In the months that
preceded Wodiczko's *Homeless Projection,* many homeless people had
been evicted from New York's parks in the cause of aesthetic gentrifica-
tion and corporate business. Wodiczko's *Homeless Projection* could be
interpreted as a transformative ritual. One commentator noted that this
"project illuminates the prevailing social relations of domination and
conflict that [urban] planning both facilitates and disavows."[29]

In this show, Wodiczko left the statues of George Washington or the
Marquis de Lafayette in Union Square intact. On top of them, he over-
laid an image that revealed these classical American heroes with crutches,

in wheelchairs, or sitting on the ground next to a garbage can. This kind of visual transformation of New York is a *mediating ritual* that in a way is reminiscent of Baudelaire's primal scenes. Wodiczko uses photography and projection as media through which a different social reality is advocated (and which, along the way, denounce other social belief systems). At the same time, though, there is more to this kind of mediation than what was present in Baudelaire's transformations. Wodiczko does not merely make use of mediation to operate social transformations. He also encourages a full participation with the medium, a constant manipulation of the method of mediation.

Despite the fact that it may enable social transformations, the *Homeless Projection* displays a different method of mediation, which becomes more obvious in later works by Wodiczko. The *Homeless Projection* and much of Wodiczko's subsequent interventions are active engagements with the practice of mediation. Mediation is not simply presented as a method through which new social and political realities can be achieved. In rituals of transformation of the romantic kind, mediation is a powerful method. But it is still a means to something else. For Wodiczko, however, precisely because mediation is such a powerful method of inscribing social meaning, mediation and those who use it must be problematized. Critical reflections cannot simply substitute one mediation for another, hoping that better social outcomes will result from this kind of transfer. Mediation itself is the locale where critical investigation must take place and where meaning is reopened.

This insistence on investigating the ritual of mediation and its power of meaning is not unique to Wodiczko's art. Several postmodern cultural/ media studies scholars have adopted a similar approach to analyzing media and mediation. Many of the essays in this volume follow this path of analysis as they explore and reconsider the meaning of mediated forms and objects (from photography to the airport) in the context of transnational cultural interactions. Marshall McLuhan, who, as some have suggested, opened up the path to the postmodern imaginary, already noted that, in a social environment saturated with media techniques and visions, signification is produced by the "system of objects"[30] rather than by a manipulating agent (the mediator) who intends to give meaning to the mediation. As McLuhan was fond of repeating, the "medium is the message."[31] Modern Man's message, his stated intention to appropriate the world, is processed by media whose forms condition social outcomes, cultural practices, and political beliefs. Social transformations targeted by the use of mediating rituals do not always take place as desired, as media forms and objects can deviate the message of the romantic self. A media(tion)-saturated society provides (post)Modern Man with a social environment that he often has a hard time mastering.[32] Transformations, then, cannot simply be the product of man's thinking (conformist or critical) enabled by the process of mediation. Transformations are undistinguishable from the rituals of mediation that construct these social realities. Thus, mediation is not simply to be used. Because mediation's form determines its content, mediating rituals need to be investigated and scrutinized.

Wodiczko's projections encourage their observers to not just remain passive consumers of rituals of transformation or representation.[33] They intimate that social meanings come from the inside, from the mediated visions that, in late modernity, have taken over the social domain within which individual subjects interact. Wodiczko's method is to "manipulate the system from within [and] interfere with [its] codes."[34] Because mediation's codes are crucial to the production of meaning and social meaning maintains relations of power, wealth, and cultural governance, the commanding force of mediation must be revealed. To reveal mediation, Wodiczko chooses to ironically mimic and exaggerate the effects of some media forms and objects (architecture, public monuments, television) by defacing and perverting them. Wodiczko's point is not to use different mediated forms to condemn mediation's excesses. His method is rather to use and reappropriate traditionally mobilized modern rituals of transformation to display their power of signification.

The problematization of mediation is not an end in itself for Wodiczko, though. Problematizing modern rituals of transformation by defacing them is necessary for him to the extent that it contributes to reopening social meaning and to freeing up cultural possibilities. Another project by Wodiczko, the *Alien Staff,* demonstrates the capacity of perverting and mimicking (re)mediations to open up (their) meaning.[35] The *Alien Staff* is a situation performance concocted by Wodiczko to reveal the *pluralizing* potential of mediation once it has been freed from transformative and representational rituals. In this art project, Wodiczko asked immigrants (in the United States mostly) to walk about the city and carry a tall stick made to look like a biblical staff (a new type of *flâneur* perhaps). The staff opens up at its top to reveal an inserted television screen. On the screen, the same individual who carries the biblical staff is shown telling his or her life story. The staff bearer is asked to meander around the city and abruptly stop in front of pedestrians. The pedestrians are then faced with the staff and its mini TV screen. The staff bearer never speaks, and in fact remains as still and stoic as can be. Only the staff is active and conveys information.

At one level, *Alien Staff* could be interpreted as a work of critical transformation and radical mobilization performed by this new kind of mediating ritual. Wodiczko, perhaps, uses the magical staff and its talking head as a metaphor for the silencing of immigrant populations in industrialized societies. Postmodern mediations do not give voice to immigrants in societies still governed by Modern Man's political power and regime of economic production. This is one possible interpretation offered by Wodiczko's art. Wodiczko does not indicate whether the problematization of postmodern media forms is the intended meaning of the display. But I think that Wodiczko, as silent as his staff bearer, refuses to tell the meaning of this art performance on purpose. Explaining the art scene would imply that one signification has been imposed. Meaning would be foreclosed and, contrary to the image that is shown, the immigrant would thus be forced to speak. By forcing the immigrant to speak (through someone else's narrating voice), the social system that "silenced" the immigrant in the first place would be reaffirmed.

At another level, this performative (re)mediation by Wodiczko is an ironic play of meaning. The contrasting image of a silent human being with this same being's talking face on a miniature TV screen mimics the blinding sight and the deafening sound of contemporary media(tions) that have no place for the immigrant. Who pays attention to television's message anyway? But instead of individual silence or the media's white noise, Wodiczko's *Alien Staff* speaks volumes. While it denounces and challenges our postmodern mediating rituals, it also offers people (immigrants in this case) vectors of speech, new methods of signification and presentation of themselves. Outside the dominant code, different forms of meaning may be accessed. Perhaps, through new mediations of meaning, new social interactions and cultural practices may be developed. Wodiczko observes: "If I could make it more playful... Laughter—all the jokes, the disruptions, the changes of topics, all the absurdity and impossibility of talking about identity. This is the new community."[36]

Wodiczko's mediated art forms reimagine subjectivities and communities but do not give them names. They enable meaning by multiplying the ways by which meaning is produced. They offer different paths through which presentation of one's body and self can be realized without having to postulate this presence from systems of representation or transformation. In fact, multiple, possibly not essential, but certainly meaningful presentations of one's selves (as immigrant, as street performer, as artist, as talking head) are facilitated. At the same time, Wodiczko's performances are not inaccessible to observers in search of more traditional representational and transformative rituals of mediation. As a ritual of representation, Wodiczko's *Alien Staff* may be taken as an allegory for the impossible passage of some individuals in democratic political systems from the status of alien to that of citizen. Similarly, *Alien Staff* could be interpreted as a ritual of transformation that denounces the unequal status of some individuals in society vis-à-vis others and thus calls for a change of condition. Although those are possible interpretations of Wodiczko's mediations, however, they may not be the most fruitful as they merely seek to impose one (their) privileged understanding of the method of mediation onto Wodiczko's own rituals.

In the end, Wodiczko provides a *pluralizing* model of mediation. Different outcomes of mediation can take place because, after all, the method of mediation is neither value-free nor the sole possession of romantic man. What Wodiczko's plural approach to the manipulation of the medium and to the use of mediation wants to avoid is *not* the fact that mediation is being used to produce social meanings. This, Wodiczko suggests, is inevitable and in a sense desirable. What it wants to avoid and what it protects against is the idea, prevalent among proponents of mediation as either representation or transformation, that desirable social meanings are decided and often established before the method of mediation even has a chance to deploy its cultural and political effects. When this happens, mediation remains an empty middle point between two distant realities or is used as a tool for something else, for some other more romantic social reality that mediation helps to substantiate. When this happens, mediation negates pluralization. The following essays show that contemporary transnational cultural interactions often mobilize mediations to do just this. The (mediating) internationals that result from such mediations are not always as open and plural as they could be.

Notes

1. See Dagobert Runes, *Dictionary of Philosophy* (Totowa, N.J.: Littlefield, Adfams & Co., 1970), p. 194.

2. See Chester Crocker, Fen Osler Hampson, and Pamela Aall, "Introduction," in Chester Crocker, Fen Osler Hampson, and Pamela Aall, eds., *Herding Cats: Multiparty Mediation in a Complex World* (Washington, D.C.: United States Institute of Peace Press, 1999), p. 7.

3. As suggested by Jacob Bercovitch, "Mediation in International Conflict," in William Zartman and J. Lewis Rasmussen, eds., *Peacemaking in International Conflict: Methods and Techniques* (Washington, D.C.: United States Institute of Peace Press, 1997), p. 130.

4. Ray August, *Public International Law* (Englewood Cliffs, N.J.: Prentice Hall, 1995), p. 444.

5. Ibid. But for a more philosophically informed interpretation of mediation as an international relations practice, see James Der Derian, *On Diplomacy: A Genealogy of Western Estrangement* (Oxford: Blackwell, 1987). Der Derian posits that mediation is not only a "connecting link," an intervention between conflicting actors that forms the starting point of peace and reconciliation analyses. Rather, mediation is crucial to the practice of diplomacy in general as, philosophically, it unfolds as a technique that resolves estrangements and separations between individuals, social groups, and political entities. Mediation, then, cannot be understood without first affirming the idea of a fundamental alienation between different object and subject positions. I believe that Der Derian's interpretation of mediation as a mode of rapprochement and as the reversal of alienation is very similar to the concept of mediation as a ritual of representation that I describe later on in this essay. In traditional international diplomatic relations, mediation as representation often necessitates the prior belief that crucial actors (units of meaning) have been alienated from one another (or from themselves) and need to be reconciled. See Der Derian, *On Diplomacy*, pp. 6–7.

6. See Catherine Bell, *Ritual: Perspectives and Dimensions* (Oxford: Oxford University Press, 1997); Tamar Liebes and James Carran, eds., *Media, Ritual and Identity* (New York: Routledge, 1998); René Girard, *Violence and the Sacred* (Baltimore: Johns Hopkins University Press, 1977); and René Girard, *The Girard Reader,* ed. James Williams (New York: Crossroad Publishing, 1996). One scholar's definition of ritual as a rite of passage blurs the distinction between ritual and mediation. William Noonan defines social ritual as "a passageway toward a new social status." Noonan continues: "This period is referred to as the 'betwixt and between' or 'limen' when reality is neither here or there." See William Noonan, "Western Hospitalization for Surgery as Rite of Passage," in Michael Aune and Valerie DeMarinis, eds., *Religious and Social Ritual: Interdisciplinary Explorations* (Albany: State University of New York Press, 1996), p. 296.

7. This view is well expressed by René Girard, for whom the notion of sacrificial rite is the model form of social mediation. Girard writes that "the key to the mystery [of rites] lies in the decisive reordering that occurs at the end of the ritual performance, normally through the *mediation* of sacrifice" (*The Girard Reader,* p. 11; emphasis added).

8. Georges Bataille, *The Accursed Share*, vol. 1, trans. Robert Hurley (New York: Zone Books, 1991), and *Erotism: Death and Sensuality* (San Francisco: City Lights, 1986).

9. Felicia Hughes-Freeland and Mary Crain, eds., *Recasting Ritual: Performance, Media, Identity* (New York: Routledge, 1998), p. 2.

10. Ibid., p. 3.

11. James Mark Baldwin, *Dictionary of Philosophy and Psychology*, vol. 2 (Gloucester, Mass.: Peter Smith, 1960), p. 59.

12. To use Arthur Lovejoy's formulation, Jesus Christ is both "this-worldly" and "otherworldly." See Arthur O. Lovejoy, *The Great Chain of Being* (Cambridge: Harvard University Press, 1933).

13. As noted in Baldwin, *Dictionary of Philosophy and Psychology*, vol. 2, p. 60.

14. Runes notes that "mediation is necessary in systems in which two forms of reality are held to be so different that immediate interaction is impossible" (*Dictionary of Philosophy*, p. 194).

15. René Descartes, *Discourse on Method*, bilingual edition, trans. George Heffernan (South Bend, Ind.: University of Notre Dame Press, 1994).

16. The etymological root of the term *mediation* (from the Latin term *medius*) also signifies "neutrality" and "indifference." A state of "mediation" is also "a neutral or uncommitted" state. See P. G. W. Glare, ed., *Oxford Latin Dictionary* (Oxford: Clarendon Press, 1990), p. 1090. As a neutral/indifferent space, mediation leaves intact the two elements it helps to connect.

17. See Robert Solomon and Kathleen Higgins, *A Short History of Philosophy* (Oxford: Oxford University Press, 1996), p. 221.

18. This is well expressed by Baudelaire, who uses the figure of the painter to exalt the virtue of the romantic mediator: "The true painter will be one who can snatch from the life of today its epic quality, and make us feel how great and poetic we are in our cravats and our patent-leather boots" (Charles Baudelaire, *Art in Paris, 1845–62*, ed. and trans. Jonathan Mayne [New York: Phaidon, 1965], pp. 31–32).

19. Charles Baudelaire, *Paris Spleen*, trans. Louise Varese (New York: New Directions, 1970).

20. Marshall Berman, *All That Is Solid Melts into Air: The Experience of Modernity* (London: Penguin, 1988), p. 153.

21. Ibid.

22. Baudelaire's rejection of lyrical style and motifs is noted by Walter Benjamin, who writes that "to Baudelaire, the lyric poet with a halo is antiquated" ("On Some Motifs in Baudelaire," in Walter Benjamin, *Illuminations: Essays and Reflections*, ed. Hannah Arendt [New York: Shocken Books, 1968], p. 192).

23. This is the title of one of Baudelaire's most representative social prose poems in his *Paris Spleen* collection.

24. See Phil Freshman, ed., *Krzysztof Wodiczko: Public Address*, with essays by Peter Boswell, Andrzej Turowski, Patricia Phillips, and Dick Hebdige (Minneapolis: Walker Art Center, 1992).

25. See Peter Boswell, "Krzysztof Wodiczko: Art and the Public Domain," in ibid., p. 15.

26. Ibid.

27. Ibid.

28. Wodiczko's *Homeless Projection* is detailed and analyzed by Rosalyn Deutsche in "Krysztof Wodiczko's *Homeless Projection* and the Site or Urban 'Revitalization,'" in Carol Squiers, ed., *Over-Exposed: Essays on Contemporary Photography* (New York: New Press, 1999), pp. 56–92.

29. Ibid., 61.

30. To borrow Baudrillard's formulation. See Jean Baudrillard, *The System of Objects,* trans. James Benedict (New York: Verso, 1996).

31. Marshall McLuhan, *Understanding Media: The Extensions of Man* (Cambridge: MIT Press, 1994), p. 7.

32. As McLuhan puts it, "[w]e are as numb in our new electric world as the native involved in our literate and mechanical culture" (ibid., p. 16).

33. This is exactly what Hal Foster notes about Wodiczko's work. Foster believes that, in Wodiczko's "situational aesthetics," "the artist becomes a manipulator of signs more than a producer of art objects, and the viewer an active reader of messages rather than a passive contemplator of the aesthetic or consumer of the spectacular" (*Recodings: Art, Spectacle, Cultural Politics* [New York: New Press, 1985], p. 100).

34. Douglas Crimp, Rosalyn Deutsche, and Ewa Lajer-Burcharth, "A Conversation with Krzysztof Wodiczko," in Russell Ferguson, William Olander, Marcia Tucker, and Karen Fiss, eds., *Discourses: Conversations in Postmodern Art and Culture* (Cambridge: MIT Press, 1990), p. 313.

35. For a discussion on Wodiczko's *Alien Staff* project, see Krzysztof Wodiczko, "Alien Staff: A Conversation with Bruce Robbins," in Anna Nabokov, ed., *Veiled Histories: The Body, Place and Public Art* (New York: Critical Press, 1997), pp. 119–45.

36. Ibid., p. 141.

Part I
Sites of Mediation

CHAPTER ONE

Site Specific

Medi(t)ations at the Airport

Debbie Lisle

> The very best kind of airport reading to be found in LAX these days
> is the triple-decker melodrama being played out all around one—
> a complex tragicomedy of love and war and exile.[1]

With the rise in postwar global travel, chances are that most of us have
entered and exited our homes via the airport. As such, we probably recognize the "triple-decker melodrama" of human interaction so evident
in the various arrival and departure lounges we have passed through.
Although we may experience feelings of loss, hope, anxiety, joy, adven-
ture, homecoming, and fear in airports, we seldom think beyond these
personal experiences and ask how contemporary forms of power are
being produced and deployed at the airport. This essay is an attempt to
think beyond our obvious experiences and ask what is *political* about
the airport. If the status and importance of the airport have increased
in tandem with the growth of global travel, surely we need new ways of
understanding these increasingly familiar spaces. What is immediately
apparent in this desire to politicize the airport is how impotent traditional
conceptions of power are in trying to analyze this site. Understandings
of power based on fixed distinctions and hierarchies suggest that airports are places where power is simply wielded "over" us by sovereign
authorities.

To counter that approach, this essay argues that, like shopping malls,
cinemas, bus stations, and motorways, airports are spaces where new
forms of mediated power are emerging. Whereas traditional understandings of power see it as something to be owned, utilized, and measured,

mediated power is something that is articulated, disseminated, transformed, and rearticulated.[2] In fact, power does not exist as a "thing" to
be measured at all. By starting with the concept of mediation, we can
begin to see that power only exists to the extent that we can identify its
practices and witness its effects. As Foucault explains, this shift from
sovereign power to mediated power requires us to ask "how" questions:

> For some people, asking questions about the "how" of power would
> limit them to describing its effects without ever relating those effects
> either to causes or to a basic nature. . . . I wish to present these questions
> in a different way; better still, to know if it is legitimate to imagine a
> power which unites in itself a what, a why, and a how. To put it bluntly,
> I would say that to begin the analysis with a "how" is to suggest that
> power as such does not exist.[3]

Foucault goes on to argue that in order to open up these how questions,
we must start with issues that are "flat and empirical," in other words,
we must start by asking, "What happens?" What we discover at the airport is that power is increasingly characterized by its complexity, speed,
and mobility. Therefore, politicizing the airport through a conception
of mediated power means tracing the power relations that are continually forged and broken between subjects, objects, spaces, and meanings.
Airports are not only sites of extreme force, surveillance, and discipline.
Rather, airports become politically interesting when they are also understood as sites of destabilization, ambiguity, and constant movement.
Just as people never stay put at airports, neither does power.

To begin, one might want to explain these new forms of mediated
power as an example of the shift from modern to postmodern—a break
with the usual "order of things" and a reimagination of life possibilities
that are not governed by the universal narratives of modernity. Mediated power does not obey any overarching authority, but rather emerges
and reemerges in spaces that exceed the modern distinctions of here/
there, inside/outside, citizen/alien. In airports, this shift from the modern to the postmodern is most evident in the architecture. The functional layouts and regimented spaces of the 1960s are being replaced by
the curved lines, maximum transparency, and sanitized space of postmodern design. As Martha Rosler explains,

> The most intensive period of airport construction coincided with
> stripped down functionalist Modernism. It would be interesting to

compare airports built in the early postwar period and more recently, when the dominant metaphors of flow dynamics shifted from water to information.[4]

But how is power embedded in these material and aesthetic changes? The emergence of postmodern architecture in airports is one of the primary indications of mediation because it has significantly changed the power relations between subjects, objects, spaces, and meaning. Think of the way that moving sidewalks now carry passengers quickly through glass-covered walkways adorned with sophisticated commercial advertising. This experience is significantly different from the functional airports built in the postwar era. However, the emergence of mediated power cannot be explained by a simple progression from modern to postmodern—employing these oppositional categories actually conceals the political questions embedded in this site. As we shall see, both approaches to the airport leave much to be desired in terms of their understandings of power.

Approaching airports from a modern framework illustrates how sovereign power works according to boundaries of inclusion and exclusion (e.g., citizen and alien). The task at hand is to decide which exclusions are necessary, just, and acceptable, and which are not. In our "enlightened" era of globalization, naked displays of sovereign authority at the airport (e.g., security checks) are required in order to safely guarantee our increased desire for travel. However, when certain forms of power are seen as "acceptable," they are effectively placed beyond question. Surely we can live with certain violations of our basic rights and freedoms (we accept being physically searched by strangers) if these violations protect our freedom of movement. Once sovereign power is accepted and its practices placed beyond question, the airport can be understood as a space of emancipation where different cultures can meet, coincide, and learn about each other. In other words, these cultural encounters are guaranteed by our civilized adherence to "acceptable" operations of sovereign power. Pico Iyer is enthusiastic in his argument that the airport is an important site for cultural encounters. In his study of LAX, he suggests that the airport is a positive space of multicultural celebration. As a recorder of the increased cultural contact that globalization produces, Iyer sees the airport as a crucial site for securing multiculturalism:

> It is commonplace nowadays to say that cities look more and more like
> airports, cross-cultural spaces that are a gathering of tribes and races
> and variegated tongues. . . . Airports are, of course, the new epicenters
> and paradigms of our dawning post-national age . . . the prototypes, in
> some sense, of our polyglot, multicolored, user-friendly future. And in
> their very universality—like the mall, the motel, or the McDonald's
> outlet—they advance the notion of a future in which all the world's a
> multiculture.[5]

For Iyer, the usual divisions between nation, culture, race, class, and
gender are now replaced by a world of hybrid travelers blissfully shopping and flying off to foreign destinations. To be sure, Iyer does not ignore the "unacceptable" operations of sovereign power that abound in
airports. For example, he is dutifully shocked at the divisions of labor
within LAX that have created an underclass of racial minorities that are
locked into an exploitative service industry.[6] In effect, Iyer gets the dialectic of modernity exactly right in his assessment of the airport. He
proves that an acceptance of sovereign authority at the airport can guarantee our freedom of movement and help ensure that this is a flourishing site of multiculturalism. Furthermore, delineating the "acceptable"
face of sovereign power makes it easier to locate and resist any excessive
operations of power (such as unequal labor relations).

From a more postmodern approach, Iyer's dialectic of modernity cannot be sustained. We cannot simply acquiesce to the practices of sovereign power in the name of multicultural celebration. Anthropologist
Marc Augé argues that the airport is a "supermodern site" where universal themes such as "emancipation" and "multiculturalism" do not
resonate.[7] Rather than provide us with these grand narratives, supermodern sites are emptied of coherent meaning because of an excess of
signification, an overload of competing signs. In Augé's approach, such
spaces as the airport are banal rather than significant, meaningless rather
than useful. The excess of information provided in supermodern sites
erodes our ability to make distinctions between signs, and therefore we
are incapable of constructing hierarchies of meaning. Augé suggests
that through the combination of excessive meaning and compressed
space, airports confuse and displace our skills of navigation in such a
way that we become passive subjects. In part, this paralysis comes from
our overfamiliarity with supermodern sites—bank machines, highways,
and supermarkets have saturated our daily lives and jettisoned any "gen-

uine" meaning. Augé argues that this overfamiliarity renders super-modern sites "non-places," in other words, spaces that are so empty of meaningful content that it is impossible for subjects to construct coherent identities. In the airport, this loss of self is augmented by the somnambulant state we find ourselves in when traveling (what time is it? what day is it? where am I?). This idea of sleepwalking is useful when thinking through the postmodern effects of hypersignification, over-familiarity, and excessive space. Our usual frameworks of understanding fall apart in supermodern sites because they are emptied of coherent narratives, stable meanings, and universal truth claims. Augé argues that within the "empire of the sign" it is impossible to locate any central organizing principle to which one could attach oneself and operate according to a fixed set of rules. Rather than a functioning grid of meaning and power, such sites as the airport only offer us a mass of competing signs and spaces through which we must pass.

Although this seems to be a useful distinction—the airport as a positive space of multiculturalism or a negative space of banality—this division is problematic because both positions make dubious assumptions about power. Not only does Iyer's modern framework attach power to sovereignty, but it also positions power as a singular, monolithic, hegemonic structure that must be either obeyed in order to avoid chaos and danger, or resisted when it becomes oppressive. Conversely, Augé's postmodern framework evacuates power entirely. Power relations in supermodern sites are wholly governed by hypersignification and excessive space. Although I am more sympathetic to some of Augé's points, he has no way of accounting for moments when significations and spaces coalesce to form an oppressive hegemonic formation.[8] Both approaches miss the emergence of mediated power and its ability to adapt, change, incorporate, and commodify. Mediated power at the airport can never be reduced to a modern equation of inclusion/exclusion, or a postmodern act of disappearance.

What is required is a reformulation of power that unlocks the sovereign concepts of space that govern our current understandings of the airport. Taking our cue from the literature on postmodern architecture, we need to understand airports as sites of flux, movement, and transition rather than as sites of fixed layouts, ordered schedules, and absolute grids. One way to foreground this shift is to imagine the airport as a "transit area":

The term "transit area" brings to mind the current trend in socio-political thought to rethink the political in terms of movement and reject the reifying tendencies of the modern political imagination. It emphasizes that IR discourse speaks more about the limits of the imaginary of its practitioners than it does about the everyday global political practices.[9]

Whereas Soguk and Whitehall are more concerned with the transit area as a metaphor for "the transversal condition of our being and becoming," I am particularly interested in the way they explain the concept of the transit area through the airport.[10] They tell the story of Iranian refugee Merhan Karimi Nasseri, who, because of bureaucratic mistakes by passport and immigration officials, was forced to live in the Charles de Gaulle airport for eleven years.[11] For Soguk and Whitehall, Merhan embodies the condition of transversality not because he has been excluded from access to sovereign power, but rather because of his resistance to the very sovereign powers that seek to erase him. Although Merhan has been forced to dwell in the "no-man's-land" of the airport rather than travel through it like everybody else, he has made extended efforts to construct this space in his own way. Rather than pass through the ultimate place of transit, Merhan has made it his permanent home.[12]

The term *transit area* is useful in reference to the airport because it allows us to analyze the constant complexity, speed, and mobility of power within a specific site. As Soguk and Whitehall explain, focusing on the mobile character of power provides a significant critique of sovereignty: "we want to suggest that all areas are experientially transit areas, sites of inexorable transversality. As Merhan's story attests, transit areas, spaces of movement, are not fully controlled by the state."[13] It is tempting to see the airport as a microcosm of sovereign power, and to trace the ways in which that power manifests itself (immigration, customs officers, baggage checks). Indeed, Iyer's work on LAX exemplifies this approach. But this perspective overlooks the complex, quick, and mobile character of power as it adapts and transforms itself in such sites as the airport. By all means, those manifestations of sovereign power are important, but to understand the airport as a transit area also requires an analysis of how power is mediated—how it is articulated, disseminated, transformed, and rearticulated. Mediated power at the airport does not simply create static inclusions and exclusions that can be traced and hopefully resisted. That kind of formulation resists the subtle ways according to which power relations instantaneously transform, adapt, and re-create themselves.

If the airport is understood as a transit area, it becomes possible to trace the circuit of mediation and counter the assumptions about power embedded in the arguments made by Iyer and Augé. Mediated power never stays still long enough to duplicate Iyer's patronizing tone, nor does it evaporate completely in the oversignification of non-places. This essay formulates an understanding of power that refuses to see the airport as simply a site of extreme control, regulation, and discipline. By analyzing the mediation of power at the airport, it is possible to see that no matter how extreme the efforts of regulation are, they are always already subverted. To illustrate how the airport works as a site of regulation *and* destabilization, this essay locates five arrangements of mediated power and traces how they are articulated, disseminated, transformed, and rearticulated.

Airport Security

Regardless of where one is traveling from or to, it is sovereign power that is the overriding force of law at the airport. The power of the state manifests itself most clearly in the agents of security who maintain the safety of the airport. These include uniformed and nonuniformed police officers, customs and immigration officers, and even private security firms. Although the obvious aim of security agents at the airport is to protect passengers, customers, and employees, their presence reinforces an important discourse of safety. Much like police officers in society, airport security personnel make us feel safe—if an incident occurs, we know there are professionals on hand to take charge. In places where a majority of revenue comes from the tourism industry, tight security at the airport ensures the continuing influx of tourist dollars. Ironically, security agents also carry connotations of danger—why do we need so many security guards here?

The haunting messages of danger that are carried by the complicated network of security forces are revealed when a terrorist incident occurs at an airport. For example, Heathrow witnessed a massive influx of security forces during an IRA mortar bombing of the airport in March 1994.[14] In order to maintain the discourse of safety at the airport (and justify the presence of security officials), it is necessary to have exemplary horror stories. Airports can be banished from international flight routes because of a *lack* of security presence. For example, the U.S. State Department banned direct flights to Murtala Muhammed Airport in Lagos, Nigeria, in 1994 because of its "inadequate security measures."[15] Therefore, one of the most important elements of security forces at the airport is the ability to enforce a discourse of safety. The presence of airport security agents convinces passengers—especially tourists—that the airport is a *safe* place to travel through. However, with the 2001 World Trade Center and Pentagon attacks, this discourse of safety is set to become the overriding force at all domestic and international airports. What the terrorists managed to do was expose the fact that no matter how secure an airport claims to be, it cannot completely arrest the flow of suspicious passengers, unclaimed baggage, and concealed weapons.[16]

What is less evident at the airport is the way security agents function as crucial subjects of state sovereignty. They patrol the boundaries of the nation. They decide who is allowed in and who is refused entry. This gatekeeping function is a crucial part of the reproduction of sovereign power. Security forces at the airport are on the front line of a national security agenda that convinces the populace of the need to protect "our" territory from outside threats. Because national security is at its most vigilant at the borders of a state, security agents at the airport can often be obstinate and inflexible in their encounters with foreigners—after all, they are only protecting "national interest." What has become very clear in the era of postwar global travel is that the gatekeeping function of the security agent is greatly facilitated by the passport. By conferring citizenship and national identity on individuals, the passport legitimates its holders and allows them the freedom to travel. Although that might sound like an opening to freedom, John Torpey argues that the institutionalization of the passport has actually increased the state's ability to control and survey our movements. As he explains, passports entrench state sovereignty under the guise of increasing our freedom of movement:

> in the course of the past few centuries, states have successfully usurped from rival claimants such as churches and private enterprises the "monopoly of the legitimate means of movement"—that is, their development as states has depended on effectively distinguishing between citizens/subjects and possible interlopers, and regulating the

movements of each. This process of "monopolization". . . has depended
to a considerable extent on the creation of documents that make the
relevant differences knowable and thus enforceable.[17]

In effect, passports materialize state sovereignty at border crossings such
as the airport. What Torpey correctly points out is that the passport is
more an artifact of state surveillance than of freedom. In other words,
the passport is a double-edged sword: it provides the freedom to travel
at the same time that it gives the state the right to track our personal
whereabouts.

If the security guard is the gatekeeper of sovereignty and the passport
the official ticket of entry, then the airport is the gateway. While analyzing the complex relationship between security, nationalism, and global
movement that manifests itself at the airport, Paul Virilio reminds us
that gateways allow flows in *both* directions. Speaking about airports
that were constructed during the height of the cold war in the 1970s,
Virilio explains how these gateways ushered in a new defense system
that had to regulate a contradiction between surveillance and freedom
of movement:

> Since the 70s and the beginnings of the world economic crisis, the
> construction of these airports was further subjected to the imperatives
> of the defense against air pirates. Construction no longer derived simply
> from traditional technical constraint. The plan had become a function
> of the risks of "terrorist contamination" and the disposition of sites
> conceived of as sterile zones for departures and non-sterile zones for
> arrivals. . . . As the last gateway to the state, the airport came to resemble
> the fort, port or railway station of earlier days. As airports were turned
> into theaters of necessary regulation of exchange and communication,
> they also became breeding and testing grounds for high-pressured
> experiments in control and aerial surveillance performed for and by a
> new "air and border control."[18]

For Virilio, the airport symbolizes the wider contradiction between movement and security that the state is currently facing. While sovereign
power makes itself felt through security agents and passports, the pressing question is that, *despite* these measures, the airport remains an
incredibly porous gateway. Understanding questions of security at the
airport through sovereign power fails to take the permeable nature of
this gateway into account. The only question sovereign power can answer is the increase in airport security as a way to counter the increase in

terrorist hijackings that emerged in the 1970s. But when we understand that security is also a form of mediation, the permeability and ambiguity of the airport must be taken into account.

What makes the question of security so pressing is that despite all the technological advances in surveillance and security since the 1970s, airports remain transit areas par excellence. When the terrorists flew out of Logan and Dulles airports on the morning of September 11, 2001, they illustrated to the world just how easy it is to circumvent sophisticated airport security measures. And this is what makes Virilio's argument so relevant in the aftermath of the World Trade Center and Pentagon attacks. His work portrays the difficulties of trying to manage global mobility with outdated concepts and practices of security. His work urges a shift from static, sovereign, and state-bounded power relations to an environment of mediation where power continually flows through "interfaces." What the recent events in the United States indicate is our inability to reimagine security in an era when we all want to guarantee our freedom of movement. The shock and surprise at how "easy" it was for the terrorists to breach security at both Logan and Dulles airports brings us face to face with the impotence of current practices of security. The aftermath of this event revealed the seduction of sovereign power, and the difficulty of reformulating security according to the flows and diversions of mediated power.

National Signification

In travel by foot, car, or boat, crossing borders is an easy process to understand: one travels through a border crossing, or one arrives at the shore of a new country. However, traveling by air means that these traditional border crossings happen in two places: several thousand feet in the air when one enters "national airspace," and when one touches down and proceeds through customs and immigration.[19] Once inside the airport, passengers are confronted with an array of national and cultural symbols. Consider the meanings generated by the national airline: Switzerland is embodied in Swissair's noble Red Cross, Australia is symbolized by the fuzzy, friendly Qantas koala, and Singapore is represented by the sarongs worn by the "exotic" flight attendants on Singapore Airlines. Often the name of the airport recognizes a great national hero, for example, JFK in New York and Charles de Gaulle in Paris. This practice has recently prompted several requests for Heathrow to be re-named as a memorial to the late Princess Diana.[20] But it is the arrival lounges at airports that have the most spectacular displays of national heritage. The use of national symbols to impress visitors is a crucial part of the lucrative tourist industry. For the most part, this involves creating the exotic from the banal and commodifying national idiosyn-crasies to the point of global recognition. For example, the souvenir shops in Heathrow carry Union Jack key chains, royal family postcards, Tower of London pens, nicely packaged tea, and "I Love London" T-shirts. But national symbols also spill out of souvenir shops: Calgary International Airport is full of pictures of the Stampede, cowboy boots, and images of the Wild West, and Dublin airport has an assortment of "Paddy Kitsch" on display. As Pico Iyer explains, national symbols help us to understand airports:

> One reason airports enjoy such central status in our imaginations is that they play such a large part in forming our first (which is sometimes our last) impressions of a place; this is the reason that poor countries often throw all their resources into making their airports sleek, with beauti-fully paved landscaped roads leading out of them into town.[21]

What is interesting about the national heritage at work in arrival lounges of airports is the "official" narratives of nation they encourage. The "first impressions" Iyer talks about are also "official" impressions designed to actively silence the complexities, difficulties, and tensions that characterize all national spaces. The "official" story of national heritage that bombards visitors and passengers in the arrival lounge is based on claims of national homogeneity. The arrival lounge offers the first triumphant shout, "THIS is what we are as a nation!" But under-neath these "official" stories is our knowledge that nations are not only imagined, but always constructed by multiple, heterogeneous, and mo-bile populations.[22]

When these "official" stories are understood as crucial to the security of national homogeneity, they seem irresistible in their simplicity. How-ever, when we understand the active silencing of difference as *itself* a form of mediation, the question of resistance cannot be avoided. Because mediation is about the constant dissemination and reassemblage of power, there is always room for alternative and resistant articulations of power.

Figure 1.1. Bill Reid, *The Spirit of Haida Gwaii.* Jade sculpture at the Vancouver Airport. Photograph by the author, August 16, 2001.

In this case, those alternatives emerge when we uncover the narratives that are drowned out by the official story of national homogeneity. One signification that embodies this tension is Bill Reid's jade sculpture *The Spirit of Haida Gwaii* on display in the newly renovated Vancouver Airport (Figure 1.1).[23] Rather than signifying unity and homogeneity, this sculpture indicates a nation whose population includes a significant percentage of First Nations groups. The centrality of this sculpture in the airport points to the ongoing contestations of statehood, national identity, and cultural heritage that characterize Canada.[24] In effect, the very presence of the sculpture prevents any "official" story of Canada from emerging. This strange monument functions as a political reminder that the presence of First Nations groups in Canada precludes any attempt to secure narratives of national homogeneity. Across the world in Belfast, the story is one of disruptive absence rather than presence. Both Belfast airports (City and International) are significant because of their evacuation of national and cultural markers. In a space torn apart by competing aspirations for statehood, the deliberate absence of national symbols is an effort to promote collective amnesia. There are no references to "the troubles" of the past three decades, and all tourist propaganda promotes Northern Ireland as a peaceful rural idyll rather than a community made famous by its violent sectarian tensions. Ironically, however, many tourists arrive in Belfast with the explicit intention of seeing "the troubles" up close.[25] The deliberate production of banality at both airports testifies to the difficulties Northern Ireland is having trying to reconcile competing national narratives. Both of these examples illustrate how the airport participates in the complex production of national identity. However, despite attempts to produce coherent, smooth, and homogeneous narratives of nation, airports also offer profound disruptions of these stories. The Haida sculpture and the empty Belfast airports are reminders that other narratives, other identities, and other symbols are always present—never more so than in spaces vainly attempting to produce national homogeneity.

The most provocative example of how complex national signification can be, is the recent British Airways (BA) "tail fin scandal." Responding to the fact that more than 60 percent of BA's customers come from overseas, Bob Ayling and the executives at BA decided to redesign the tail fins of the company's fleet to reflect this diversity. Gathering ethnic designs from such places as Africa, Canada, Hong Kong, the Netherlands, and Ireland, BA began the expensive job of repainting all of its airplanes (Figure 1.2).[26] What followed was not only a marketing disaster, but a revealing misjudgment about the power of recognized national symbols. The disaster began when air-traffic controllers had difficulty distinguishing the newly painted airplanes from other lesser-known carriers, which resulted in huge runway delays. In market surveys, customers thought the designs looked like a "relatively cheap" airline. It was soon nicknamed Air Bongoland, the vomit comet, and graffiti with wings. The culmination of the marketing blunder came when, at a Tory party convention, Margaret Thatcher famously covered up a model of one of the tail fins with her handkerchief.[27] With a corporate deal with American Airlines pending, BA was under pressure to turn this "uncoordinated jumble of meaningless primitivism" into an airline that "looked more British." The "cleanup" is currently under way, and BA is spending £60 million repainting the tail fins with a historic Union Jack design used by Admiral Nelson (Figure 1.3).[28] Although business commentators speak of the "tail fin scandal" in terms of BA's failure to understand the power of brand recognition, this incident reveals a great deal more

Figure 1.2. British Airways tail fins. Reprinted with permission of Adrian Meredith Photography.

about the power of national symbols of identity. Whereas Vancouver's Haida sculpture indicates a more open approach to diversity, the BA tail fin scandal gives a more depressing message. The fact that one of the biggest airline companies in the world caved in to the argument that Britain is a homogeneous nation illustrates the ongoing seduction of sovereign power.

Figure 1.3. Nelson's flag. Reprinted with permission of Newscast.

Functionalism

Despite the airport being a "porous gateway," as Virilio suggests, the architectural arrangement of technology and space is governed by the requirements of functionalism. The choreography of arrivals and departures must be timed exactly because the consequences of confusion are too horrific to contemplate. As Rosler explains, this overarching functionalism is embedded in the very architecture of airports:

> As an invitation to theorizing, the airport suggests the meeting point of theories of time and of space, of schedules and of layouts. The airport is

a multi-dimensional, multifunction system whose overriding concerns are operational. To state the obvious, airport design requires a consideration of a set of flow trajectories in vertical space, a dimension normally regarded as more or less stable.[29]

Control, regulation, and surveillance are encoded at the basic material level of the airport as a way to manage large numbers of people efficiently and effectively. The functional imperative of the airport can be seen most obviously in the logic of its layouts, usually explained as the hub-and-spoke layout, or as piglets suckling on their mother. This layout maximizes the use of land (a majority of which will be given over to runways) and gives prominence to the Panopticon-like control tower. Although these basic structures remain, many theorists have argued that airport architecture has changed significantly from the austere modernism of the postwar period to something else altogether.[30] The sleek aerodynamic features of newly built airports encourage the flow of everything— steel, air, glass, people. In effect, these new buildings are the architectural realization of Virilio's gateway. For example, the new Kansai airport built on the island off Osaka, Japan, prides itself on flow and transparency primarily so that passengers can actually see the airplane they are about to board.[31] However, although this new postmodern architecture is an attempt to reorient the position of the subject vis-à-vis the structure, at no point is the rule of functionalism disobeyed. Increased attention to transparency actually aids in practices of control, regulation, and surveillance by airport authorities and security staff. Despite the changes in airport architecture, the overriding objective remains the control of people in transit.

One of the ways we can sense ambiguity in this overriding functionalism is to explore the airport's relationship with the city. Whereas Iyer argues that airports look like small cities, Virilio claims that our increased desire for mobility is completely transforming our understanding of both airports and urban space:

> The airport today has become the new city. At Dallas-Fort Worth they serve thirty million passengers a year. At the end of this century there will be one hundred million. People are no longer citizens, they're passengers in transit. They're in circum navigation. . . . When we know that every day there are over one hundred thousand people in the air, we can consider it a foreshadowing of future society: no longer a society of sedentarization, but one of passage; no longer a nomad society, in the

sense of the great nomadic drifts, but one concentrated in the vector of transportation. . . . the city of the future is not the inertia of immobility, but the dictatorship of movement.[32]

As the airport and the city become intertwined in Virilio's "dictatorship of movement," it is difficult to tell where one space ends and the other begins. What emerges in this zone of indistinction is a voice of resistance to growing urbanization generally, and to the ever-expanding airport specifically. If an airport is successful at regulating the movement of people, one of the inevitable outcomes is that it will seek to expand its capacity for that regulation and increase its profit. The necessity of increasing the size of airports to meet the growing needs of international travelers has been fiercely resisted by local groups opposed to the environmental damage that airports bring. Their concerns include noise pollution, increased traffic (including more motorways), changes to public transport, and endless urban expansion. This resistance has recently emerged in response to the proposed Terminal 5 at Heathrow (to be built on what is currently a sewage plant). The public inquiry about T5 has been ongoing for several years because local residents have organized numerous petitions and protests against the expansion.[33] From the point of view of Heathrow and the British Airports Authority (BAA), which runs Heathrow, the proposed cost of T5 is £2 billion, and it is hoped that the projected 20 million people moving through the terminal each year will alleviate pressure from the other terminals.[34] However, as a result of successful resistance and the long public inquiry, the earliest possible date for construction of T5 is now 2003, which means that the earliest date of completion will be 2007.[35]

Other moments of resistance occur when the expansion of an airport threatens areas of national and historical importance, more specifically, when urban expansion comes face-to-face with efforts to preserve sites of cultural heritage. These protests are particularly interesting because they introduce a contradiction at the heart of the tourism industry: a bigger airport will bring more tourists and tourist dollars, but destroying sites of cultural heritage will destroy the very objects tourists come to see in the first place. For example, the construction of a private airport in Crete has been halted to protect the remains of a Neolithic fort and a fifteenth-century church. Likewise, an airport at Billund in Denmark has been altered to accommodate the remains of Danish king "Amlet," thought to be the character made famous by Shakespeare.[36]

Another interesting example of the complex relations between airports, urban expansion, and environmental protest is Manchester airport. On the one hand, Manchester airport has resisted governance by the BAA and instead developed a consortium of municipal borough councils to run the airport as a local enterprise. As a result, it has been cited as one of the most convenient, cleanest, and efficient airports in Europe.[37] On the other hand, during its recent expansion, the airport was the focus of environmental resistance as the proposed runways required the destruction of surrounding forests. The complex relationships between the airport and the city are the manifestation of an eternal tension between those who wish to modernize (and increase airport capacity and size) and those who wish to arrest technological progress (and restrict airport expansion, and possibly air travel). As Virilio suggests, what remains to be seen is the extent to which the overriding functionalism of the airport encroaches upon and governs our urban space.[38]

The Commercial Imperative

The rule of function at the airport is currently giving way to the forces of commercialism. In other words, the successful regulation of the flow of passengers at the airport is substantially aided if the consumer desires of those people are targeted. For example, passengers awaiting flights can browse through the duty-free shops on their way to the departure gate. By using the functionalism of the airport to its own ends, commercialism transforms individuals into passengers *and* valuable consumers. The increasing force of commercialism performs several functions: it hides the naked functionalism of the airport; it helps to create "docile bodies" willing to be directed through airport space; and, above all, it generates profit. Most of the airports in the United Kingdom are run by the BAA, which is now the world's largest *commercial* operator of airports. As a result of the privatization of the BAA in the 1980s under Thatcher, Heathrow now derives more than half of its revenue from retail, but retail currently takes up only 12 percent of terminal space.[39] The BAA pursues the commercial imperative with advertisements such as "Everything you needed and quite a few things you didn't even know you needed are now available." From an economic perspective, this arrangement is mutually beneficial. Airports derive much-needed revenue by renting out retail space, and retailers capitalize on the large amount of time people spend waiting in these spaces.

Along with the traditional duty-free shops, airports are host to four main retail concentrations: luxury goods (chocolates, diamonds), travel goods (personal hygiene, sunglasses, convenience foods, magazines), refreshments (cafés, bars, restaurants), and traditional products (these are the souvenir shops). As Jennifer Rowley and Frances Slack explain, departure lounges in airports are considered "low load servicescapes" that are designed to target the international clientele who "are suffering dislocation in place and time." Not only are retailers guaranteed a constant number of potential customers, but the "dislocation" of these shoppers means that they do not need much convincing to purchase items.[40] Rowley and Slack argue that customers (most commonly "lone male shoppers") are likely to feel under pressure to make a purchase when traveling through an airport. These purchases are impulsive and often triggered by browsing. Price is less of an issue than in the usual retail experience, and international brands take on a special significance in the context of the airport. Very simply, this is an ideal site for commercialism to flourish—regular customers with time and money to spend.

In an interesting reaction to the encroaching commercial imperative at airports, Sir Terence Conran (inventor of the Habitat furniture chain) argues that Heathrow is an "appalling orgy of consumerism":

> An air terminal should be an air terminal—a pleasant, efficient, relaxed place for boarding passengers on to planes with a minimum of fuss. I cringe at the thought that the last impression many people take home with them when leaving the UK is of a cluttered, frenzied, shopping mall, a bargain-basement bazaar from which there is no escape. . . . I am not against airport shopping per-se; it is just the scale of the BAA's operation that appalls me.[41]

Conran is disgusted because there is no escape from the commercial imperative. Shopping is no longer confined to the High Street and suburban malls, but confronts us in *every* part of our lives. As scholars in cultural studies have argued, we know that the overwhelming power of consumerism is radically changing the way we ascribe meaning to our everyday lives.[42] The growing commercial imperative at the airport only adds to this confusion. Every possible site at the airport has been given over to enticing our consumer desires—billboards on the approaching motorway, advertisements on moving walkways, and slogans on the brakes of luggage trolleys. As the BAA understands, it is the combination of functional *and* commercial imperatives that makes airports like

Heathrow lucrative. In the end, the elision between shopping malls and airports is not just architectural. Both are important sites in the circuit of consumer culture. Airports are simply one more place we can entrench our growing consumer desires, which makes Conran's lament seem ludicrous. Consumerism is no longer segregated because we now live in a twenty-four-hour consumer society. Surely this would come as delightful news for the owner of one of the most successful furniture shops in the United Kingdom? Perhaps he is just cross that Heathrow passengers are unable to purchase duty-free sofas and coffee tables to take with them on their journeys.

Subjectivity

What is politically interesting about these four arrangements of power is their effect on subjectivity. One could argue that all these different mediations of power produce passive subjects who must be continually categorized and accounted for (through customs, with tickets and seat numbers, over public announcements). But this approach fails to get at the multiple ways in which subjectivity is constructed at the airport. When airports are understood as transit areas characterized primarily by movement, static conceptions of identity do not offer any political insight. The most important aspect of mediated power at the airport is that it does not produce stable, fixed, and absolute subjects. Rather, mediated power offers us multiple and shifting subject positions. As Iyer explains:

> everywhere I went in the airport I felt myself in an odd kind of twilight zone of consciousness, that weightless limbo of a world in which people are between lives and between selves, almost sleepwalking, not really sure of who or where they are. . . . People are at the far edge of themselves in airports, ready to break down or through. You see strangers pouring out their life stories with other strangers here, or making new life stories with other strangers. Everything is at once intensified and slightly unreal.[43]

Mediated power at the airport defeats any notion of a stable autonomous identity and produces subjects that exist "at the far edge of themselves." The airport cuts through all of our usual guarantors of identity and unhinges the self from its usual spatiotemporal moorings.

The indeterminate status of the subject at the airport produces opposing effects: a desire to announce one's identity by embracing national stereotypes, and the contrasting desire for anonymity. If ever there was a site where national stereotypes are on display, it is at the airport. It is as if we need obvious national and cultural markers to convince us who we are and where we come from. At the airport, it is commonplace to identify Canadians by the maple leaf flag sewn on their heavy-duty rucksacks, Asians because they have the largest suitcases, Americans by their bright white tennis shoes, and Brits returning from the Mediterranean because they all have sunburns.[44] Although national stereotypes can have humorous connotations, we must always remember that they are not divorced from the decisions of who gets stopped at customs and immigration. But mediated power also has a countereffect on subjects who desire anonymity rather than the comfort of national markers. The most symbolic creature in this respect is the elite global business traveler who lives on planes, in boardrooms, and in airport lounges—the traveler par excellence. These travelers usually own a copy of the recently published guidebook on how to live while between planes in Chicago's O'Hare airport, and some have special permission to carry two passports of the same nationality as they get filled up so quickly.[45] Collecting an impressive amount of frequent-flyer points, these subjects pose interesting questions about belonging and loyalty in a universe more geared to corporate than to sovereign power. But the most telling indicator of anonymity rests with air-traffic controllers. These subjects are "able to handle their jobs only through de-realization: if they thought of the radar blips as *planes* with *people* in them . . . they would not be able to last a single day."[46]

Never comfortable with indeterminate subjectivity, the United States reacted to the breakdown of stable identities at the airport by introducing the system of "passenger profiling" in 1997. Initially introduced to increase security by matching passengers with their luggage, the profiling system prevented any unaccompanied bags from being loaded onto aircraft. This way, any dangerous device could be attached to a specific passenger who would then be held responsible. But recently, the profiling system has developed to the point where passengers themselves are matched with certain "profiles" of known terrorists. With this system, "secret algorithms" are used to "match personal data to profiles of likely terrorists."[47] This has reintroduced debates between proponents of privacy and civil liberties (such as the American Civil Liberties Union) and those favoring increased security at airports. Although these debates emerged after the TWA 800 crash in 1996, it is not difficult to see that they are framing questions of airport security after the World Trade Center and Pentagon attacks. What is of political concern is the way the profiling system continues to unfairly single out certain national, ethnic, gender, and racial groupings. This has certainly been the case with Americans of Arab descent—so much so that recurring incidents of racism at the airport have developed into what commentators call "Arabophobia."[48] The Arab American Anti-Discrimination Committee believes that the profiling system will

> unfairly single out people who appear to be of Arab descent and recent Middle East immigrants. . . . It is based on looks, accent, dress, national origin. When we go to the airport we want to check our luggage not our civil rights.[49]

These examples of "Arabophobia" are the reason the Web site for the Arab American Anti-Discrimination Committee has a computerized complaint form for passengers to fill in when they have been harassed at an airport.[50] According to some Arab Americans, "This is out-and-out discrimination, which is rooted in the stereotype that all Arabs are terrorists."[51] Unfortunately, with the finger-pointing at Islamic groups for the terrorist attacks on America, the civil rights of many Arab Americans will be ignored as the pressure increases to prosecute the terrorists. What is more, any debate about the violation of civil rights will be silenced by the overwhelming discourses of American nationalism, revenge, and justice.

Rosler argues that the rule of technological functionalism—exemplified by passenger profiling—is pursued at the expense of the subject: "technical efficiency . . . is venerated by the airport and has resulted in structures whose experiencing subjects are atomized."[52] For Rosler, atomization is a political concern because it results in "human docility, homogeneity, replicability, transitoriness."[53] The consequence of this functional atomization is that people are effectively prevented from treating the airport as a private space (like a home) or a public space (like a square or a park). As more people spend more time in airports, the demand for private space grows. This has led to the development of the Ziosk: "private spaces within public places." For a small fee, families and groups can now hang around in comfort in cocoon-like booths equipped with comfortable couches, telephones, and color televisions. They are available for hire by the hour, but are currently only available in certain

American airports.[54] The question of public space at the airport is more difficult. Airport authorities are concerned with directing people *through* a system rather than allowing people to adopt the kind of behavior pursued in spaces geared to leisure activities. This tension is what the BBC documentary *Airport* explores every week at Heathrow.[55] Cameras follow several Heathrow staff as they try to control the constant flow of bored and irritated passengers. They stop impromptu choral performances, they break up unruly Manchester United fans, and they quickly usher incompetent passengers onto their delayed airplanes. This fly-on-the-wall documentary is part of a discourse that convinces subjects that spontaneous "public space" behavior is inappropriate for the functional space of the airport.

But the *Airport* documentary also offers an important destabilization of subjectivity. Rather than being watched by the surveillance cameras at the airport, we are now in the privileged position of the voyeur. We watch the fascinating interactions between staff and passengers at Heathrow on television. Our voyeurism is further encouraged through the Heathrow Visitor Center, which organizes guided tours of the airport.[56] And, as we become voyeurs, the airport becomes a coveted media and tourist attraction in itself—a Disneyland for travelers. Rosler's claim that the airport creates atomized individuals is persuasive, but it fails to take into account the possibility of multiple and resistant subject positions. More important, focusing on atomization neglects the ways in which our identities are constantly transforming in a site of such intense mediation. As power moves through the circuit of mediation, our subject positions are also in transit. Atomization is only one possibility for subjects in a transit area. As the *Airport* documentary reveals, we just as easily resist that atomization when we do not play by the rules.

Conclusions

One of the consequences of the postmodern architecture is that airports all over the world are starting to resemble one another. The focus on transparency in these buildings is what alerts us to different relationships of power. In other words, transparency is the hallmark of mediated power. The practices of surveillance maintained by sovereign power now operate in conjunction with other measures that push the destabilizing effects of mobility. We have seen how narratives of security, national signification, functionalism, commercialism, and subjectivity include efforts to make the airport a more controlled, regulated, and disciplined space. However, when understood through a framework of sovereign power, the only relevant relationship here is one of discipline and resistance. That is to say, power is only ever enacted over subjects who can either acquiesce or resist. By shifting the framework to mediated power, a whole series of power relationships becomes possible. Within this framework, the scope for politicizing the airport becomes much greater: this is a site overflowing with multiple and shifting power relations that exceed the grasp of sovereignty.

Mediated power allows us to explore much more than state intervention and surveillance at the airport. It allows us to locate different hegemonic formations of power (commercialization, for example) and trace how these formations continually move through a circuit of mediation. Thus, the most important aspect of mediated power is that it allows us to see the clever ways in which power changes and adapts to its surroundings. What we discover is that in every space of the airport, power is exercised in increasingly complex, quick, and mobile ways. It is not just a force for coercion, nor is it a force for freedom. To go back to Foucault, power is nothing but its practices and effects, in this case the practices and effects of mediation. Augé's claim that airports are banal and empty makes some sense in terms of postmodern architecture, but it makes no sense in terms of politics. Power does not just disappear when space is altered through transparency. Rather, power is articulated in the way it adapts to these changes. For this reason, it is necessary to look underneath the banal facade of the airport and pay careful attention to the ways in which power is increasingly mediated. The airport is not banal or empty. It is one of the most important sites where we can witness the continual transformation from sovereign power to mediated power, and thus from international relations to world politics.

Notes

This essay originated in April 1998 at a workshop titled "Territory and Identity" at the University of Newcastle. Thanks to Martin Coward, Rob Walker, Tarak Barkawi, and Hackan Seckinelgin for pushing the argument beyond that initial stage. I would also like to thank Michael Dillon for generous, extensive, and helpful comments on an earlier draft presented at the International Studies Associaton conference in Chicago, February 2001. His comments encouraged me to look beyond the simple formulations of power I was originally working with. The final draft was completed in the week of the terrorist attacks on the World Trade Center and the Pentagon on September 11, 2001. It remains to be seen what the wider implications of this event will be for international relations, but it is clear that airport security will be transformed. With that in mind, any comments on the event in this essay are necessarily speculative.

1. Pico Iyer, "Where Worlds Collide," *Harper's Magazine*, August 1995, p. 52.

2. This formulation marks the beginning of a larger debate I am pursuing between those who use a post-Gramscian conception of hegemony to theorize power (e.g., Laclau, Mouffe, Foucault) and those who place power directly on the terrain of mobility (e.g., Deleuze, Virilio, Baudrillard). What concerns me specifically is how all these thinkers understand power as a complex and mobile formation. Although it is tempting to create a distinction between these two approaches, it strikes me that both manage to hold on to a productive tension between *(a)* reimagining a politics of resistance and *(b)* understanding how contemporary formulations of power operate by constant dissemination and redissemination.

3. Michel Foucault, "The Subject and Power," in Hubert L. Dreyfus and Paul Rabinow, eds., *Michel Foucault: Beyond Structuralism and Hermeneutics* (Brighton: Harvester Press, 1982), pp. 216–17.

4. Martha Rosler, "In the Place of the Public: Observations of a Traveller," in Ole Bouman and Roemer Van Toorn, eds., *The Invisible Architecture* (London: Academy Editions, 1994), p. 431.

5. Iyer, "Where Worlds Collide," p. 51.

6. Ibid., p. 54. Not only does Iyer point out the inequalities of the airport service industry, he is also careful to narrate the stories of those passengers from the third world as they arrive at LAX, bewildered to see that the faces they encounter in the airport are more like those they left behind rather than the airbrushed movie stars they are expecting.

7. Marc Augé, *Non-Places: Introduction to an Anthropology of Supermodernity* (London: Verso, 1995).

8. For further critiques of Augé's argument, see Grant Boswell, "Non-Places and the Enfeeblement of Rhetoric in Supermodernity," *Enculturation* 1.1 (spring 1997); Samuel Collins, "Head Out on the Highway—Anthropological Encounters with the Supermodern," *Postmodern Culture* 7.1 (1996); and D. X. Raiden, "Soft-Where Specifics of Site," *New Age*, issue 10 (winter 2000).

9. Nevzat Soguk and Geoffrey Whitehall, "Wandering Grounds: Transversality, Territoriality, Identity and Movement," *Millennium: Journal of International Affairs* 28.3 (1999): 677.

10. Ibid., p. 678.

11. Ibid., pp. 675–81. For more newspaper articles on Merhan's story, see Elizabeth Neuffer, "A Man without a Country," *Boston Globe*, December 25, 1997; Adam Sage, "Kafkaesque Exile Cleared for Take-off," *The Times*, July 13, 1999; Susannah Herbert, "Fear of Flying," *Sunday Times*, lifestyle section, July 18, 1999; and Suzanne Daley, "11 Years Caged in an Airport; Now He Fears to Fly," *New York Times*, September 27, 1999.

12. Soguk and Whitehall, "Wandering Grounds," p. 677.

13. Ibid., p. 680.

14. David Cornett and Martin Whitfield, "Heathrow Bombing: IRA Exposes Airport's Vulnerability," *Independent*, March 11, 1994, p. 2.

15. Simon Calder, "Airport 94: Nigeria," Weekend Travel Section, *The Independent*, June 11, 1994, p. 35.

16. For early analyses of how airport security is likely to change as a result of the terrorist attacks, see Roger Bray, "Why Your Journey Will Take Longer," *The Guardian*, travel section, September 15, 2001, and Joanne O'Connor and Joanna Walters, "Flying into an Uncertain Future," *The Observer*, Escape section, September 16, 2001.

17. John Torpey, *The Invention of the Passport: Surveillance, Citizenship and the State* (Cambridge: Cambridge University Press, 2000), pp. 1–2.

18. Paul Virilio, "The Overexposed City," in Paul Virilio, *The Lost Dimension* (New York: Semiotext[e], 1991), p. 10.

19. For a discussion on the relationship between sovereignty and airspace, see Malcolm Anderson, *Frontiers: Territory and State Formation in the Modern World* (Cambridge: Polity Press, 1996), pp. 163–65.

20. Louise Jury, "Call for Heathrow Airport to be Named after Diana," *Independent*, September 9, 1997, p. 3.

21. Iyer, "Where Worlds Collide," p. 54.

22. Two of the most important texts in this respect are Benedict Anderson, *Imagined Communities: Reflections on the Origin and Spread of Nationalism* (London: Verso, 1983), and Homi K. Bhabha, ed., *Nation and Narration* (London: Routledge, 1990).

23. For more information on this sculpture, see www.canadianembassy.org/embassy/haida.html.

24. James Tully uses Bill Reid's sculpture to begin his argument about multiculturalism in Canada in *Strange Multiplicity* (Cambridge: Cambridge University Press, 1995).

25. See Debbie Lisle, "Consuming Danger: Re-Imagining the War/Tourism Divide," *Alternatives* 25.1 (January–March 2000): 107.

26. Copyright permission granted by Adrian Meredith Photography, August 2001. The author would like to thank Queens University Belfast for assistance in securing copyright permission of this image.

27. Simon Jenkins, "Tailfins in a Spin," *The Times*, September 25, 1998, p. 28; Stephen Bayley, "The British Flag: Not Waving but Drowning," *Independent*, June 8, 1999, p. 11. See also John Wilcock, "People and Business: More Bad News on BA Tailfins," *Independent*, February 10, 1999, p. 21; Jonathan Leake and David Parsley, "Tailfin Art: On the Way Out," *Sunday Times*, July 12, 1998, News, p. 1; and "British Airways £60,000,000 Paint Job" at www.aviation-uk.com/graffiti.htm.

28. Copyright permission granted by British Airways Press Office, September 2001.

29. Rosler, "In the Place of the Public," p. 431. Another artistic approach to the airport is *Jet Lag*, a multimedia art project by Diller + Scofidio and The Builders Association; see www.thebuildersassociation.org/index.html. See also *ArtCrash*, Journal 3 (October 1998): 6, also available at www.artcrash.dk/content/journal/journal3/page6/jour3p6.html.

30. See Christopher Blow, *Airport Terminals* (Oxford: Butterworth, 1991); and Brian Edwards, *The Modern Terminal: New Approaches to Airport Architecture* (London: E.&F.N.Spon, 1998).

31. Peter Buchanen, "Going with the Flow," *The Independent on Sunday*, The Sunday Review, September 4, 1994, p. 18.

32. Paul Virilio and Sylvère Lotringer, *Pure War* (New York: Semiotext[e], 1997), pp. 6, 43, 64–65; Virilio gives a historical reading of this "dictatorship of movement" in *Speed and Politics*, trans. Polizzotti (New York: Semiotext[e], 1986), pp. 29–30; see also Edward Soja's comments on LAX and its relationship to an "outer-city" on the Pacific slope of L.A., in "Postmodern Geographies: Taking Los Angeles Apart," in Roger Friedland and Dierdre Boden, eds., *Now Here: Space, Time and Modernity* (Berkeley: University of California Press, 1994), pp. 127–62.

33. See Philip Sherwood, *Heathrow: 2000 Years of History* (Gloucestershire: Sutton Publishing, 1999), p. 125. One of the most vocal groups protesting T5 is HACAN (Heathrow Association for Control of Aircraft Noise). See www.hacan.org.uk.

34. For British Airway's point of view on the T5 controversy, see www.britishairways.com/tfive/.

35. Sherwood, *Heathrow*, pp. 113–26.

36. John Carr, "Greeks Battle over Neolithic Fort at Site of New Airport," *The Times*, February 12, 1997, p. 14; Harvey Elliot and Glyn Genin, "Hamlet's Tomb Foils Airport Expansion," *The Times*, December 5, 1996, p. 34.

37. See Simon Calder, "Manchester: Gateway to the World," *Independent*, March 28, 1996, pp. 1–3.

38. For more on this argument, see Virilio, "The Overexposed City."

39. See http://www.baa.co.uk/main/corporate/about_baa_frame.html.

40. Jennifer Rowley and Frances Slack, "The Retail Experience in Airport Departure Lounges: Reaching for Timelessness and Placelessness," *International Marketing Review* 16.4/5 (1999): 363–75.

41. Terence Conran, "What Is an Airport For?" *Independent*, August 17, 1996, p. 13.

42. See Mike Featherstone, *Consumer Culture and Postmodernism* (London: Sage, 1990); Celia Lury, *Consumer Culture* (Cambridge: Polity Press, 1996); and Don Slater, *Consumer Culture and Modernity* (Cambridge: Polity Press, 1996).

43. Iyer, "Where Worlds Collide," p. 53.

44. For more examples of national stereotypes and their traveling habits, see Benetton Magazine, *Colours*, vol. 11 (June–August 1995): 14–19.

45. Pico Iyer, "The New Business Class," *New York Times Magazine*, March 8, 1998, p. 39.

46. Rosler, "In the Place of the Public," p. 429.

47. Declan McCullagh, "You? A Terrorist? Yes!" *Wired News*, April 20, 1999, p. 1, available at www.wirednews.com/news/politics/0,1283,19218,00.html.

48. Brian Whitaker, "Arabophobia in the Air," *Guardian*, December 15, 2000.

49. Nihad Awad, executive director of the Council on American-Islamic Relations, quoted in www.avweb.com/newswire/news9638.html.

50. See www.adc.org/legal/fbifrm.html.

51. Cindy Rodriguez, "Arabs Say Airport Checks Single Them Out," *Boston Globe*, September 2, 2000.

52. Rosler, "In the Place of the Public," p. 431.

53. Ibid., p. 434.

54. Anonymous, "Real Life: The Airport Rent-a-Refuge (Credit Cards Only)," *Independent on Sunday*, March 19, 1995, p. 22.

55. See www.bbc.co.uk/airport.

56. See www.baa.co.uk/main/airports/heathrow/about_heathrow_frame.html.

CHAPTER TWO

Spatializing International Activism

Genetically Modified Foods on the Internet

Jayne Rodgers

These days it seems like activism has become truly international. We see it in antiglobalization protests from Seattle to Genoa, in antimissile protests in Yorkshire, and in the internationalization of food safety concerns such as the genetically modified foods (GMO) issue.[1] Some forms of contemporary political protest can still be explained with reference to traditional models of politics and political communication that are based on largely territorial assumptions. Others, most notably Internet-led protests, challenge—if not defy completely—traditional spatial assumptions. These forms of protest raise a key question that will be explored in this essay: how do Internet mediations pluralize classical models of political communication and, in so doing, redefine the meanings of both political protest and political activism?

As the Introduction to this volume has shown, the study of international politics has been subject to highly proscriptive interpretations of its metaphoric boundaries. These boundaries apply not only to conceptualizations of what political participation actually is but also to the places where politics is assumed to happen. The Internet does not necessarily bring "new" actors into the political arena, though it can build upon existing networks. Nor can we assume that connections made between activists constitute "new" forms of political practice, though it is incumbent upon us to investigate any changes wrought by access to the technology. What the Internet undoubtedly does, by simplifying the process of transmitting and exchanging information, is internationalize the connections between activists to such a degree that their relevance to analysis of political communication can no longer be ignored.

This essay focuses on the GMO issue as a test case, as this case provides insights into the use of the Internet as a tool for lobbyists. It also provides us with some clear evidence on Internet practices that can be used to help us to develop appropriate analytical tools. As will be shown, there is now a vast range of actors and practices that can, through the use of the Internet, be understood to be engaged in international politics. As a consequence, definitions of what constitutes "international politics," and who it involves, require broader definition and more flexible interpretative frameworks. The intellectual divisibility of "the cultural" from "the political" becomes untenable where, as in the case study examined here, consumers use communications technologies to influence governments, multinational corporations, the mass media, and other consumers. The boundaries are, as it were, quite clearly blurred.

The essay is divided into three sections, each addressing different aspects of the Internet activism debate. The first section looks briefly at some of the dilemmas involved in analyzing Internet use in the political arena. The second section examines the ways some nongovernmental organizations (NGOs) and other political activists are using the Internet in relation to the GMO issue.[2] After examining how the Internet is being used in this context, the third section proposes theoretical approaches drawn from the work of Henri Lefebvre that may help us to engage more effectively with changing practices that the Internet may engender (or indeed to identify if the underlying patterns of political interaction remain intact).

Theoretical Dilemmas

In all research into the effects of the Internet, the multilayering of social and political processes presents problems. In particular, the difficulties of applying existing theoretical approaches to multidimensional, relational practices is evident. In analyzing the use of the Internet as a political tool in the case of GMOs, a wide range of actors and overlapping institutions come into play.[3] These include the individual as both political actor and consumer, nongovernmental organizations, less formal social movements, governments, agricultural professionals, food production companies, and international organizations. None of our existing approaches to the analysis of international politics can accommodate all of these actors and the complex and multifaceted dynamics of their interrelations.

The main difficulty in analyzing the Internet and its effects lies in the dramatic pace of change and the increasing overlaps not only between social and political spheres, but also between real and virtual worlds. At this juncture, where these real and virtual worlds meet, where broad- and narrow-casting can reach the same audience, and where traditional patterns of political communication are fractured, the mediating role of the Internet becomes apparent. The complexities of this "techno-social restructuring" mean, however, that a great deal of frustration can be experienced in attempting to apply conventional theories to understanding of the social relations of cyberspace, not least because attempts to apply extant approaches *as they have previously been applied* generally prove fruitless.[4] It seems incumbent upon scholars, therefore, to completely revise ontologies of political power and process and to develop new mechanisms for analyzing the forms of social and political change wrought by the Internet. All these "problems" and "dilemmas" make research into the Internet appear to be something of a Sisyphean labor. This need not necessarily be the case, of course, and this area of research is providing some of the most stimulating debates in recent years in international relations and most other disciplines.

When addressing Internet use, it is evident that the complex interweaving of its technological capabilities with social and political structures forces us to reexamine many of the core assumptions that underpin academic disciplines. Since the introduction of the Internet, scholars have been arguing that it challenges material and metaphoric boundaries. It disrupts, too, our constructions of the social and the political, and creates new forms of economic inequalities, leading us to question many of the basic assumptions that form the foundations of our analytical approaches.[5] Consequently, a technology such as the Internet creates a form of "ontological insecurity" that, despite seemingly negative connotations, is actually a rather valuable asset. This concept allows us to reassess the strengths and weaknesses of different approaches and helps us to identify what we take for granted and what remains valid, and provides starting points from which to move forward. Effectively, this insecurity provides us with an "ontological awareness" of the disciplinary assumptions that impose constraints on research.[6]

In assessing the use of information and communications technologies (ICTs) in political activism, the discursive centrality of the state in international relations (IR) is problematic. This is mainly because both the definitions of politics and the assumptions about the manner in which politics can be conducted have different manifestations in the socio-political sphere of online activism than they do in the more institutionally oriented world of IR. Although there has been much discussion in recent years of the ways politics is spatialized in the discourse of IR, very little attention has been paid to the role of nonelite individuals as political actors in their own right.[7] This is where a development of links between IR theories and contemporary political practices becomes necessary, as it is evident that Internet technology is being used as an international networking tool for activists. For example, the Internet is widely acknowledged as the key communicative tool for the large-scale anti-capitalist protests that took place in Davos and Genoa in 2001. These forms of activism, which obviously affect "official" political actors but which also may have their origins in less formal political networks, require some form of analytical framework that can accommodate the overlapping dimensions of such protests.

Unfortunately, theoretical approaches that *appear* to be useful frequently have the disadvantage of respatializing the field of analysis as restrictively as the state-centric approach. One current favorite, the global civil society approach, promotes individuals, NGOs, and less formal collectives as political agents, and is having a demonstrable impact on the ways politics is now being understood in IR. The interpretations of politics in the global civil society approach challenge, albeit often implicitly, the concept of the state as central to political practice, and acknowledge the significance of nonterritorial forms of political association more fully than the dominant discourse of IR does. However, as R. B. J. Walker has argued, the concept of civil society provides another "spatial container" that can be viewed as comparable to state-centric norms in its discursive closure;[8] that is, this approach substitutes one vision of politics for another. In this sense, the concept of global civil society, while taking analysis in IR an important step away from state centrism, effectively posits another, potentially equally limiting, version of politics. Thus, although this approach addresses some of the problems associated with the diffusion of contemporary political practices, it ontologically privileges nonstate actors as key to analysis, replicating the myopia of state centrism.

As politics becomes an increasingly multilayered enterprise, theoretical approaches from other disciplines may have something to offer. New social movement (NSM) theories, for example, have much to say on evolving sociopolitical practices and the mobilization of social networks.[9] NSM theories can be used to identify some of the ways in which Internet technologies may be applied to the formation and consolidation of activist groups, and could therefore provide a mechanism for analyzing this aspect of the GMO issue. NSM theories will not show, though, how more "formal" NGO networks interact with NSMs, and can tell us virtually nothing about how governments and multinational corporations (MNCs) relate either to nonstate activists or to each other.[10] NSM approaches *do* have much to offer to Internet analysis, particularly in establishing parallels between social and electronic networks. The example of NSMs is used here simply to highlight the problems of finding a single theoretical approach that can be applied to Internet research. It would be useful at this point, therefore, to describe some of the ways the Internet has been used by political activists prior to attempting to identify a theoretical approach with sufficient flexibility to address the local–global, public–private, individual–institutional continuums that Internet use operates along.

GMOs and the Internet

Genetic modification involves the transfer of traits between genes in plants and seeds, a technological development that has produced a furious, and extremely polarized, debate. The biotechnology companies that develop and produce GMOs claim that they will help to maximize productivity and increase yields. Seeds and crops will also have greater resistance to some common pests, resulting in savings on insecticide costs. Widespread use of GMOs should, for the biotech companies, also improve the supply of livestock feeds, which will have a knock-on effect for the whole of the food supply chain. Overall, the issues of cost efficiency and increased productivity are central to the case for GMOs as promoted by commercial producers.

Those lobbying against genetic modification argue that there has been insufficient testing of genetically modified crops, that there is a danger of damage to other species through cross-pollination, and that increased resistance to herbicides will actually result in *more* pesticide residues entering water supplies. There is also a fear of the power of multinational companies to control global food supplies and, linked to this, the fear of reduced consumer choice. These fears represent one dimension of broader concerns about the spread of global capitalism and the lack of accountability of MNCs. At the heart of the anti-GMO case is the claim that genetically modified crops are not "natural" and that their introduction into the food chain will result in irreversible, as yet unquantifiable, damage. As one commentator put it, "society—at least European society—is beginning to view genetic science as a market-impelled juggernaut out of control and wearing moral blinders."[11]

GMOs only really became a major political issue with the import of modified soya beans to Europe in the late 1990s, following the decision by U.S. providers to stop separating such crops from those grown using more conventional methods. Prior to this, genetically modified crops had been grown in the United States and elsewhere for almost a decade with little comment from the food-buying public. It has been argued that the apparent lack of interest on the part of U.S. consumers can be attributed to the Food and Drug Administration's 1992 policy, which deemed that such foods were "substantially similar" to other foodstuffs and should not therefore be subject to special legislation or more rigorous labeling.[12] The implications of this decision for the *global* food market are obvious. The United States is a strong supporter of its biotech industries and does not consider labeling of such foods a "material fact" for consumers.[13]

This has had a serious knock-on effect for the global distribution of U.S.-grown foodstuffs; as different legislative systems set different standards, clashes between U.S. biotech companies and overseas regulators were inevitable. The United States has dealt adroitly with these confrontations by treating them as *trading* disputes rather than as food safety or environmental issues, and by using the World Trade Organization (WTO) as a settlement mechanism. The combined strength of the United States and its biotech companies has, however, been subject to some dramatic challenges from what was apparently viewed as an unlikely source—the consumer.

Given the timing of the debate and the extremes of opinion, the Internet was the obvious place for the debate to be played out. There are thousands of Web sites addressing these issues, with some of the most interesting being posted by three of the key groups of actors involved in the debate—biotech companies, "formal" lobbyists, and "nonformal" activists. It is interesting to note that states are most emphatically *not* the key players in this debate (though the role of the United States in supporting biotech companies is significant).[14] By and large, the debate is being played out between corporations and consumers, with most governments vacillating between seeking national economic advantage and avoiding controversy at home and abroad.

The GMO debate can be seen as the first real test of the power of the Internet as a tool for political lobbying. The Internet can transmit vast amounts of information, is available as a means of monological, dialogical, and multilogical communication, and is available to actors at any point on the political spectrum.[15] It has the advantage of being (usually) extremely rapid and of being a difficult medium to censor. The Internet is thus potentially as useful to the individual consumer as it can be to a multinational corporation, at least in terms of the information that can be accessed and distributed online.

If we accept that the introduction of Internet technologies produces material change and that globalizing tendencies inevitably affect the power dynamics of politics, it is reasonable to argue that opportunities for political action adjust accordingly. However glib and facile the term *globalization* sometimes seems, the (albeit uneven) spread of communications technologies clearly reflects the concepts of increased connectedness that underpin almost all definitions of the term. This is not to suggest that access to the Internet *induces* political change, but simply that the mechanisms for debate and dissent may be extended with its availability, as the potential for communication with other actors on the global stage increases.

The Internet's role as a facilitator for political communication is becoming increasingly obvious. Political activism can be understood to emanate from two key sources: existing networks and "moral shocks."[16] Existing networks come into play where people become involved in political activity through family, friends, and other social groups. "Moral shocks," such as the Chernobyl disaster or localized pollution scares, have the effect of raising awareness of a social or political issue, and generally result in significant rises in NGO membership and direct political action.[17] In relation to both of these sources, the Internet appears to have a role in extending activist networks, first as a means of diffusing information more rapidly, and, second, as a means of publicizing details of "morally shocking" issues as widely as possible. There are some as yet untested areas in this debate, most notably assessment of the role of the Internet in "creating" new political communities.[18] To a significant degree, however, the GMO issue provides evidence that an extension of already-existing communities is in progress.

The Internet is used in a variety of different ways, according to the ways information providers situate this issue. For example, much of the material posted by the biotech companies involved in production and development of seeds, crops, and pesticides both promotes a "healthy" image of genetically modified foods and tends to use terms such as "enhanced flavor," "plentiful supply," and "improved nutrition." In essence, the biotech companies use the Internet as an information board that frames their activities as socially responsible and is designed to contribute to sustainable agricultural development. One company, AgrEvo, suggests that genetic engineering can be regarded as a form of accelerated evolution, which supersedes some of the rather lengthy processes plants go through naturally.[19] Most of these sites provide e-mail lists for company updates, and Monsanto, one of the largest biotech companies, provides a "send comments" facility. On the whole, however, these sites are monological and are used purely as an informational tool, applying the patterns of sender–receiver practices employed by broadcast media.

In contrast, both "formal" and "informal" lobbyists make much greater use of the interactive potential of the Internet. Some of the lobbyists are major international NGOs, such as Greenpeace and Friends of the Earth, high-profile organizations with well-structured campaigns. Information available on these sites tends to offer a "scientific" explanation about the risks associated with genetic modification, alongside fairly emotive discussions about environmental and food hazards. The standard terms applied on these sites include *scandal, danger, concern,* and so on. The terms vary between organizations, of course, with some more measured than others. On the whole, however, there is a tendency to emphasize that risk requires action. To this end, the major NGOs that address this issue provide a wide range of targeted links to politicians, governments, and international institutions. In this respect, the electronic petition has come into its own, as these organizations focus their activity on achieving change through existing hierarchical political structures. Electronic letters to presidents, prime ministers, and parliaments are common on these sites, as well as e-petitions to biotech companies and international policy-making bodies such as the World Trade Organization.

Although some smaller activist groups use these same techniques on a smaller scale, many others operate on a much less formal basis and appear to use the Internet to promote political action at the grassroots level.[20] The Internet thus becomes both a public forum where ideas and information are exchanged, and a technology applied specifically to facilitating direct-action campaigns. The most successful example of this is the UK-originated GenetiX snowball movement, which has effectively established the groundrules for anti-GMO activism.[21] The GenetiX sites provide an activists' handbook that details how to establish a diffused activist network and includes information on how to conduct and publicize actions such as supermarket "decontamination" (that is, removing genetically modified foodstuffs with maximum impact) and the destruction of genetically modified crops.

Between these formal and informal organizations, their use of the Internet has prompted direct action in countries such as Argentina, China, India, Italy, Brazil, Mexico, Korea, Austria, the United States, and the United Kingdom.[22] The various forms these actions have taken, including crop burning, the dumping of genetically modified crops at U.S. embassies, and the mass protest at the WTO meetings in Seattle in November 1999, have, in turn, prompted coverage by the mass media. This highlights the interplay between different media, a feature of Internet use that is often overlooked in media analysis. The relationship between the old media of broadcasting and the new media of the Internet signals a point of mediation between the "real world" of reporting and the "virtual world" of information used by activists, another dimension of political practice that has yet to be fully comprehended.

It is evident that the Internet, as both the newer and more information-intensive media, has the potential to extend existing networks and to be used to effectively "create" moral shocks; that is, although many people are not connected to existing activist networks (one of the preconditions for political activism), they may be prompted to engage in debate by the shock factor (the other precondition) of mass media coverage. Note that the mass media generally provide very little opportunity for political debate, as the technology mitigates against interactivity, and press and programming conventions allow little room for nonelite political opinion. The links between the Internet and the mass media are something that at present political activists seem to be employing much more effectively than the larger, wealthier, seemingly more "powerful" multinational biotech companies.

There is a possibility that the novelty of Internet use means that what appears to be a surge in consumer activism may be little more than a coincidence of the GMO issue with interest in the new technology. It could be argued, therefore, that although the Internet is providing a tool for political engagement, it may simply be encouraging "armchair activism" where e-mailing political institutions becomes a substitute for more proactive forms of protest and debate. Two issues are pertinent to this claim. First, the use of the Internet may indeed encourage armchair activism. However, because a key aim of major NGOs is to increase their visibility and their relative political power, "e-activism" can be a valuable tool in this process. For these organizations, any activism is better than none. In addition, given the proliferation of Web sites addressing the GMO issue, the familiarity of organizations such as Greenpeace, and the ease of access to political institutions that they offer, armchair activists may gravitate toward these, rather than other, organizations. Second, there is little evidence that the GMO issue has been characterized simply by electronic protest. On the contrary, the amount of direct action the debate has prompted—from crop burning at one extreme to a simple refusal to buy genetically modified foods at the other—is indicative of the value of the Internet in encouraging political *activity,* rather than simply promoting discussion.

Theorizing the Spaces of Political Protest

To address how the use of the Internet in the GMO debate may be affecting political practice, it is useful to turn to the work of Henri Lefebvre, and in particular his insights on the organization of space in society. Although his writings covered a wide range of topics, most notably urban theory and practice, it is his spatial theories that are most valuable to an analysis of international politics, as this work provides some loose categories for interpretation of social phenomena that do not abide by exclusionary dichotomies.[23] Lefebvre suggested that "space is nothing but the inscription of time in the world, spaces are the realizations, inscriptions in the simultaneity of the external world of a series of times."[24] Using Lefebvre's ideas on inscriptions of time, it is possible to argue that the world *as it has been* is not necessarily the world *as it is now.* In this respect, the historical inscriptions on which understanding is based are supplemented, reaffirmed, erased, and altered over time, adjusting the foundations on which understanding depends. Consequently, both the assumptions of what knowledge is and how it can be interpreted change over time. It is possible to see, therefore, why it is necessary for the discourses of IR and other academic disciplines to change to reflect the nature of contemporary political practices. Lefebvre's spatial theories provide an approach that moves beyond the traditional spatial assumptions of political analysis.[25]

In recent decades, the inscriptions of international politics have been altered and a state-centric discursive framework is no longer justifiable. In addition, methods of gathering and disseminating information are changing with the use of new communications technologies, adjusting the ways links and divisions between political actors are created and maintained. Related to this is the impression that the dynamics of political relations are manifold and there can be no justifiable assumption that "politics" is the exclusive province of states and international institutions. As a consequence, a need to develop analytical approaches that look at the *actions* of political actors, rather than at the structures within which they operate, is evident.

Lefebvre outlined a tripartite conceptualization of space—spatial practice, representations of space, and the spaces of representation—which offers an alternate framework for analysis.[26] These three elements of spatial process are closely interrelated: it is possible to distinguish between them, though the nature of each critically influences the others. By providing a mechanism for addressing the material conditions, the discursive influences, and the opportunities for dissent in the lives of individuals, Lefebvre's categories provide a loose structure through which some of the more complex characteristics of contemporary politics can be interrogated. This loose structure, moreover, directly addresses the contrasting political practices of individual actors.[27]

Spatial practice relates to the ways in which societies are organized, both by the material environment and through the social behaviors of people within them. Spatial practice encompasses the relations between people, their environment, their modes of interaction, and the nature of the work, leisure, social and political opportunities, and so on available to them. These are, for Lefebvre, the *perceived* spaces of human existence.

As a consequence, spatial practices differ from society to society, and to greater or lesser degrees from person to person.

The key adjustment to spatial practices in the Internet era is access to the technology. In the case of anti-GMO activism, it is possible to see the twofold influence of access to the network technologies. First, access to the information available online encourages the extension of activist networks—networks that may not be available in "real life." The growth of online networks, where links between distant actors are created, suggests that a new dimension is being added to the prerequisites of political activism. Thus, where activism is more likely when kin and friendship ties to other activists already exist, it is possible that the introduction of the Internet to the range of available political tools can extend the formation of networks. The role of the Internet in providing links, both to information and to other activists, is evident.

Second, online norms of behavior are not subject to the same constraints on freedom of expression experienced in the "real world." This is not to suggest an anarchic free-for-all. But this point does suggest that opportunities for expressing views that contradict the values of policy-making bodies are increasing. It is possible, for example, for Indian farmers to talk to a potentially global audience about the "inferior cotton variety and related pollution" that result from genetic modification.[28] In this manner, a voice rarely given airtime by the international mass media gains access to a wide audience and is provided with the opportunity to promote opinions that the gatekeeping mechanisms of conventional media would frame or filter out. In this sense, political communication is pluralized by the inclusion of voices that previously would have lacked a platform beyond their immediate physical environs.

For Lefebvre, *representations of space* relate to conceptualized spaces that constitute control over knowledge, signs, and codes. The ways societies represent space are articulated in dominant discourses and theories, through the vocabularies of academic research, through media representations, through accepted codes of social behavior, and so on. Representations of space effectively define our perceptions of ourselves and the worlds we inhabit. Consequently, representations of space are "the dominant space in any society" and, as Edward Soja suggests, they constitute "a storehouse of epistemological power."[29] For these reasons, representations of space are obviously an important tool of hegemony and authority as they define the accepted limits of social and political activity within societies. They are viewed by Lefebvre as the *conceived* spaces of human existence.

Applying the concept of representations of space to activist use of the Internet, it is possible to see how the defining codes of political practice no longer relate solely to institutional norms. This continues trends that have been evident for some time, such as the rise of the NGO movement in recent decades, and the growth of issue-based transnational social movements.[30] The Internet cannot therefore be seen as a catalyst for political change, but it does provide a mechanism through which the evolving politics of dissent can be aired more effectively. In this respect, it provides a key dimension of pluralized political communication: a tangible infrastructure for the sharing of information. In the GMO issue, the ways the politics of protest reached the "ordinary" consumer, against the interests of more powerful actors such as the biotech companies and the U.S. government, is a case in point. Since the introduction of the Internet, control over the accepted limits of political behavior, which in the past was largely determined by institutional values, has become more difficult. This is not to dispute the power of governments or multinationals—many people are still, often unwittingly, eating genetically modified foods. It does suggest, however, that hierarchical control over the codes of political practice cannot be managed as effectively when the Internet is used as a tool for lobbyists. Furthermore, concepts of political legitimacy—that is, who best serves the public interest—are complicated by the multilayering of actions and interests manifest in Internet use.

Lefebvre's third category, *spaces of representation,* relates to concepts of agency and to practices of resistance, struggle, and opposition to dominant values. The suggestion here is that spaces of representation are the *lived* spaces of human action, both distinct from the other two spaces and encompassing them. Individuals exist within and through spatial practice, and are constrained within representations of space. The social and political choices made in relation to these real and metaphoric demarcations constitute the spaces of representation of each individual. These lived spaces of representation relate to resistance to the dominant order on the part of those in subordinate, peripheral, or marginalized positions.[31] Most political activity that is not related directly to governmental processes involves some degree of marginalization.

The GMO issue highlights how the Internet has been used to create links between marginalized actors, raising both their profile and their power to resist dominant political values. More formal organizations that conduct highly structured campaigns have used the Internet to gather public support and consequently increase their leverage over political institutions and major economic actors. Less cohesive collectives have used the Internet to promote the political autonomy of individual actors, and have targeted their activities more specifically at the GMO producers. For these actors, the whole concept of politics is rooted in their own definitions of (in)appropriate practices, and not in institutional norms or values.

In addition, the spatialization of politics in the GMO debate has posed profound challenges to state-determined definitions of politics. Some protests are organized on a local basis using international technology, with the outcomes in turn being detailed online. In this sense, protests are fed back into the networks as part of the informational archives available to other activists. The destruction of genetically modified crops in Croatia, for example, was undertaken by local activists using tactics detailed online by the GenetiX Snowball group in the United Kingdom.[32] It appears, therefore, that both the metaphoric spaces of politics (that is, what politics is conceived to be) and the "real" ones (where politics can be understood to take place) are being adjusted by the mediation of political protest through the Internet.

Conclusion

This essay began by asking how Internet mediation is pluralizing political communication. Of course, political activism is and always has been about individual choice: to act or not to act. The Internet does not alter this fundamental principle. It does, however, extend the range of information available to actors, and thus adjusts the basis of political communications, in three significant ways. First, the absence of a gatekeeping function comparable to that embedded in mass media communications makes a dominant discourse harder to determine and maintain. News values that establish hierarchies of relevance are almost entirely meaningless in cyberspace and, though the merits of such unmediated provision of information are hotly debated, there can be little doubt that Internet communications allow s/elective access to information in a way that broadcast technologies cannot.[33]

Second, the equation of politics with institutions, politicians, and governmental processes, already challenged by new social movements, is further undermined through the use of the Internet as a tool for activists. The GMO issue clearly illustrates that governments are only one of several relevant actors. Even then, governments are by no means the most influential players on the field, in the eyes either of the multinational biotech companies or of activists. The significant tensions in this debate clearly reside in the divergent opinions of these nonstate actors and, although some of their activity is filtered through policy makers, a considerable proportion takes place through Internet debate and information exchange.

Third, if information binds networks together, and if political protest can be seen to require collective action, it is evident that the nature of activism is being adjusted both geographically and qualitatively;[34] that is, the Internet can have an impact on both the geographies of protest and the forms such protest may take. Again, the GMO issue clearly illustrates how mass activism collectives may now be more widely dispersed than ever before and how the individuals, networks, and organizations that constitute these collectives can cherry-pick from more information than has ever been available to them.

In some senses, the Internet can be seen as something of a mega-mediator, in that its use can affect not only the political structures within which individuals operate but also, through information provision, the politics of the individual. In addition, the power of the nonelite individual, uniformly ignored in IR, becomes a feature of international politics as the Internet activist is rarely simply a receiver of information but is also often a sender. This, of course, challenges assumptions of the homogeneity of the audience (typical of mass media analysis) and the voting public (typical of political analysis). In its mega-mediating role, the Internet is implicated in affecting the relative positions of different actors and in influencing the content and scale of information available to them. Thus, when the Internet is included in political processes, traditional assumptions about power, hierarchy, and control cannot be taken as givens.

The flexibility offered by Lefebvre's spatial theories, which recognize changes to both agency and structure, can offer a useful starting point for respatializing and "deinstitutionalizing" conceptions of international politics and provide opportunities for due recognition of the role of the individual as international actor. The Internet and Lefebvre's particular form of theorizing space both respond to the dichotomies at the heart of most interpretations of international politics, forcing us to broaden our understandings of what politics actually *is* and what analytical tools can best be applied to its interpretation.

As we attempt to develop new ways of spatializing politics, it becomes evident that a discursive flexibility, rather than a new form of closure, is required. Research into Internet use has provided some surprises for IR scholars, as the limitations of the discipline's spatial imagination have become apparent. Looking from the outside in,[35] it should have been easy for a discipline dedicated to analysis of the international to address this space-transcending, deterritorializing technology. That positioning the Internet has proven so problematic for many IR scholars suggests a need to shift the line of vision from the structures of politics toward the agents that constitute them. The Internet does, of course, have structures and hierarchies of its own, most notably in recognizable patterns of information provision and reception, and in distribution of technological artifacts. It is not possible, however, to analyze these patterns through the top-down, structure-led models most common in extant theoretical approaches in IR. Nor is "bottom-up" necessarily the way forward, as the overlapping of institutions, agencies, and practices is more complex than a unidirectional theoretical framework can permit.

The spatial categories applied in this essay have been developed with Internet analysis in mind and require further research. Much of the impact of the Internet on international politics to date has come from the "bottom up." However, there is a need to develop mechanisms for addressing how this form of protest can best be analyzed in IR. The categories applied here, while requiring further work, do appear to provide a useful tool for addressing the effects of nonstate, nonhierarchical political practices and, for this reason, warrant further investigation.

Notes

1. GMO refers to "genetically modified organisms" and is the term used in this essay. GMOs are also sometimes referred to as GM foods and occasionally in the United States as LMOs (living modified organisms).

2. This is too vast and complex an area for a single chapter to cover all of the political actors involved. NGOs and other, less formalized, activist groups have been chosen because their use of information and communication technologies (ICTs)

to debate the GMO issue has been exclusively related to its potential as a tool of political dissent.

3. No judgments are made here about the merits or safety of genetically modified foods. Detailed information on GMOs can be found on the following Web sites: www.oecd.org/subject/biotech.edinburgh.htm, www.gmissues.org/frames.htm, www.foe.co.uk/camps/foodbio/queries, www.greenpeace.org, www.monsanto.com, www.novartis.com, www.dupont.com, www.agrevo.com.

4. It is tempting to use the "you can't put your hand in the same river twice" adage here, as the social and political relations that we analyze today may not prevail tomorrow, particularly in relation to the rapid spread of Internet use. See Brian D. Loader, "The Governance of Cyberspace: Politics, Technology and Global Restructuring," in Brian D. Loader, ed., *The Governance of Cyberspace* (London and New York: Routledge, 1997), p. 7; David Lyon, "Cyberspace Sociality: Controversies over Computer Mediated Relationships," in Loader, *The Governance of Cyberspace,* pp. 23–37.

5. See Tim Jordan, *Cyberpower—The Culture and Politics of the Internet* (London and New York: Routledge, 1999); Brian D. Loader, ed., *Cyberspace Divide: Equality, Agency and Policy in the Information Society* (London and New York: Routledge, 1998); Jayne Rodgers, "NGOs, New Communications Technologies and Concepts of Political Community," *Cambridge Review of International Affairs* 12.2 (summer 1999); James Slevin, *The Internet and Society* (Cambridge: Polity Press, 2000).

6. Helen Jones of the University of Huddersfield is credited with the invention of the term "ontological awareness," which develops from Anthony Giddens's concept of ontological security. See Anthony Giddens, *Modernity and Self-Identity: Self and Society in the Late Modern Age* (Stanford, Calif.: Stanford University Press, 1991). It should be noted, of course, that gender theorists have been questioning the ontological foundations of IR and other disciplines for decades.

7. See, for example, John Agnew, "Mapping Political Power beyond State Boundaries: Territory, Identity, and Movement in World Politics," *Millennium* 28.3 (1999): 499–521, and Alexander B. Murphy, "The Sovereign State as Political-Territorial Ideal," in Thomas Biersteker and Cynthia Weber, eds., *State Sovereignty as Social Construct* (Cambridge: Cambridge University Press 1996), pp. 81–120. See also Jayne Rodgers, *Spatializing International Politics* (London and New York: Routledge, 2002).

8. R. B. J. Walker, "The Concept of the Political," in Ken Booth and Steve Smith, eds., *International Relations Theory Today* (Cambridge: Polity Press, 1995), p. 312.

9. See Donatella Della Porta and Mario Diani, *Social Movements: An Introduction* (Oxford: Blackwell, 1999), for a comprehensive overview of NSM theories.

10. Agnew highlights the way IR posits dyadic relationships as central to power relationships in IR (person/person, state/person, etc.) ("Mapping Political Power"). This point is pertinent to Internet analysis as it illustrates how political actors are understood to operate in mutually exclusive spaces rather than being interactive in any meaningful way.

11. James Walsh, "Brave New Farm," *Time,* January 11, 1999; www.time.com/time/magazine/articles/0,3266,1/698,00.htm.

12. See *Multinational Monitor* 21.1–2 (January–February 2000); www.essential.org:80/monitor/mm2000. *Multinational Monitor* claims that more than half of all soybeans and one-third of corn crops in the United States are now grown from genetically modified seeds, data confirmed by the DuPont biotech company Pioneer (see

www.pioneer.com). Note too the survey in *Time* magazine from January 1999: 81 percent of people surveyed in the United States said that genetically engineered food should be labeled, but 58 percent said they would not buy it if it was. See www.time.com/time/magazine/articles.

13. The Food and Drug Administration position on genetic modification—that it does not change food in any material way—was upheld by the U.S. District Court in the District of Columbia in October 2000. See www.gene.ch/genet/2000/Oct/msg00039.html and www.bio-integrity.org/press_release-Oct4-2000.html.

14. Press reports claim that the U.S. government has put pressure on the European Union and the British government to allow greater trade in genetically modified foods. See Bob Hencke and Rob Evans, "How US Put Pressure on Blair over GM Food," *The Guardian,* February 23, 2000, p. 6.

15. This is one of the most significant differences between the Internet and any other form of communications technology. The mass media, for example, are essentially monological and therefore of only limited use in promoting debate. The telephone, while now potentially multilogical (though few of us have experienced this), can carry only a fraction of the information the Internet allows.

16. See Jenny Pickerill, "Spreading the Green Word? Using the Internet for Environmental Campaigning," *ECOS* 21.1 (2000): 14–24.

17. Ibid.

18. See Rodgers, "NGOs, New Communications Technologies."

19. See www.agroevo.com/biotech/QA/qa_ge2.htm.

20. An example of the former is Organics Direct, a UK-based company that actively lobbies supermarkets to sell non-genetically modified foods (www.organics-direct.co.uk). An example of the latter is the artactivist and purefood sites that publicize direct actions against biotech companies and provide information on crop test sites, forthcoming actions, and so on (www.artactivist.com and www.purefood.org).

21. See www.genetix.org.

22. Greenpeace records details of the actions of governments, MNCs, and protesters on these issues in various countries on its Web site: www.greenpeace.org/~geneng.

23. See Henri Lefebvre, *Writings on Cities* (Oxford: Blackwell, 1996).

24. Ibid., p. 16.

25. Many scholars (such as Agnew in "Mapping" and Walker in "The Concept") argue that the spatialization of politics in IR is inappropriate. Few have attempted to move beyond this critique, though, and to develop spatial theorizing as a methodology.

26. See Henri Lefebvre, *The Production of Space* (Oxford: Blackwell, 1974–1984) and *Writings,* and Edward Soja, *Thirdspace—Journeys to Los Angeles and Other Real-and-Imagined Places* (Oxford: Blackwell, 1996).

27. Lefebvre's categories can, of course, be extended to address the actions of collectives.

28. See the artactivist site.

29. Soja, *Thirdspace,* p. 67.

30. See Margaret E. Keck and Kathryn Sikkink, *Activists beyond Borders: Advocacy Networks in International Politics* (Ithaca, N.Y.: Cornell University Press, 1998), and Jackie Smith, Charles Chatfield, and Ron Pagnucco, eds., *Transnational Social Movements and Global Politics: Solidarity beyond the State* (Syracuse, N.Y.: Syracuse University Press, 1997).

31. See Soja, *Thirdspace,* p. 68.

32. See the GenetiX Web site.

33. The major debates on free speech in cyberspace center, of course, on the problems of regulating access to material that would be restricted or prohibited in the "real" world. The term *s/elective* is used to connote processes of selection and election (that is, opting in and out of services at the user's leisure) that Internet browsing permits.

34. See Keck and Sikkink, *Activists,* p. 18.

35. This is a rather feeble play on R. B. J. Walker's *Inside/Outside: International Relations as Political Theory* (Cambridge: Cambridge University Press, 1993), one of the first, and still one of the most important, works on the restrictive spatial imagination of IR.

CHAPTER THREE

Postcards from Aztlán

Patricia L. Price

The Delicious, Maddening Line

The border, conceived both literally as the geopolitical line separating the countries of the United States of America and Los Estados Unidos Mexicanos, and more generally as those lines or zones where differences come together, overlaps the diverse connotations of "mediation." Aztlán, the mythical homeland of modern-day Aztecs, has emerged as a particularly appropriate construct for approaching the dual impulse to spatially fix collective identities in a homeland, while recognizing the difficulty of doing this in a way that explicitly calls into question the fixity of other lines. In this essay, I will literally and figuratively depart from Aztlán as an unsettled, and unsettling, metaphor for grappling with the growing intolerance for difference that sadly characterizes the hegemonic national imaginary of the United States, and for signaling defiant, creative, more inclusive paths toward a less bordered future.

The notion of Aztlán arose in the 1960s with the Chicano movement, which was nurtured within the broader context of civil rights and anti-war struggles in the United States in the 1960s. The Chicano movement, or "el movimiento," brought together Mexican-descended rural, urban, poor, and working-class peoples living throughout the United States. It highlighted empowerment of the individual and the social collective through improved education, labor conditions, and support of bilingualism.[1] At the most visible political forefront of the early stages of "el movimiento," the United Farm Workers organized strikes and boycotts to protest the dangerous, degrading working conditions of Chicano farmworkers in California's Central Valley. Across the United States, numerous political strategies to promote Chicano nationalism developed in large cities and urban barrios (neighborhoods), universities, and smaller communities, and Chicanos engaged in boycotts, protests, walkouts, and street militancy.[2] A short-lived and fractured political party, the Raza Unida Party (RUP), held "brown power" and the taking back of the U.S. Southwest through the electoral process as central platform issues.[3]

Although the material political organizing occurred in concrete geographic places, the Chicano imaginary became firmly rooted in Aztlán, a mythical homeland that defies the territorial limits of the nation-state. According to pre-Columbian lore, the Aztecs had come from the north to settle Mexico's central valley and to found the city of Tenochtitlán (present-day Mexico City). The northern birthplace of the Aztecs was a "white region of seven caves," an earthly paradise from which the Aztecs had been expelled and to which they must return.[4] The physical location of Aztlán is guesstimated as being somewhere north of the Gulf of California, yet for most Chicanos Aztlán exists as a "spiritual reality" or a "living myth."[5] "Whosoever wants to find Aztlán, let him look for it, not on the maps, but in the most intimate part of his being."[6]

In the Chicano national imaginary, the border between the United States and Mexico, set by the Treaty of Guadalupe Hidalgo in 1848, had in effect ceded Aztlán to the gringos and placed an artificial barrier between modern-day Aztecs and their rightful homeland. Thus Mexican migration to the United States, and in particular to the U.S. Southwest, constitutes a reverse diaspora. Far from illegally invading foreign lands in the United States, modern-day Aztecs are merely returning to their rightful homeland.[7] In the Plan Espiritual de Aztlán (the Spiritual Plan for Aztlán), a founding ideological document of the Chicano movement written in Denver in 1969, this antiborder sentiment is poetically invoked: "Aztlán belongs to those who plant the seeds, water the fields, and gather the crops and not to the foreign Europeans. We do not recognize capricious frontiers on the bronze continents."[8]

If the legal-institutional scaffolding known as the state is in fact nearing the end of its useful life, being quickly abandoned in the wake of transnational corporations, global capital flows, internal and international migrants and refugees, multinational mafia, and terrorists as the true arbiters of power in the world, then the U.S.–Mexico border crystallizes the death throes of this transition. Indeed, the notion of Aztlán is at once so profoundly unsettling for some, and so energetically promising for others, precisely because it questions the fixity of the contemporary border between the United States and Mexico. Aztlán signals the slipperiness and malleability of spatial constructs such as international borders, and hints at a time before there was a United States of America and a United States of Mexico and a border dividing them. It picks at the wound that is the state in late modernity.

The contemporary U.S.–Mexican borderland has given birth to a rich range of aesthetic production.[9] Expressed in song, film, performance art, poetry, dance, fiction, painting, and the plastic arts, borderlands artists work creatively with the contradictions of existing on both sides of borders between nations, races, languages, genders, sexualities, and even fragmented selves. In much of this work, the border emerges as a productive sort of liminality, a space that allows for new identities to emerge, identities that defy either/or choices and instead forge new subjectivities that straddle borders.

Yet the U.S.–Mexico border has also hardened of late, and became an increasingly brightened and muscular place through the 1990s. Fiberglass panels left over from the 1991 Gulf War were upended to form a wall along the border at Nogales, while landing mat material "from Guam to Guantánamo" was recycled to build a similar wall at El Paso.[10] Thermal-imaging cameras, night-vision scopes, aerostat balloons stationed along the border, and state-of-the-art computer processing of entrants at border checkpoints have erected an ephemeral fence, a high-tech silicon border to buttress the physical walls already in place.[11] The late 1990s saw the institutional scaffolding arise to buttress this infrastructural buildup, ranging from San Diego's "Gatekeeper" operation to Nogales, Arizona's "Operation Safeguard," and El Paso, Texas's "Operation Hold-the-Line" (formerly "Operation Blockade"). Concerned citizens, too, are doing their part. In San Diego, residents park their cars along the line at night and shine their headlights to "light up the border." There are rising levels of gun ownership by ranchers and property owners along the U.S. side of the border. Anti-immigrant vigilantism and do-it-yourself justice on the part of "concerned citizens" is mounting. The nativistic political rhetoric of Ross Perot, Pete Wilson, and Pat Buchanan echoed these local concerns nationally. Pertinently, José Saldívar asks:

Will the politics of backlash and the Reagan-Bush-Clinton doctrine
of low-intensity conflict target new and old U.S. Latino/a ethno-racial
populations in California? Will ugly, chauvinistic "Light Up the Border"
campaigns and nativist legislation like Proposition 187 continue to go
unchecked, like weeds, along the U.S.–Mexico *frontera?* Will California
sheriff's deputies . . . keep clubbing with their erect batons defenseless
undocumented border-crossers like Alicia Sotero, Enrique Funes, and
José Pedroza? Will our own home-grown *intifada* . . . be fueled by a
generation's collapsing hopes in the future?[12]

It is this ability to bring into conversation hatred and beauty, limitation and possibility, violence and the sacred that has led writer Paula
Gunn Allen to write of the bordered desert straddling Mexico and the
United States as a magically real landscape, a "geospiritual reality."[13] In
this essay, I wish to highlight the dangers and possibilities for forging
pathways across the unstable, reworked terrain of late modernity. To do
so I will suggest that the border can be approached as a trickster figure
of sorts. In the oral storytelling tradition of native Southwestern peoples,
the figure of the trickster often plays a pivotal role. Tricksters also appear
in classical mythology, West African folktales and their diaspora (Brer
Rabbit in African-American stories is a trickster figure), Krishna the
butter thief, and Chinese street theater. In Native American stories, trickster is typically an animal, often a coyote or a hare in the Southwest, or a
raven in the Pacific Northwest.

In stories that center on the origins and development of Native American peoples, the trickster figure is literally tricky, a master of deceit,
one who slips across boundaries normally not crossed. Yet trickster is
not simply evil—another manifestation of the Devil, for example; for
the trickster ultimately releases needed goods—fire, the arts of agriculture, souls—from the gods in order that humans may survive in the
world. The trickster may also be a healer, as in the coyote stories of the
Navajo. The telling of the story of coyote as "eye-juggler," a tale told to
Lewis Hyde as he hitched a ride through the desert one night, plays a
central role in any Navajo healing ritual used to cure diseases of the
eye. Thus, Hyde argues, trickster tales do not simply entertain, or teach
people how to behave; they can also "knit things together again after
disorder has left a wound."[14]

In suggesting that the border as such be approached as a trickster, I
am pointing to the capability for action on the part of a largely spatial

construct. This is important, as we attempt to move beyond contentions of the spatial as synonymous with the dead and the fixed. It also builds on Donna Haraway's ideas of the world itself as a trickster figure, as possessing the capacity for witty agency.[15] The border is transverse, it defies orthodox notions of scale. It exists not just as a line on a map, it also runs through the human imaginary at the level of individual and collective alike. The border is a shape-shifter, historically moving south and west to gobble up nearly half of Mexico's territory in 1848. (But Mexico has fought back, and Los Angeles is now the second-largest Mexican city.) The border is a dual sort of character, existing as both presence and absence, separator and bridge, aporetic and open. Its duplicity, its shape-shifting qualities, and its fluid transversality all point to a profound disruption in the geo-imaginary status quo.

The U.S.–Mexico border mediates the past and the future of the European nation-state as primary arbiter of power in the world. The border points both to a long-standing reluctance to think beyond the nation and to a looming imperative to do just that, difficult as it may be. Geopolitical borders today both define and defy the power of the state. They are at once the most visible, physically present delimiters of the state and as such saturate the landscape itself with the power of the state. Yet they also constitute the receding horizon of the state as it is imagined and practiced. Borders are the places where the power of the state becomes most tenuous, most challenged, most dissipated. The U.S.–Mexico border has become a space of both fear (of confronting an uncertain future without the nation-state) and possiblity (of crafting human collectives that may rework existing social relations of power in less oppressive ways). The line itself signals this uncertainty: do we choose violence when our fears cannot be resolved, or do we push beyond the border, and our fears, to search for new alternatives? The barbed-wire fence mocks us and invites us at once.

Thus, like trickster figures in native American storytelling practices, the border may wreak a great deal of havoc, but it also has the potential to teach, to heal, and to open doors to new futures. As Hyde writes of the coyote, so too of the border:

> When he lies and steals, it isn't so much to get away with something or get rich as to disturb the established categories of truth and property and, by so doing, open the road to possible new worlds.[16]

In what follows, I will introduce three iconic figures—the ripper, the Virgin, and the twins—who distill the anxiety and exuberance that characterize the U.S.–Mexico border. In operational terms, they lend the vacuous spatiality of "the border" as such its dynamic, trickster-like personality. They act on the border and they enact the border. They are characters in the narrative space of the border, and as such signal the deep performativity and fluid textuality of the border. They continually cross the lines between the United States and Mexico, between grim reality and the fantastically mythological, between death and life, sacred and profane, past and future. In doing so, they at once define and defy the border.

They also both define and defy the idea of mediation. The ripper, the Virgin, and the twins are allowed to exist because they go between. The ripper may cross the border to kill women, then cross back again to escape his punishment. He enacts the very border between life and death for the women who are his victims. The Virgin of Guadalupe is by definition a border crosser, existing because she mediates between heaven and earth, the Old World and the New, Spaniard and Indian, and the United States and Mexico. The twins are time travelers, mediating the transition from a global order composed of a tightly jigsawed surface of nation-states to an uncertain postnational future. They go between the nation and whatever might come after.

Yet these figures can also be conceived as denizens, and products, of a third space. They spring from liminality, not hybridity. The ripper uses the chaotically crisscrossed space of the border itself, and of the emerging new world order of production, as the perfect hiding place. He is allowed to continue to exist because his use of this slippery space defies structures of accountability that stop at international boundaries. The Virgin of Guadalupe conjures the imaginative region of "Greater Mexico." Through her evocation-in-mobility, she defies the anachronism-in-practice that is the border between the United States and Mexico and blurs it irretrievably with her embroidered slippers. The twins, for their part, are cut from wholly theoretical cloth. They outrun the strictures of expository social-science writing. They play with a future beyond the nation-state that relies on a quantum understanding of manifold possibilities in time and space. They explore alternate futures and as such can perhaps help to will them into being.

The ripper, the Virgin, and the twins are members of a larger (and growing) pantheon of personages that populate the late modern borderscape. They act as guides (and sometimes as baleful harbingers) to how we might think ourselves across the unstable terrain of tomorrow, and of today.

The Ripper

A grim, magically real sort of figure, a serial killer—the border ripper—appears to have a taste for diminutive young women with cinnamon skin and straight, dark, shoulder-length hair. Nearly three hundred such women have died in Ciudad Juárez from early 1993 to date, some of them raped and strangled, their bodies left to mummify in the desert or putrefy in irrigation canals. Seventeen-year-old Adriana Avila Gress was found about a week after her death in 1995, mummifying in a desert tract on Ciudad Juárez's southern perimeter. She worked six days a week in a multinational factory making turn signals for cars. Adriana earned five dollars per day.[17] Irma Angélica Rosales, thirteen, was raped and smothered in a plastic bag and left in a drainage ditch, hours after she lost her four-dollar-a-day job in an American-owned factory, Electrocomponentes de México, in February of 1999. She was fired for talking.[18]

The list goes on and on, almost three hundred times more (and counting). But, as journalist Debbie Nathan writes, "by now, the murdered women of Ciudad Juárez are such an old story that the locals hardly pay attention any more."[19] This is echoed by journalist Charles Bowden, who admits:

> After all, I would rather smile and feel the sun against my face than think about Juárez or all the places like Juárez that are growing quietly like mold on the skin of the planet. When I go to the United States, no one ever mentions this place. It simply ceases to exist, even if I only travel to El Paso. I used to wonder about this fact.[20]

Most of the murdered women worked in Ciudad Juárez factories performing labor-intensive jobs on the assembly lines of U.S. and Japanese electronics, garment, and automotive firms.[21] These factories took root in the 1960s, reaching deep into fertile soil tilled by tax holidays, industrial parks, and permissive legislation that allowed the labor-intensive parts of the productive process to be spun southward to take advantage of cheap, docile, female labor along the Mexican side of the border. These *maquiladoras* bloomed like poison desert flowers, and have quickly spread into cities in the Mexican interior, as well as into Mexico's farm sector, nourished in the 1990s by the North American Free Trade Agreement (NAFTA), ever-cheaper labor, and astounding reforms to Mexico's revolutionary constitution.

Suspect after suspect has been jailed for the Juárez murders, but the killings have not stopped. In 1995, Egyptian chemist Sharif Abdel Latif Sharif was booked and jailed, but the bodies kept turning up. "The Rebels," a group of men jailed for these crimes in 1996, apparently were not the culprits either, because a gang of fourteen-to-sixteen-year-old boys, who supposedly held raffles among themselves to see who would get to kill women, were jailed in 1998. The latest gang, dating from spring 1999, was composed of *maquiladora* personnel bus drivers operating cast-off U.S. school buses. Incidentally, far more common in the lives of Juárez women are the beatings, stabbings, and rapes received at home. Domestic violence reports in Ciudad Juárez are higher than anywhere else in Mexico.[22]

Unfathomable, so much violence? Perhaps, though perhaps, as Debbie Nathan has argued, the assembly-line nature of killings is but a chilling, yet somehow understandable, counterpart to the violently sexualized work and home lives of women in the new global (dis)order, distilled so purely in border electro-boom towns like Juárez.

The Virgin

The borderscape of the ripper is a dark and violent place. Indeed, a veritable borderama blurring the line between reality and myth haunts the bordered desert. The *chupacabra,* or goat sucker, is rumored to stalk rural areas of the border at night, preying on the blood of livestock. The faceless crying woman, La Llorona, who first appeared to Moctezuma as an eerie portend of the fall of the Aztec empire to the Spaniards, still haunts the fence along the border, wailing and looking for her lost children. Recent tales of a mass grave hiding the bodies of hundreds of victims of drug lords in northern Mexico were never substantiated, but authorities continue to scour the desert for signs.[23]

In the midst of the despair that these stories evoke, there have been a rash of appearances of the Virgin of Guadalupe. She has appeared in a water heater in Tucson, in a stain of mole sauce poured in Los Angeles, and to Santiago Quintero as he fixed his car in Elsa, Texas. Holy water, holy mole, and the holy Camaro. Assisted apparitions abound, too. Images of the Virgin of Guadalupe are writ large and small in tattoos, on hubcaps and stick-shift knobs, on computer mousepads and long-distance phone cards.[24] These are fast virgins, mobile virgins, virgins connected intimately to the new information economy. Such virgins bring a refurbished yet stable, modern yet timeless sense of fixity to the flux of the new world border.

The Virgin of Guadalupe provides an enduring vision of Mexican Catholicism and Mexican national identity. In a larger sense, her image can be seen as jumping the border between the United States and Mexico, defying geopolitical niceties to connect people despite separation in space and time. Virgin images form an extensive circulatory system that helps to build an imagined transborder nation and to root identity through the assimilation (literal and figurative) of her image. Writing of recent apparitions of the Virgin Mary in Falmouth, Kentucky, Angela Martin and Sandra Kryst have also noted the fluid, debordered spatiality involved in apparitions of the sacred:

> a blurring or breakdown of boundaries can be found in the fundamental principles underlying Mary's ability to appear to earthly, mortal individuals.... Conceptually, the symbol of the Virgin Mary exists at the boundaries, on the edges of the world that human beings are able to know. Mary belongs in Heaven, but somehow she keeps slipping physically back into the lives of individuals on earth. Mary's ability to appear involves a blurring of boundaries between this world and the other world, between sacred and profane places.[25]

For Mexicans and people of Mexican descent in the United States, the Virgin of Guadalupe has always been a mediatrix, working hard to heal and building bridges across difference. She first appeared to the peasant Juan Diego in December of 1531, a mere ten years after the Iberian conquest of Mexico. On her fourth and final apparition, her image was literally divinely tattooed onto Juan Diego's *tilma* (rough-woven cape), as he released a miraculous winter bouquet of roses in the presence of an astonished Bishop Zumárraga. Her image embodies one of the many ways that two profoundly distinct cultures—Aztec and Iberian—began the ongoing task of making sense of one another. As La Virgen Morena, or Brown Virgin, she embodies a wealth of symbology that blends her indigenous identity with that of Catholic Iberians. Guadalupan scholars continue to analyze and debate her image and its symbolism today.[26]

Initially, then, the Virgin of Guadalupe provided an exercise in mediation, an attempt at healing and understanding following the violent rupture of conquest. She has subsequently appeared with intense frequency during Mexico's independence from Spain, during the Mexican Revolution, and in contemporary Mexican hard times of debt crisis, neoliberal economic reforms, and massive out-migration to the United States. Much as her image has long served to salve the wounds of violent rupture, her present-day presence in apparitions both spontaneous and assisted along the U.S.–Mexico border may well be in keeping with this tradition. In much the same way as the original tattoo on Juan Diego's carrying cloth helped Mexicans and Iberians understand each other, her image today helps *mexicanos* stabilize a coherent Self within an enduring collective, despite an often hostile Anglo majority culture and devouring assimilationist rhetoric.

Yet through her repetitive, mimetic appearances on both sides of the U.S.–Mexico border, she is also stabilizing a rethought region born of performativity, practice, and nostalgic longing. Drawing on Americo Paredes's conceptualization of the U.S. Southwest as simply a northward component of the region he called "Greater Mexico," I suggest that the Virgin of Guadalupe is, through her appearances on both sides of the border, repeatedly signaling the irrelevance of the line.[27] This somersaults both backward, historically, to a time when this area was a northern outpost of the viceroyalty of New Spain and forward to a time when culture erases the lines etched by treaties and purchases and political accords. Her apparitions are ephemeral passport photos that defy the need for any proof of nationality. She both predates the border and outlasts it. She is at home wherever she shows up. She is, to use Rubén Martínez's phrase, an "undocumented virgin."[28]

The Twins

Consider a pair of twins. Suppose that one twin goes to live on the top of a mountain while the other stays at sea level. The first twin would age faster than the second. Thus, if they met again, one would be older than the other. In this case, the difference in ages would be very small, but it would be much larger if one of the twins went for a long trip in a spaceship at nearly the speed of light. When he returned, he would be much younger than the one who stayed on earth. This is known as the twins paradox, but it is a paradox only if one has the idea of absolute time at the back of one's mind.[29]

The following is a piece of creative fiction based on this "twins paradox." By working with fiction in an academic venue, I attempt to practice the sort of "writing differently" that has been so clamored for, yet so rarely practiced, in contemporary critical scholarship. It is tempting to dismiss or discount fictional work as somehow less true than "real, material analyses," and I will doubtlessly be criticized for straying into territory best left to raconteurs housed somewhere in the humanities wings of our ivory towers. Yet it is important to ask: is the tale of the twins any more fantastic than the stories of the border ripper or the Virgin of Guadalupe?

The twins are trickster figures who traverse space and time and signal alternate views of the future in a "world without borders." They inhabit the third space leveled by the ripper and the Virgin of Guadalupe; the geographic smooth space of the desert and the political smooth space of a world without borders. Their reality illustrates the difficulty of thinking ourselves beyond the nation, while their stories, dreams, and parallel worlds signal the durable desire to break beyond borders of all sorts. The story is set in the desert Southwest (or desert Northwest, if viewed through Mexican eyes), in a postnational not-too-distant future, where that which was solid has dissolved into the desert wind and all that is fleeting is caught in postcards sent from Aztlán.

The newspaper curled in her hands and fell to the floor as her arms went slack. The twilight shaded into indigo, and one by one generators chugged on, twinkling lights up like fireflies across the night.

Headlines from the *Desert Daily* were as foreboding as ever: 330 total perished this week attempting to leap the rift, mass graves going years back had finally been uncovered but the bones belonged to politicians and cross-border businessmen instead of the victims of drug lords, a twenty-seventh border ripper had been jailed but still the killings of women continue, an eight-foot-tall vampire-like figure was said to assault travelers at night and tattoo their backs with strange figures, and the terrible wails of a woman who had lost her children could be heard along the arroyos on quiet moonless nights. On and on. Frankly, she was no longer amazed by such stories. In fact, she found them oddly soothing in their repetitiveness.

Mei Ling was an old woman. She reckoned her age at about ninety years, give or take a few (it didn't really matter anymore). Every day now she could feel her body becoming drier, lighter. The frequent urge to sleep was the only thing that filled and weighed her and kept her anchored to the earth, saved her from being swept up in the strong, hot desert wind and blowing over the edge. Her skin had shrunk faster than her bones, slowly curling her body forward. Strong sunlight at midday shone right through her, glowing a translucent porcelain orange. She avoided it. Even so, the skin on the bridge of her nose had stretched too tight. It split abruptly the other day, spraying a fine mist of blood before her like fireworks. And, of course, that brought her back to the starting place, bowed her back in time to their own personal Big Bang, she and Pei Ting. Fireworks and her twin sister Ting-ting were almost the only things she remembered about Before.

Before the Waste, but after the nation (a time not too far from now, in fact). Before when The Place Formerly Known as China had been scoured by the ominous agrochemical cloud that felled everything in its tracks, even village and field and home and a Mother whom the girls could not remember almost from the start of her end. All of the fixity in their narrow world had dissolved in an instant, rendered mute and sterile. Only the children had been spared, little witnesses to the Waste. Mei Ling heard, later, in the cold cargo hold of the plane that had taken her and her sister and all of the children away from that cursed place, a whispered conversation between the guards, frightened talk of "fatal blooms" and "genetically altered vengeance" and "killer tomatoes." The glow from the sleeping bodies of children that packed the cargo hold kept the guards awake for the entire trip.

The children had dissolved into the fabric of postnational need, dispersed like milkweed across the Continent Formerly Known as North America. They worked in sweatshops, they cleaned office buildings, they sowed and reaped in the vast pod-plots that dotted the desert. This post-Waste generation, some one million in all, had provided the blood and sweat and hard work for a thirsty continent, a continent hungry for leisure and eager to keep the rough edges of getting there hidden from view. Indeed, that was what drove them, at the height of fury before the Nation was declared illegal, to wage that heroically stupid war against plate tectonics, prizing open the continent still then known as North America along the Rio Grande and through the desert to the Pacific. The titanium rods did their job well, holding the continent apart a hundred years later, a great dark chasm marking where the border between Mexico and the United States had been. It was preserved as a global memorial of sorts, demonstrating in the flesh of the rent earth what hatred between nations could carve.

It was also utterly fascinating to the twins, and they felt drawn to it as if to a vortex. Most of the local children were frightened solid of the great yawning gulch, but not Ling-ling and Ting-ting. Most afternoons, when the crop tending was done for the day, the girls would sit at the rim and watch the sun set. Sometimes they would stay for the coming of twilight, transfixed by the deepening opalescent lavender of the desert night.

One night, a man approached them. He came upon them so softly across the empty desert floor that he was right behind them before they looked back and up in unison to see the rising full moon shooting its cool rays through his wispy, long hair. Ting, always the braver of the two, had to steady Ling from falling over the edge of the abyss. They had heard stories of the border ripper, to be sure, yet they were not afraid of this quiet man. He lowered himself to a sitting position behind the twins and the three of them waited, utterly still, as the moon slowly sailed higher and higher, shedding the lower layers of the atmosphere and the softened glow that these imparted. When the moon was high and bright and round above them, the man rose slowly and walked forward, directly over the lip of the gulf and into the blackness beyond.

Every evening after this, the man visited the girls. He told wonderful stories, tales that brightened their lonely hearts. The man spoke of lovely green fields that were not fenced and of the marvelous animals that roamed free there, unafraid of the women and men and children who worked together raising families and crops. The land and the people were part of a greater way of life that pulsed to the coming and going of seasons and the longer rhythms of birth, growth, and death. There were seven fabulous cities of gold. Sometimes he told funny stories about wily coyotes and foolish hares. Other times, he spoke of a glowing, good-hearted woman, and the twins began to piece together fragments of memories about their mother and this warmed their souls. All of his stories began with "Long ago, this is what happened, and here is how it was told to me by my father, and to him by his father, and so on through time." Of course, this time had to be before the Waste, before the Nation had been abolished, certainly before Mei Ling and Pei Ting had been born. He had a name for the chasm, he called it "Aztlán," saying that this dark and mysterious gap was in fact a place, and that it was his home, and the home of his father, and his father's father, and so on through time. They should not be afraid for him when he marched into the darkness each night, he said, for it was merely a doorway to a brighter and kinder world than they could ever imagine.

The twins called him "el Chicano" because he had asked them to, though when they asked him to explain the meaning of this name they did not understand, because he spoke in an old tongue of Mexico and Los Angeles and a long journey in search of an eagle in a cactus eating a snake. It was a good story.

Like his name, some of the stories he told were confusing, and the girls mulled them over together long after bedtime but could not make sense of them. He spoke of mysterious people not of this world, who came and went so fast they made time flow differently. These people came in all colors of the rainbow, and did their work through elaborate dreams that the people of Aztlán translated into bright, sprawling murals. El Chicano tried to explain that Aztlán was not just a place, but that it was also a time, and it moved so fast as to weave a curved edge from the very threads of time and space.

After many nights of these stories it became clear to Mei Ling that Ting-ting had begun to understand them at a deep and unspeakable level. Ting had also grown irresistibly curious about what lay beyond the darkness of the chasm. She spoke of it even in her sleep. And for the first time in their lives, the twins diverged.

Thus Mei Ling was hardly surprised when, three days later, Pei Ting rose with the man after the stories were done, took his hand, and walked with him into the darkness. Ting had turned briefly and smiled at her sister, and in that secret language that twins speak, her eyes said she would be gone for only a minute. Yet though Mei Ling had returned to the same spot night after night, she never saw her again.

All of this reminiscing about those cool desert nights long ago and the stories that had been told made her think she was still dreaming when she felt the warm, moist child's palm as it insistently shook her awake. "Ling-ling, Ling-ling! Wake up!" Mei Ling opened one eye, then another, and with a start she felt the dreaming and the awakening melt into one vision: her sister, Ting-ting, all twelve years of her returned intact and identical to the day she had disappeared.

"The stories, they are true," she said with a child's breathless enthusiasm. "Come with me and you will see for yourself." Mei Ling rose from her chair, took her twin sister's hand, and slowly walked into the night and over the threshold.

I said that Mei Ling had never seen her sister again. But she had heard from her. A dozen postcards had arrived over the years. There was no writing on them, but the bright mural scenes shifted and told stories of their own accord, tales that bore a familiar similarity to those told by el Chicano so many nights ago.

When the workers arrived for her the next morning, they found these postcards on top of the newspaper that covered the chair where Mei Ling usually sat, waiting for them to go into the fields and begin the day's labors. What they made of them is another story, one that has yet to be told.

Notes

1. Rodolfo Acuña, *Occupied America: A History of Chicanos,* 3d ed. (New York: Harper and Row, 1988).

2. Ignacio M. García, *Chicanismo: The Forging of a Militant Ethos among Mexican Americans* (Tucson: University of Arizona Press, 1997).

3. Acuña, *Occupied America,* pp. 366–68.

4. Rudolfo A. Anaya, "Aztlán: A Homeland without Boundaries," in Rudolfo A. Anaya and Francisco Lomelí, eds., *Aztlán: Essays on the Chicano Homeland* (Albuquerque, N.Mex.: Academia/El Norte Publications, 1989), pp. 230–41.

5. Michael Pina, "The Archaic, Historical and Mythicized Dimensions of Aztlán," in Anaya and Lomelí, *Aztlán,* pp. 14–48.

6. Luis Leal, "In Search of Aztlán," in Anaya and Lomelí, *Aztlán,* pp. 6–13.

7. Anaya, "Aztlán."

8. The "Plan Espiritual de Aztlán" is reprinted in Anaya and Lomelí, *Aztlán,* pp. 1–4.

9. For overviews of borderlands aesthetic production, see (among many others) José Manuel Valenzuela Arce and Néstor García Canclini, *Intromisiones compartidas: Arte y sociedad en la frontera México-Estados Unidos* (Tijuana: Programa de Fomento a Proyectos y Coinversiones Culturales del Fondo de Cultura y las Artes/ INSI, 2000); Denis Lynn Daly Heyck, *Barrios and Borderlands: Cultures of Latinos and Latinas in the United States* (New York and London: Routledge, 1994); José E. Limón, *American Encounters: Greater Mexico, the United States, and the Erotics of Culture* (Boston: Beacon Press, 1998); David R. Maciel and María Herrera-Sobek, eds., *Culture across Borders: Mexican Immigration and Popular Culture* (Tucson: University of Arizona Press, 1998); and José David Saldívar, *Border Matters: Remapping*

American Cultural Studies (Berkeley, Los Angeles, and London: University of California Press, 1997).

10. See "Go Back to Mexico!" produced by Galan Productions, Inc., for *Frontline*, distributed by PBS Video (Boston: WGBH Educational Foundation, 1994).

11. See Peter Andreas, "Borderless Economy, Barricaded Border," *NACLA Report on the Americas* 33.3 (1999): 14–21; Timothy Dunn, *The Militarization of the U.S.– Mexico Border, 1978–1992: Low-Intensity Conflict Doctrine Comes Home* (Austin: University of Texas, Center for Mexican American Studies, 1996); Verne G. Kopytoff, "A Silicon Wall Rises on the Border," *New York Times*, January 14, 1996, pp. D1, D5.

12. Saldívar, *Border Matters*, p. 129.

13. Paula Gunn Allen, "*Cuentos de la Tierra Encantada:* Magic and Realism in the Southwest Borderlands," in David M. Wrobel and Michael C. Steiner, eds., *Many Wests: Place, Culture and Regional Identity* (Lawrence: University Press of Kansas, 1997), pp. 342–65.

14. Lewis Hyde, *Trickster Makes This World: Mischief, Myth, and Art* (New York: Farrar, Straus and Giroux, 1998), p. 12.

15. See Donna J. Haraway, *Simians, Cyborgs, and Women: The Reinvention of Nature* (New York and London: Routledge, 1991) and *How like a Leaf: An Interview with Thyrza Nichols Goodeve* (New York and London: Routledge, 2000).

16. Hyde, *Trickster Makes This World*, p. 13.

17. Charles Bowden, "While You Were Sleeping," *Harper's Magazine*, vol. 293, no. 1759 (December 1996): pp. 44–52.

18. Sam Dillon, "Feminist Propels Outcry at Brutal Mexico Killings," *New York Times*, February 28, 1999, p. A3. As of November 2002, the official number of murders of women since 1993 stood at 282. Approximately ninety of these are thought to be serial killings. Since I first wrote this piece, the Juárez murders have become big news. A good online source of Ciudad Juárez coverage can be found at Frontera NorteSur, New Mexico State University, http://frontera.nmsu.edu. An excellent series on the slayings, authored by Diana Washington Valdez, appeared in the *El Paso Times*, June 23–24, 2002.

19. Debbie Nathan, "Work, Sex and Danger in Ciudad Juárez," *NACLA Report on the Americas* 33.3 (1999): 24–30.

20. Bowden, "While You Were Sleeping," p. 52.

21. Melissa W. Wright, "The Dialectics of Still Life: Murder, Women, and Maquiladoras," *Public Culture* 11.3 (1999): 453–74.

22. Nathan, "Work, Sex and Danger." Researchers at El Colegio de la Frontera Norte in Ciudad Juárez have suggested that there may be little "serial" pattern at all to the murders, and highlight the fact that murders of men in Ciudad Juárez have far outpaced those of women, yet escalating male deaths have largely gone unremarked (personal conversations with César Fuentes and Alfredo Rodríguez, July 2001).

23. Ricardo Sandoval, Christopher Marquis, and Daniel Vasquez, "U.S., Mexican Police Search for Bodies," *Miami Herald*, December 1, 1999, pp. 1A and 16A.

24. For some of these images, see Jacqueline Orsini Dunnington (photographs by Charles Mann), *Viva Guadalupe! The Virgin in New Mexican Popular Art* (Santa Fe: Museum of New Mexico Press, 1997).

25. Angela K. Martin and Sandra Kryst, "Encountering Mary: Ritualization and Place Contagion in Postmodernity," in Heidi J. Nast and Steve Pile, eds., *Places through the Body* (London and New York: Routledge, 1998), pp. 222–23.

26. See, for example, Virgil Elizondo, *Guadalupe: Mother of the New Creation* (Maryknoll, N.Y.: Orbis Books, 1997); Jacqueline Orsini Dunnington, *Guadalupe: Our Lady of New Mexico* (Santa Fe: Museum of New Mexico Press, 1999); Jeanette Rodriguez, *Our Lady of Guadalupe: Faith and Empowerment among Mexican-American Women* (Austin: University of Texas Press, 1994). In July 2002, Juan Diego was canonized, an elevation to sainthood.

27. See Americo Paredes, *A Texas-Mexico Cancionero: Folksongs of the Lower Border* (Urbana: University of Illinois Press, 1981).

28. Rubén Martínez, "The Undocumented Virgin," in Ana Castillo, ed., *Goddess of the Americas/La Diosa de las Américas: Writings on the Virgin of Guadalupe* (New York: Riverhead Books, 1996), pp. 98–112.

29. Stephen Hawking, *A Brief History of Time: The Updated and Expanded Tenth Anniversary Edition* (New York: Bantam Books, 1998 [1988]), p. 34.

Part II
Sights of Mediation

CHAPTER FOUR

Salgado and the Sahel
Documentary Photography and the Imaging of Famine
David Campbell

In memoriam: Mary J. Geske, 1960–2001

The Famine Icons of Africa

Africa is a continent already imprinted with its own peculiar photographic iconography.[1]

The African food crises of the 1980s fundamentally transformed the academic consensus on the nature of famine. In place of timeworn assumptions about the naturalized occurrence of shortages, famines were recognized as human productions, engendered as much by asymmetrical power relations in the economic, political, and social environment as by the continent's ecology.[2]

What did not change in this period, however, were the images of African famine. In the European imagination, "Africa" (itself a mythical unity) has been produced as a site of cultural, moral, and spatial difference, populated by "barbarians," "heathens," "primitives," "savages," and the generally underdeveloped. With a historical pedigree ranging across various media and stretching from the first encounters to contemporary international relations scholarship, this discursive economy makes available the interpretative resources for subsequent imagery.[3] In particular, the nineteenth-century intersection of anthropology, colonialism, and photography gave a powerful technological boost to already-existing conceptions hospitable to the new power relations.[4] When these resources intersect with a disaster such as famine, the end result is a "global visual field of often quite standardized representational practices"—either lone individuals or a seething mass, victimized, hungry, staring blankly for a pitying audience far away.[5]

These images portray a particular kind of helplessness that reinforces colonial relations of power. With their focus firmly on women and children, these pictures offer up icons of a feminized and infantilized place, a place that is passive, pathetic, and demanding of help from those with the capacity to intervene.[6] They are manifest most obviously in the mother-and-child images that have dominated both still photography and video footage of famines.[7]

The imaging of famine remains controversial, as the remarks of Claire Short, the British Secretary of State for International Development, in April 1998 indicate. In pressing for a political response from the international community to war and famine in the Sudan, Short lambasted those British aid agencies that had authorized a public appeal to raise funds for emergency relief. This appeal, with its well-established imagery of starvation, was, in Short's view, counterproductive. Speaking at a seminar on disasters and the media, she protested that "the pictures hurt and upset [the public] but they feel it keeps coming around and it seems to be hopeless and they flinch and turn away."[8] The end result, Short claimed, was despair and hopelessness among the donor public, confirming the position of Africa as a place of hunger and misery, in which political solutions to the crisis cannot be found.

Short's attack on the aid agencies' visual strategies, and her call for them to engage only in "positive advertising," provoked a flurry of media comment. Journalists reflected on the constraints of reporting, and the way difficult choices might have unintended consequences. For example, the BBC's Fergal Keane recounted his experience of filming a starving thirteen-year-old girl in southern Sudan as the centerpiece of a story. Going beyond what he calls "the ritual guilt to our trade," Keane laments what he did:

> It is a sense that perhaps I have taken away her individuality; her right to be seen as something other than another starving African. I had believed that by focusing on this one child I could actually make people identify with the crisis in south Sudan. Give her name, her age, her story. The people will see that skeletal creatures are in fact individual human beings. . . . I now wonder if the opposite did not turn out to be the case. Yes, my report contained all the "necessary" facts. . . . But I fear that in

my report the context was overshadowed by the image of a child in agony. With four minutes to tell the story (and that is a lot of time in a 30-minute news bulletin) that harrowing image was bound to be the defining one.[9]

Although this report might have made some sad and others give, like Short, Keane wonders if "others may have simply looked and turned away, depressed and alienated by yet another image of starving Africa." As Keane concludes, "we have become used to viewing the continent through a prism of misery. The relentless tide of bad news from Africa has reinforced cultural stereotypes that date from the colonial era: the African as savage; the African as buffoon; the African as helpless, starving shadow."[10] The only solution, he argues, is to place the image of misery in its context, which is something that can only be determined by the individual reporter.

Despite that plea, Keane's concern about the power of the imagery of suffering individuals overshadowing any attempt at contextualization is well founded. In large part, the changing political economy of news gathering is exacerbating the problem. With major media corporations employing fewer dedicated foreign reporters and regional experts, the stories and images that are being submitted from the field are increasingly generic, and thus increasingly determined by already-existing representations of events. For the electronic media, the proliferation of news channels, with their insatiable appetite for dramatic live reports with accompanying images, means the shorthanded staffs are tied to their satellite dishes rather than out in the field.[11] For the print media, crisis coverage will not run without good pictures, and the priority of stories is being determined by the availability of images.[12] This is helping to change, to some extent, the nature of news photography, which has "begun to take on aesthetic qualities, borrowing freely from the formal innovations of artists in an attempt not only to seize the eye but also to hold it. What used to be called 'stoppers'—pictures that made page-turners pause—have been replaced by more complex and self-conscious images intended to be 'keepers.'"[13] But with print resources as stretched as the electronic counterparts, stock pictures (those already taken and on file with an agency) are sometimes substituted for context- and time-sensitive reporting, and the reporting that does take place is more often than not a product of three global news agencies working to scripts rather than individual photojournalists pursuing issues. All of which means "the BB" image (Bloated Belly, the journalist's shorthand for a "starving child" picture) continues to have salience.[14]

Interlude: Imaging the Event

> The construction of the event (the humanitarian emergency) becomes the event—for the purposes of public opinion and policy flow.[15]

The obvious and numerous shortcomings associated with the dominant way in which famine in Africa is imaged should not be taken to suggest that a form of representation that would be "closer to the truth" could or should be found. Relevant to this conclusion is François Debrix's discussion of mediation in the Introduction to this volume. Debrix argues that mediation should be regarded as a social practice located between subjects and objects that guarantees their existence as subjects and objects, thereby making social meanings possible. Although it might be heuristically correct to observe—as Debrix does—that mediation thereby protects subjects and objects from an *immediate* encounter, no such encounter devoid of mediation is phenomenologically possible. This impossibility derives from the fact that events, particularly political events, and especially humanitarian crises, do not possess a naturally given meaning or significance. For them to reach us in some way, they have to be constituted as an event, and this process of constitution is inseparable from their event-ness.

In the context of the construction of humanitarian crises, such as a famine, the pictorial can play a particularly important role. For happenings to become events worthy of the name "disaster," a standard calculus is operative whereby the numbers of victims and their proximity (or lack of it) combine to effect a sense of urgency. The visual can reinforce and underscore that calculus, but it can also work to disrupt it by embodying a power that through images generates an affective and effective demand from those otherwise outside the sphere of concern.[16] And yet, this possibility is often constrained by a double bind—although an event can only be an event if it can be reproduced (and then only a particular sort of event when it can be re-presented in a particular way), the reproductibility of the event can prevent us from experiencing and understanding the event.[17] This double bind is even more marked within the specific pictorial domain of photography, which honors yet marks and fixes its subjects, gives a name and a face to an event while stigmatizing and holding it at bay.[18] This doubling of meaning in photography embodies one form of the "double contradictory imperative" integral to deconstruction's affirmative and radical possibilities.[19]

Although a "better" form of representation, insofar as that means getting closer to the unmediated (or immediate) truth, is not possible, better forms of representation are not impossible. The established modes of imaging African famine do not exhaust the interpretative possibilities for the pictorial representation of the event. Alternatives exist, and insofar as they might be amenable to readings and responses that challenge the pathetic subjectivity of victimhood made possible by the established modes, by embodying a power that transgresses colonial relationships, those alternatives could be considered better. The photojournalism of Sebastião Salgado might constitute one of the better alternatives.

Alternatives: Salgado's Sahel Photographs

Hunger lies. It simulates being an insoluble mystery or a vengeance of the gods. Hunger is masked, reality is masked. Salgado was an economist before he found out that he was a photographer. He first came to the Sahel as an economist. There, for the first time, he tried to use the camera's eye to penetrate the skins reality uses to hide itself.[20]

Now regarded as one of the foremost documentary photographers and photojournalists, Sebastião Ribeiro Salgado, born in Brazil in 1944, began his working life as an economist. Trained at São Paulo University, he emigrated to Paris in 1969 to escape the political repression of the Brazilian military junta. Having half-completed a doctorate in economics at the University of Paris, he was employed for two years by the International Coffee Organization (ICO) in London.[21]

Salgado discovered photography relatively late in his working life, taking his first camera on field trips for the ICO. But what he encountered in the process was that the photographic image involved a practice of mediation at odds with the formal relationships of a social science such as economics: "It was a completely different way to put yourself in relation to that person that was in front of you. . . . The way I presented myself to people as an economist dealing with social problems was completely different than with the camera. I saw that with photography I could probably have a connection with my work that I didn't have until then."[22] With his background of Latin American Marxist economics and photography, Salgado has been pithily described as being "nothing less than André Gunder Frank with a Leica."[23]

Having abandoned his economics career and become a freelance photographer, Salgado's first assignment in 1973 was to photograph the situation in the Sahel for the World Council of Churches.[24] Despite having produced the well-known images of the attempted assassination of Ronald Reagan in 1981, Salgado does not do and does not care for news photography. Instead, he undertakes "lengthy, self-initiated and generally self-financed voyages."[25] With the income from the universally syndicated Reagan pictures, and aided by his then agency, Magnum, but without a specific assignment, Salgado ventured back to the Sahel in 1984 in order to make the lives of people there visible. Working for fifteen months in the region, he produced a series of photographs that many regard as markedly different from the standardized "starving child" images.[26]

Published under the title of *L'Homme en détresse,* as a book for Médecins sans Frontières in France and Spain, Salgado's images of the Sahelian famine of 1984–85 embody many of the pictorial themes that would run through his later work.[27] That these images are not reproduced here means that this argument confronts the problem of "ekphrasis"— how to achieve the verbal representation of visual imagery.[28] Confronting ekphrasis is in many ways to be faced with an impossibility. As W. J. T. Mitchell writes, "no amount of description, as Nelson Goodman might put it, adds up to a depiction. A verbal representation cannot represent— that is, make present—its object in the same way a visual representation can. It may refer to an object, describe it, invoke it, but it can never bring its visual presence before us in the way pictures do. Words can 'cite,' but never 'sight' their objects."[29]

What, then, can be said directly of Salgado's Sahel images? From the selection of this series available at Salgado's Web site, the photographs' uncompromisingly portray the situation, with abundant images of death and deprivation.[30] At the same time, these images disclose more than the standardized icons of famine. People are shown in "more active and clear-cut situations: caring, fleeing, hiding, grieving, and burying their dead."[31] Ethiopians are not just helpless; although in need of assistance, they are seen working for one another in the provision of aid, and the observed rituals surrounding the deceased demonstrate that life is not regarded as cheap, or that the severity of the circumstances has curtailed culture.

The form of these images marks them off from the work of many news photographers. Salgado declines to use color photography on the grounds that "it is too much real. It doesn't allow you to have a single degree of imagination," and he eschews the use of the flashlight as being too harsh.[32] Instead, he photographs only in black and white, with elegant contrasts and texture achieved by the plentiful use of black and shadows. Relying on natural light, and often shooting against the light, he achieves a luminosity that can be surprising. Anna Cataldi, who accompanied Salgado to refugee camps in Croatia as part of a later project, recalled that everything she observed was "gray, dark, formless," and yet Salgado's images emitted light.[33] In Eduardo Galeano's (somewhat unfortunate) analogy, "light is a secret buried under the garbage and Salgado's photographs tell us that secret."[34] In the Sahel series, the image of Tigrean refugees clustered under trees hiding from Ethiopian surveillance flights, with shafts of sunlight streaming through the leaves, is an obvious example of this.[35]

Salgado's use of light, especially when combined with the blurring of life and death in and among the content of his images, has led many to tag him as a photographic practitioner of "magical realism."[36] The concept of magic realism is most often applied to aesthetic forms that emanate from the global periphery and seek to challenge the dominant and totalizing modes of intelligibility propagated by the imperial center. As a feature of much postcolonial fiction—such as the novels of Gabriel García Márquez, Ben Okri, or Salman Rushdie—it involves the hybrid intersection of the real and the fantastic.[37] The effect of this intermixing is to highlight the contradictions in the social that the magical seeks to transcend, and to resituate the real as an incomplete and even misplaced account of the totality of life. As Michael J. Shapiro observes, magic realism thus shows "how all forms of the so-called real are simply the result of a more concerted and institutionalized set of fantasies."[38]

In this context, the interpretation of Salgado as photography's magic realist is a powerful and suggestive reading. However, the manner in which it is readily asserted but rarely explored means that it can function less as an account of his work's significance and more as a means of inscribing it as an "aesthetic form of exotic otherness."[39] Sometimes Salgado's own pronouncements on the uniqueness of a Southern perspective, or the influence of Brazilian culture with its everyday violence and attendant death on his imaginary, might encourage this.[40] Nonetheless, if the category of magic realism is taken to include more than the aesthetics of the global margin—something that an appreciation of the literature of first-world minorities, such as the novels of Toni Morrison and Keri Hulme, warrants—and it is situated as part of an effort to foster what Foucault called "the critical ontology of ourselves," the affirmative, liberatory qualities of a postcolonial stance can be multiplied.[41] That said, as with many, if not most, other aesthetic forms, a progressive political stance is not guaranteed by magic realism's disturbance of governing genres. Rather, it offers radical possibilities in its disturbance of the seemingly natural through the disclosure of contradictions, yet permits passivity by only drawing attention to the aesthetic paradox. In this sense, "magic realism has been shown both to engage with history, by manipulating narrative conventions as symbolic acts of resistance or empowerment, and to reject history for a more static vision, but resisting precisely an engagement with the political."[42] Insofar as Salgado's photographs embody pictorially this double possibility, their status as problematizing alternatives, though achievable, is not intrinsically given.

Another feature of Salgado's photographs that chimes with the appellation of magic realism is the presence of apparently religious themes. Indeed, the aura that is produced by the intersection of form and content in Salgado's Sahel images leads some to see them as part of "the long Christian tradition of the iconography of suffering."[43] Photographs of men with their arms in crosslike positions; people with shrouds around their heads; children being held and carried by their parents—all combine to leave an unmistakable impression of the sacred.[44] If taken as a series—and Salgado insists that his work be taken as a series rather than as a collection of individual images—the feminization and infantilization of famine dominant elsewhere are far from prevalent.[45] Nonetheless, a number of the individual images of mothers with children recall the pietà images—those representations of the Virgin Mary holding the body of Christ, with their name derived from "piety"—that often lead observers to speak of the famine as a "biblical" event.[46] And yet Salgado rejects the notion that either he or his work is religious, noting instead that what interests him "is the spiritual side of man."[47] In marking off spirituality from religion, and wanting to see dimensions to humans other than materiality, Salgado's reasoning has affinities with William Connolly's notion of a "non-theistic reverence for being."[48]

The overriding reason for the difference between Salgado's Sahel images and the iconic famine images is the sentiment that the intersection of form and content can produce. Compassion is not Salgado's aim: "If the person looking at my pictures only feels compassion, I will believe that I have failed completely. I want people to understand that we can have a solution."[49] As David Levi Strauss observes, "Whereas those other images end at pity or compassion, Salgado's images begin at compassion and lead from there to further recognitions. One of the first is that starvation does *not* obliterate human dignity. . . . Salgado did not photograph passive victims, and pity does not suffice."[50] The focus on dignity, this construction of dignity in place of pity, is perhaps Salgado's leitmotiv. As he has remarked: "Sometimes we from the Southern hemisphere wonder why you in the North think you have the monopoly of beauty, dignity, of riches. Ethiopia is a country in crisis, where the people are suffering so acutely, yet Ethiopians are probably among the most beautiful, most noble people in the world. There is really no point in going there to deny this reality."[51]

This reality, for Salgado, is not one easily apprehended. He encountered in his first days in an Ethiopian camp something "beyond my imagination." So many people dying and so many people in distress left him incapable of making photographs. Yet, after the passage of some time, and after reflecting on the fact that he came like the doctors or the engineers with a job to do, he began to work. "So you start to photograph, and after a few more days you start to see the human qualities of the people, not just their pain. You see that they have hope. That is the most human quality for me—hope. And maybe after three weeks in the camp you even begin to smile, like the old people in the camp who smile through their desperation. They have hope to go ahead and fight for their lives. Hope becomes your way of life."[52] Given this, even the famine camp is not a reality in which the people are miserable: "Sometimes people say to me, 'Sebastião, you take pictures of such misery.' I take pictures of people that have less material goods than others. Misery is human, misery is the spirit. Misery is not lack of material things."[53] In this context, Salgado maintains that he does not find the project—as one interview put it, of photographing "the wretched of the earth"—a depressing exercise:

> No, it's not really depressing in the sense you mean. It is exceptional to see people who are in the process of struggling to maintain their living conditions, not just for their survival, but for the dignity of their lives, and to protect their community. When you see this courage, this will to struggle, you realize that history is not finished, that they have not laid

down their arms and given up the struggle. One must show that. When an English or French or German person sees that he or she sees part of themselves, that we are all part of the human species.[54]

Having deployed elements of the sacred, tapped in to a particular tradition of iconography, and acknowledged agency, beauty, and dignity amid disaster, Shawcross and Hodgson argue that Salgado achieves a repositioning of concern, one that attempts to overcome estrangement: "By placing the Sahel within a tradition we know, Salgado refuses to allow us to claim distance or strangeness as a reason for not understanding."[55] As a result, "Salgado's photographs are more than the cold docketing of disaster. By using images that recall others long familiar to us, he forces us to contemplate seriously what we see. He allows us to bridge the abysmal gap between the unimaginable (but very real) and ourselves by interposing photographs that ask for reaction from the eyes first and only then from the conscience."[56]

This means that "Salgado's photos are not a historical record; they are of the present, and they are of the future. Their message is that humanitarianism is not enough."[57] Indeed, Salgado's Sahel photographs embody a humanitarian critique of much conventional humanitarian activity. Hugo Slim observes that humanitarian activity can be understood in terms of prophecy versus the priesthood.[58] The priesthood includes those elements of institutionalized humanitarianism (such as the International Committee of the Red Cross) that have limited the principle of humanity to standardized practices within formal international parameters. The prophets are those who see themselves as confronting convention with the truth and a demand for transformation. In the realm of humanitarian aid, Médecins sans Frontières, for whom Salgado did the Sahel series, regularly enacts the prophetic function.[59]

Although Salgado's images may serve the prophetic function of humanitarian critique, much of his thinking and the work it produces are predicated on notions of a common humanity: "humanity is just one humanity. We must save ourselves, the human species. We've done such bad things to each other."[60] However, this commonality both incorporates a complex sense of difference and involves not a pre-given sense of human being, but a shared sense of what constitutes being human in the contemporary world. In the introduction to his project on migration, Salgado says:

More than ever, I feel that the human race is one. There are differences of color, language, culture, and opportunities, but people's feelings and reactions are alike. People flee wars to escape death, they migrate to improve their fortunes, they build new lives in foreign lands, they adapt to extreme hardship. Everywhere, the individual survival instinct rules. Yet as a race, we seem bent on self-destruction.[61]

For Salgado, pictures alone cannot change much. Nonetheless, he does think that they can provoke contemplation, increase sensitivity, inspire a debate, further understanding, and move beyond compassion, all without giving "anybody a bad conscience."[62] Despite being read and appreciated in aesthetic terms, Salgado insists that his pictures be valued differently: "What I want in my pictures is not that they'll look like art objects. They are journalist pictures. All my pictures. No exceptions. They are published in the press. If a person wants to buy my picture, that's fantastic. The money will help fund my projects. What comes from photography, stays in photography."[63]

Salgado's intentions notwithstanding, the political economy of photojournalism and publishing has meant that his images are not as widely seen as he would like. Indeed, his images are better known in the world of fine art than in the mass media. This outcome is part and parcel of the decline of news-related photo magazines. Even where illustrated magazines remain—as with the color supplements of most of Britain's weekend broadsheets—their focus is primarily directed toward consumer culture and lifestyle issues rather than documentary reportage. Given that, as Stallabrass contends, serious photojournalism "seems unsuited to a neoliberal climate"; the displacement of documentary photography from the mass media to the art gallery and coffee-table book is less an aesthetic choice than a publishing necessity.[64]

These strictures were particularly apparent with regard to Salgado's Sahel photographs. Although published as a book for Médecins sans Frontières in France and Spain (both Salgado and the printer provided their labor free of charge, and twenty thousand copies were sold), the images were not widely published elsewhere. Salgado offered the portfolio to several American aid groups, but they declined to sponsor publication on the grounds that the pictures were too strong for a book to succeed. Likewise, a literary agent who viewed them, and was moved to tears by the images, concluded there was no market for them.[65]

Aside from one spread in a photographic journal, the color magazines also turned them down.[66] *Life* magazine, which, as Susan Edwards observes, "has been known to publish entire photo-spreads consisting of the pathetic, begging images of famine and disease," rejected Salgado's efforts to portray those in the Sahel differently. This led her to conclude that when it comes to famine, "it seems we cannot deal with such images without distancing ourselves somehow." Whereas the dominant iconography of African famine meets this existential desire for moral distance, "Salgado's images confront us with a complex humanity, perhaps too painful to be realized on a global scale."[67] Eventually, some of the Sahel images were seen in the United States, albeit in a retrospective museum exhibition that toured in 1990–91 under the title *An Uncertain Grace*. Reviewing the exhibition for the *New York Times*, Michael Brenson wrote that Salgado's photos, like the people in them, "carry a sense of smoldering energy, of passion too big to be held in check by any body, any job, any relationship or any political system." The photos "are immediate and physical. Their contrasts are sharp, their light hard. They are controlled: form serves content, restraining energy, dignifying death, bringing children up almost into the lens, turning African tribesmen and women into biblical kings and queens."[68] This praise notwithstanding, the belated showing of the Sahel images, after the passage of time had distanced people from the events in the Sahel but increased Salgado's reputation, confirms what Fred Ritchin calls "an unfortunate tendency to elevate the messenger while denying the message."[69]

Methods: Photography as Ethnography

Charity, vertical, humiliates. Solidarity, horizontal, helps. Salgado photographs from inside, in solidarity.[70]

If Salgado's famine images differ from the iconography of pathetic victimhood commonly produced, that difference can in large measure be attributed to his photographic method, and its contrast with one of the most famous declarations of method: Henri Cartier-Bresson's notion of "the decisive moment." In 1952, Cartier-Bresson stated that "photography is the simultaneous recognition, in a fraction of a second, of the significance of an event as well as of a precise organization of forms which give the event its proper expression."[71] This gave him a particular modus operandi: Cartier-Bresson "liked to pop up, as if out of nowhere, take a picture, and then innocently walk on as if nothing had happened."[72] This reasoning meant that in Cartier-Bresson's view, Magnum photographers—those belonging to the agency he helped found in 1947— were "witnesses of the transitory."[73]

Salgado's photographic method, at first glance, might be thought of as similar to Cartier-Bresson's. As in the idea of the "decisive moment," Salgado regards the photograph as a unique conjunction of the spatial and the temporal. In the first instance, the photograph is a product of a complex set of often obscured relationships: "A picture, for me, is like the point of an iceberg. What you see in it is one point of contact, one relation, one preparation."[74] The key relationship is that between photographer and subject: "An image is your integration with the person that you photographed at the moment that you work so incredibly together, that your picture is not more, your camera is not more, than the relation that you have with your subject. Your camera is just a movement inside all these movements that happen, that keep going. I trust in this. I'm probably wrong, but that's my own view."[75] And this relationship of photographer and subject, in which both work together, occurs in but a short time: "Photography is the one medium in which you have all your emotions during a short lapse of time integrated with the person that's in front of you. In a few moments you can get something together that represents all these together. Only photography can get this."[76]

Despite the initial similarities, at least insofar as the photograph inevitably involves a particular temporality, Salgado's self-understanding of his photographic method—which he articulates despite protesting that he has no explanation for it, and only works in a "very, very instinctive" way—is differently conceived, and even styled in deliberate contrast, to Cartier-Bresson's.[77] Instead of the instantaneous click of a shutter creating a short-lived relationship between an unknown photographer and his subject, Salgado's decisive moment, the moment in which an image is inscribed on film, only comes *after* the photographer and subject have developed a mutual relationship. If Cartier-Bresson's photographs can be likened in geometric terms to a tangent balanced on top of a circle, Salgado "feels he must enter the circle, almost, in a sense, 'becoming' those he photographs, at the very least working to understand the existence of those he depicts."[78] The geometric analogy is Salgado's, and illustrates what he describes as the "photographic phenomenon": "When I go to photograph a person or a family, or an event, or workers in

a factory, I create certain conditions which I experience as a phenomenon. You live in a certain time, a short time or a long time, inside of this
phenomenon."[79]

It is because of this understanding that Salgado is regarded as a "photo-
ethnologist," one who works in a critical anthropological manner, embodying the ethos of participant-action research (PAR).[80] Having become
a photographer to overcome the distance produced by social-science
analyses, Salgado believes that his ethnographic style helps transcend
the tendency of photography itself to remove or detach the photographer (and viewer) from the subject. In contrast to the usual routine of
simply snapping the "photographic phenomenon" in front of one,

> there's an entirely different way of working . . . you don't have preconcep-
> tions about the life in front of you. What you know is simply automatic—
> you have a camera that's part of your hands, part of your eyes. And
> then you go inside without judging anything. You don't come with your
> American or your Brazilian or whatever culture in order to presume . . .
> you come because you must come, it's your way of life. You're there to
> see, hear, listen, understand, integrate. Of course, you're a photographer,
> and you take pictures. And you'll probably arrive at the same point as
> the guy who takes things from the outside. But now you can touch it
> from the inside. And then the photos have another reason, another
> meaning. Because in the end it's not really the photographer who takes
> the pictures; it's the persons in front of the camera who give the photos
> to you.[81]

Because "the picture is a gift," the relationship with the subject is the
key. Photography for Salgado is a humanist project rather than a series of
technical issues. "The purpose of photography . . . is to have the strongest
relation with a person, to go inside the intensity of a person."[82] As an instrument of communication, it tells the story that "man is made to live
socially," and the prerequisite for fantastic photographs is to "respect the
people you photograph, and . . . see the nobility and dignity of your subjects."[83] This rationale can change the experience of being photographed
for the subject. One of the oil workers in Kuwait whom Salgado pictured
observed that he "melts away" the normally aggressive act of taking a
picture.[84] It can also mean that many images go unrecorded: Salgado refused to take a photograph of a crazed man tied to a tree like a dog because "I would have been using his humiliated position. I wouldn't have
been 'given' the photograph; I would have stolen it."[85]

Not surprisingly, given the commitment to live amid the photographic phenomenon he wishes to picture, Salgado derides the all too common practice of journalists flying in and out of disaster zones. Without time to appreciate the situation and its people, he says, those journalists take back only what they brought with them.[86] Eduardo Galeano paints an acerbic picture of the contrast:

> Salgado photographs people. Casual photographers photograph phantoms. . . . Consumer-society photographers approach but do not enter. In hurried visits to scenes of despair or violence, they climb out of the plane or helicopter, press the shutter release, explode the flash: they shoot and run. They have looked without seeing and their images say nothing. Their cowardly photographs soiled with horror or blood may extract a few crocodile tears, a few coins, a pious word or two from the privileged of the earth, none of which changes the order of the universe. At the sight of the dark-skinned wretched, forsaken by God and pissed on by dogs, anybody who is nobody confidentially congratulates himself: life hasn't done too badly by me, in comparison. Hell serves to confirm the virtues of paradise.[87]

It is thus the relationship to the other embodied in Salgado's photographs that encapsulates the difference between his imaging of others and other representations of difference. If photography can be regarded—especially through its symbiosis with anthropology—as having a formative role in our understanding of the other, can we regard Salgado's documentation of "a world of differences within the singularity of humanity" as a reworking of the documentary tradition and the established colonial relationships of power it has made both possible and visible?[88] If Salgado's photographs do represent such a reworking, is it because they restore faith in the universal humanism of the "family of man" that drew the ire of Roland Barthes, or is it because, at their best, they escape "the orbit of United Nations 'family of man' internationalism . . . and evince some profound human empathy that nevertheless refuses to reduce the sense of utterly different life experience"?[89] Do these photographs manifest the I–Thou relationship of Martin Buber, or the ethical first philosophy of Emmanuel Levinas?[90] Or is it the case that at the heart of Salgado's powerful imagery there is a productive ambiguity that makes definite answers to these questions impossible? Perhaps, as David Levi Strauss argues, "this extraordinary balance of alterity and likeness, of metaphoric and documentary function, is part of the Salgado signature. It allows his subjects to be at once themselves and more than themselves."[91]

Although Salgado is in no doubt that he is engaged in developing a "militant photography, for the best comprehension of man, a valorization of the human effort," the nature of this project is equally ambiguous.[92] On the one hand, it can be argued that his use of photographic content, his visual rhetoric, is radical, especially in relation to the established iconography of African famine. On the other hand, given his "strikingly realist sense of the camera," Salgado is less radical when it comes to the form or medium of photography.[93] This more conventional stance is evident in his understanding of how the photographer participates in the photographic phenomenon, the relationship with his subject. On the one hand, Salgado invokes the documentarian's oath that he does not "interfere with anything in reality or with the people that I photograph."[94] On the other, he readily acknowledges that, through his ethnographic style of work, "I create certain conditions which I experience as a phenomenon," and that this means "I interfere in the reality of the situation to get my pictures."[95] The source of this interference, however, is not derived from a conscious act of manipulation. It flows, rather, from the unavoidable impact of the photographer's ideology, which Salgado understands not as a political worldview—despite the many reviewers who read it solely in terms of his supposed Catholicism, humanism, Marxism, universalism, and the like—but as "the imaginary," "the apparatus of ideas that we all have, all the formations we have, all the family, all the friends, all the culture inside."[96]

Problems: The Beauty of Disaster

That Salgado's Sahel photographs were not widely disseminated in the media, because they were regarded as too disturbing and too harrowing, is something of a surprise given the fact they they are normally singled out for their beauty. For Salgado's many admirers, the beauty of these images, achieved through a representation of human dignity, is what sets them apart from the iconography of anonymous victimhood found in most reporting on third-world disasters.[97] As Galeano observes:

> Salgado's photographs, a multiple portrait of human pain, at the same time invite us to celebrate the dignity of humankind. Brutally frank, these images of hunger and suffering are yet respectful and seemly.

Having no relation to the tourism of poverty, they do not violate but penetrate the human spirit in order to reveal it. Salgado sometimes shows skeletons, almost corpses, with dignity—all that is left to them. They have been stripped of everything but they have dignity. That's the source of their ineffable beauty. This is not macabre, obscene exhibitionism of poverty. It is a poetry of horror because there is a sense of honor.[98]

Even though he is dealing with horrors, the evident beauty positions Salgado's work as the antithesis of a concern with the abject.[99] One photograph of patients at a leprosy clinic is marked by the proud posture of a woman at the center of the image.[100] In large part, the beauty of the images is for Salgado derived from the aesthetic qualities of the subjects rather than being something he imposes on them. However achieved, the emphasis on beauty and dignity is designed to fuel identification. Speaking of the Sahel images, Salgado notes: "I wanted to respect the people as much as I could, to work to get the best composition and the most beautiful light. . . . If you can show a situation in this way—get the beauty and nobility along with the despair—then you can show someone in America or France that these people are not very different. I wanted Americans to look at the pictures of the people and see themselves."[101]

These intentions and rationales notwithstanding, Salgado's photographs are often derided for being "markedly aestheticising."[102] In a caustic review of Salgado's increasing and popular prominence (prompted by the dual showing of the *Uncertain Grace* retrospective and the postwar Kuwaiti oil photographs), Ingrid Sischy—a former editor of *Artforum*—lambastes his work as being contrived, gimmicky, meretricious, self-aggrandizing, sentimental, and sloppy with symbolism.[103] Although she acknowledges that the presence of beauty in the midst of poverty is a means to challenge the usual clichéd representation, Sischy feels that beauty has become equally a cliché in Salgado's images. His strategies "consistently add up to aestheticization, not reportage," the end result being that "this is photography that runs on a kind of emotional blackmail fuelled by a dramatics of art direction."[104]

Sischy's critique is driven by her evident commitment to naturalism. Salgado's subjects are said to be too much in the service of his desires to be capable of appearing simply as individuals or representatives of the masses, as though subjects could be represented without mediation. Salgado's images are said to be flawed because his work "is not photography in which the facts are allowed to sing for themselves, which is how Lincoln Kirstein once described Walker Evans' work."[105]

Although criticisms of the aesthetic as being out of place in the picturing of disaster are largely driven by a surprisingly robust faith in photography's capacity for naive social realism, it is a concern for the political impact of aesthetic images that is most prominent. Sischy sums up this position well: "the beautification of tragedy results in pictures that ultimately reinforce our passivity toward the experience they reveal. To aestheticize tragedy is the fastest way to anesthetize the feelings of those who are witnessing it. Beauty is a call to admiration, not to action."[106]

Sischy's critique draws attention to one particular photograph from the Sahel series, an image of a shrouded woman with diseased eyes, her hand touching her face, the clothes wrapping her body almost indistinguishable from the near black background. Although she recognizes that Salgado's strategy is to counter fear and horror through the use of what one reviewer called a "dark, necrogenic beauty,"[107] Sischy concludes that "Salgado's strategy here fits into a long and convenient tradition of coupling human suffering and God's will . . . the photograph suggests that the woman's blindness is holy—in other words, that it needn't be seen as something to cure."[108] Although it is not an intrinsically invalid interpretation, Sischy's reading is nonetheless highly contestable, not least because it is dependent on a particular sense of religiosity being read into a single image extracted from a large series. It is a reading, moreover, that pays little heed to the secular explanation of the caption: "With dead eyes worn out by sand storms and chronic infections, this woman from the region of Gondan has managed to survive."[109]

Sischy's concern for the political impact of aesthetics is widely shared, for it is commonly felt that when it comes to disaster, beauty affords distance.[110] But if, as George Steiner has famously argued, "the aesthetic makes endurable," then the beauty ascribed to Salgado's famine images should have permitted some emotional or moral distance for the viewer, and therefore made them more palatable for a mass media audience.[111] However, given that the Sahel photographs were overtly excluded from the mass media because they were considered too disturbing, we can conclude that there is perhaps something unsettling in the particular beauty of his disaster imagery that challenges the idea that the aesthetic necessarily anaesthetizes.

The blanket claim that aesthetics has no place, or a dangerous place, in the representation of disaster has a couple of serious limitations. The first is that there is an implicit assumption—again related to an outmoded faith in the capacity of technologies of representation to achieve a naive social realism, as well as involving a particular ontological claim—that disasters per se are not beautiful, or in any way hospitable to the aesthetic, and that to represent those dimensions thus involves a heavy-handed imposition on the facts. As Stallabrass asks, "should one show such events using an anti-aesthetic form of photography, one which strove to be as ugly as famine itself?"[112] Sischy believes that Salgado's pictures are insulting to those he portrays, and less than they deserve.[113] But are those subjects less insulted by the starving-child images of conventional representations? Assuming it is possible, do these individuals deserve an antiaesthetic portrayal? Of course, the idea that only ugly pictures were possible depends upon viewing the world in distress as without aesthetics. Although the reverse is not necessarily true (i.e., the claim here is *not* that disasters are beautiful per se), the reduction of all forms of life in their complexity to an antiaesthetic dimension seems equally problematic.

A second limitation is that, in critiques such as Sischy's, "beauty" is taken to be a one-dimensional and universally recognizable phenomenon, that beauty is the same whenever or wherever it is used, regardless of context. There is the suggestion, for example, that the aesthetic qualities of Salgado's photographs are not qualitatively different from those found in, say, *National Geographic*. But, as Andy Grundberg has pointed out, the beauty embodied in that journal's images of the third world is of a very particular kind: they are "the apotheosis of the picturesque. That is, they embody many of the same conventions of color and form as *plein air* painting. *They aim to please the eye, not to rattle it.*"[114] In contrast, Salgado's aesthetics are hardly picturesque, even if they do represent a particular beauty. And they certainly do not aim to please the eye. Indeed, Salgado's aesthetics might be regarded as a key element in his effort to overcome the anaesthetizing effects of the iconography of African famine. Instead of, or in addition to, the simple shock that comes from a photograph of an atrocity, the mixture of the beautiful and the repugnant in Salgado's images disconcerts and disturbs, thereby inviting us to be more attentive and even awestruck by the situations depicted.[115]

Although Salgado's images are themselves often without context (an absence that gives them their universal air), it is the social and political context in which his photographs appear, and the traditions against which they are situated, that helps make them significant.[116] This is not to deny either the validity or the importance of asking whether we should be unsettled by the appearance of beauty in the midst of disaster, or whether Salgado negotiates the inevitable tension between the moments of magic versus social realism in his images. Given the complexity of the problems and the subtlety of the images, finding an answer is not going to be easy. Perhaps, though, it is not even desirable. Perhaps the greatest achievement of Salgado's photographs is that they unashamedly raise these questions pertinent to the politics of representing disasters. In the space these images and the discourse about them open up—a space made possible by the double contradictory imperative—comes the possibility of thought and action.

Reprise: Alternatives Other Than Salgado

By way of conclusion, a reflection on one famous famine photograph, and another alternative to the iconography of famine, can help situate this discussion of Salgado. In March 1993, the *New York Times* published a single image taken by Kevin Carter in Sudan. Showing an emaciated child, alone and hunched over, with a vulture lurking in the background, it shocked the paper's readership. Without a context, and representing the famine through the classic image of a lone individual as a victim of nature with death imminent, Carter's photo embodied suffering.[117] Questions of beauty and dignity were absent. The response to the picture focused less on the child and her circumstances and more on the photographer and his actions. Did he aid the girl? Did he help others? Although the newspaper later responded to this deluge of questions with an editorial statement that the child made it to a feeding center and was unharmed by the vulture, their accusatory tone eventually helped drive Carter to suicide.[118] Although the image has become what David Perlmutter calls an "icon of outrage" (winning for the *New York Times* its first Pulitzer Prize for photography), its impact, aside from the consequences Carter bore, was minimal. One of the paradoxes of such images is that the outrage they foster "may stir controversy, accolades, and emotion, but *achieve* absolutely nothing . . . the little girl in Carter's picture was not plucked away by some special Western relief effort, nor did intervention stem the causes of her suffering. . . . Far from a metonym, the photograph should be taken as an anomaly precisely because the human disaster of the Sudan, then as now, is largely ignored by the Western media."[119]

Although not wrong about the specifics of the Carter photograph, Perlmutter's conclusion is too sweeping when we consider other attempts to document the famine in Sudan. Tom Stoddart's 1998 series from the Sudan bears comparison—as a series done with the assistance of Médecins sans Frontières, as well as for their uncompromising content and visual style—with Salgado's Sahel photographs.[120] They represent a committed form of photojournalism that persists, even with the limited opportunities for publication, with the importance of an engaged visual narrative going beyond the conventional clichéd images. Like Carter, Stoddart found himself criticized by some viewers for his actions; they wanted to know whether he had intervened to prevent the robbery of food one of his photographs portrayed. Unlike Carter, Stoddart used his photographs for a particular purpose, insisting that the phone numbers of Médecins sans Frontières and UNICEF accompany their publication. When some of the images first appeared in the *Guardian*, Médecins sans Frontières alone received some seven hundred phone calls pledging forty thousand pounds. Later published in the *Guardian Weekly, Le Figaro, Stern, U.S. News & World Report*, and magazines in Holland, Spain, and elsewhere, they similarly prompted further financial support for aid agencies. In the process of doing so, they refuted Claire Short's notion that the public instinctively shied away from such documentary photography. As John Sweeney concludes, the response to Stoddart's photographs "suggests that the idea of compassion fatigue is a convenient myth for those who hold political power."[121]

Serious questions can and should be asked about whether the act of giving is sufficient, and whether the aid it purchases is beneficial, but the response invoked by the photographs of Salgado, Stoddart, and others demonstrates clearly that viewers do not automatically flinch at and shy away from images that challenge many of the prevailing visual clichés. Photographs are a modality of power, and the bulk of contemporary famine images conform to colonial economies of representation. In contrast to the depoliticization of disasters through such pictures, Salgado's

comportment vis-à-vis his subjects functions as an ethical and respon-
sibilizing practice in which the aesthetic repoliticizes, making it possible
to envisage a humanitarian ethos.

Notes

This essay has benefited greatly from the critical comments, readings, and suggestions provided by Martin Coward, Marieke de Goede, Mick Dillon, Mark Duffield,
Kate Manzo, and Michael Shapiro. For providing the time and space that made this
research possible, I am grateful to the Leverhulme Trust for the award of a Leverhulme Research Fellowship in 1999–2000.

1. Michael Watts and Iain Boal, "Working-Class Heroes: E. P. Thompson and
Sebastião Salgado," *Transition* 68 (winter 1995): 105.

2. Michael Watts, "Heart of Darkness: Reflections on Famine and Starvation
in Africa," in R. E. Downs, Donna O. Kerner, and Stephen P. Reyna, eds., *The Political Economy of African Famine* (London: Gordon and Breach Science Publishers,
1991), pp. 23–24.

3. See Sander L. Gilman, *Difference and Pathology: Stereotypes of Sexuality, Race,
and Madness* (Ithaca, N.Y.: Cornell University Press, 1985); V. Y. Mudimbe, *The
Invention of Africa: Gnosis, Philosophy, and the Order of Knowledge* (Bloomington:
Indiana University Press, 1988); and Jan Nedeerveen Pieterse, *White on Black: Im-
ages of Africa and Blacks in Western Popular Culture* (New Haven: Yale University
Press, 1992). For a discussion of international relations scholarship in this context,
see Roxanne Lynn Doty, *Imperial Encounters: The Politics of Representation in
North–South Relations* (Minneapolis: University of Minnesota Press, 1996).

4. James R. Ryan, *Picturing Empire: Photography and the Visualization of the
British Empire* (Chicago: University of Chicago Press, 1997).

5. Liisa Malkki, "Speechless Emissaries: Refugees, Humanitarianism, and De-
historicization," *Cultural Anthropology* 11.3 (1996): 386.

6. Erica Burman, "Innocents Abroad: Western Fantasies of Childhood and the
Iconography of Emergencies," *Disasters* 18.3 (1994): 238–53; Margaret Kelleher, *The
Feminization of Famine: Expressions of the Inexpressible?* (Cork: Cork University
Press, 1997).

7. A report by Oxfam on British media coverage of the 1984 famine in the Sahel region of northeastern Africa demonstrated that these photographs featured
mother-and-child images more than any other theme. See Nikki van der Gaag and
Cathy Nash, "Images of Africa: The UK Report," mimeo, November 1987.

8. "Final Plenary—Conclusions, Claire Short's Speech and Debate," presentation to the Dispatches from the Disaster Zone seminar, London, May 27–28, 1998.
Although Short criticized the agencies for eventually making an appeal, the same
agencies were criticized by a BBC TV reporter for not making the appeal sooner.
See George Alagiah, "Hungry for the Truth," *Guardian (Media Supplement)*, May 25,
1998.

9. Fergal Keane, "Another Picture of Starving Africa. It Could Have Been Taken
in 1984, or 1998. How Can We Change the Imagery of Despair?" *Guardian (Media
Supplement)*, June 8, 1998.

10. Ibid.

11. See Jim Akhurst, "Live and Dangerous," presentation to the Dispatches from the Disaster Zone seminar, London, May 27–28, 1998; and Nik Gowing, "New Challenges and Problems for Information Management in Complex Emergencies: Ominous Lessons Learnt from the Great Lakes and Eastern Zaire in Late 1996 and Early 1997," background paper for the seminar, London, May 28, 1998. Despite the increase in the number of news channels—or perhaps as part of the "ghettoization" of international news to a larger number of infrequently watched news channels—the overall amount and quality of international coverage on British TV is in serious decline. See Jennie Stone, *Losing Perspective: Global Affairs on British Terrestrial Television 1989–1999* (London: 3WE–Third World and Environment Broadcasting Project, 2000).

12. Susan D. Moeller, *Compassion Fatigue: How the Media Sell Disease, Famine, War and Death* (New York and London: Routledge, 1999), p. 37.

13. Andy Grundberg, *Crisis of the Real: Writings on Photography, 1974–1989* (New York: Aperture, 1990), p. 240.

14. Moeller, *Compassion Fatigue*, 27 and 35; Edgar Roskis, "The Tarnished Image," *Le Monde diplomatique*, February 2000. Accessed at http://www.monde-diplomatique.fr/en/2000/02/16roskis,22/2/00.

15. Don Redding, "Time for Scrutiny," presentation to the Dispatches from the Disaster Zone seminar, London, May 27–28, 1998.

16. Jonathan Benthall, *Disasters, Relief and the Media* (London: I. B. Tauris, 1993), p. 8.

17. Eduardo Cadava, *Words of Light: Theses on the Photography of History* (Princeton, N.J.: Princeton University Press, 1997), p. xxvii.

18. Andrea Liss, *Trespassing through the Shadows: Memory, Photography, and the Holocaust* (Minneapolis: University of Minnesota Press, 1998), p. 4.

19. See David Campbell, *National Deconstruction: Violence, Identity, and Justice in Bosnia* (Minneapolis: University of Minnesota Press, 1998), especially pp. 189–91.

20. Eduardo Galeano, "Salgado, 17 Times," trans. Asa Zatz, in Sebastião Salgado, *An Uncertain Grace* (New York: Aperture, 1990), p. 15.

21. Amanda Hopkinson, "Salgado, Sabastião *[sic]* Ribeiro," in Martin Marix-Evans, ed., *Contemporary Photographers,* 3d ed. (New York: St. James Press, 1995).

22. John Bloom, "Interview with Sebastião Salgado," *Photo Metro* 9.84 (November 1990): 8.

23. Watts and Boal, "Working-Class Heroes," p. 101.

24. Peter Hamilton, "One Man's Struggle," *British Journal of Photography* 7 (May 1997): 15.

25. Fred Ritchin, "The Lyric Documentarian," in Salgado, *An Uncertain Grace,* p. 145. For a discussion of the Reagan assignment, see Russell Miller, *Magnum: Fifty Years at the Front Line of History* (London: Pimlico, 1999), pp. 253–56.

26. Mark Harris, "Sebastião Salgado," *Camera and Darkroom Photography* 14.11 (1992): 28.

27. *L'Homme en détresse: Photographies de Sebastião Salgado,* Introduction by Jean Lacouture, text by Xavier Emmanuelli (Paris: Prisma Press, pour Médecins sans Frontières, 1986). For a critique of Médecins sans Frontières and its media actions, see François Debrix, *Re-Envisioning Peacekeeping: The United Nations and the Mobilization of Ideology* (Minneapolis: University of Minnesota Press, 1999), chapter 5.

28. See the discussion of this problem in W. J. T. Mitchell, *Picture Theory: Essays on Verbal and Visual Representation* (Chicago: University of Chicago Press, 1994), chapter 5.

29. Ibid., p. 152.

30. See "Famine in the Sahel 1984–85" under the section "The Majority World: Three Photo Essays 1977–92," at http://www.terra.com.br/sebastiaosalgado/.

31. Julian Stallabrass, "Sebastião Salgado and Fine Art Journalism," *New Left Review* 223 (1997): 141. Of course, Salgado's photographs are not the only images to achieve this, but this feature is nonetheless rare. In the Oxfam report compiled after the 1984 famine, only one publication was highlighted in these terms: *Fighting the Famine*, text by Nigel Twose, photographs by Mike Goldwater (London: Pluto Press, 1985). See van der Gaag and Nash, "Images of Africa," pp. 60–61. Insofar as Goldwater's images are progressive, it is largely because of their subject matter. They portray dimensions of African life (labor, education, agriculture, political assemblies, and the like) not normally photographed within the ambit of representing famine, and do not attempt to represent overtly the consequences of famine.

32. Matthew L. Wald, "The Eye of the Photojournalist," *New York Times Magazine*, June 9, 1991, p. 72.

33. Anna Cataldi, "Seizing the Light," *Rolling Stone*, February 23, 1995, p. 67.

34. Galeano, "Salgado, 17 Times," p. 8.

35. See the photograph captioned "Ethiopia 1985" in "Famine in the Sahel 1984–85," at http://www.terra.com.br/sebastiaosalgado/.

36. Ritchin, "The Lyric Documentarian," p. 147; Helen Innis, "The Photography of Sebastião Salgado," Public Lecture at the Australian National Gallery, Canberra, July 14, 1994; Watts and Boal, "Working-Class Heroes," p. 107.

37. Folke Lindahl, "Rewriting the Caribbean: Identity Crisis as Literature," in Michael J. Shapiro and Hayward R. Alker, eds., *Challenging Boundaries: Global Flows, Territorial Identities* (Minneapolis: University of Minnesota Press, 1996), pp. 87–109.

38. Michael J. Shapiro, "Introduction to Part II," in Shapiro and Alker, *Challenging Boundaries*, p. 84. As such, the link between Salgado and magic realism intersects with the argument that the documentary photography of Gilles Peress "derealizes" the world and its realist portrayals. See François Debrix, "Post-Mortem Photography: Gilles Peress and the Taxonomy of Death," *Postmodern Culture* 9.2 (1999). Accessed at http:muse.jhu.edu/journals/postmodern_culture/v009/9.2.r_debrix.html, January 31, 2000. However, Debrix's critique of Peress as offering an aesthetic, comforting, and palatable representation of death—which seems to depend on the idea that representation could better approach the materiality of death by dispensing with the mythical—differs from the argument here.

39. Bruno Bostells, Louis Mirella, and Peter A. Schilling, "The Politics of Totality in Magic Realism," in Shapiro and Alker, *Challenging Boundaries*, p. 111.

40. One of the reasons he focuses on what others (mistakenly) term misery, Salgado argues, is that he comes "from a place where death is a part of life" (Jonathan Cott, "Sebastião Salgado: The *Rolling Stone* Interview," *Rolling Stone*, December 12–26, 1991, p. 141). For a powerful ethnographic account of Brazilian life in these terms, see Nancy Scheper-Hughes, *Death without Weeping: The Violence of Everyday Life in Brazil* (Berkeley and Los Angeles: University of California Press, 1992).

41. Bostells, Mirella, and Schilling, "The Politics of Totality in Magic Realism," pp. 116–20, who align magic realism with Foucault's ethos at p. 111. For my discussion of the importance of Foucault's ethos to the rethinking of international relations, see David Campbell, "Political Prosaics, Transversal Politics, and the Anarchical World," in Shapiro and Alker, *Challenging Boundaries*, especially pp. 19–21, and *National Deconstruction*, chapter 1.

42. Bostells, Mirella, and Schilling, "The Politics of Totality in Magic Realism," p. 112.

43. William Shawcross and Francis Hodgson, "Sebastião Salgado: Man in Distress," *Aperture* 108 (fall 1987): 3.

44. In the book version of the Sahel series, a photograph of a German-run surgery at Abeche Hospital shows a Sudanese man on an operating platform, his arms extended to the side as though he were lying flat on a cross. See *L'Homme en détresse*, p. 40. On Salgado's Web site, the images captioned "Ethiopia 1984," with a shrouded woman and two children, and "Sudan 1985," with a father carrying his son to the Wad Sherifay camp, illustrate this. See "Famine in the Sahel 1984–85" at http://www.terra.com.br/sebastiaosalgado/.

45. See Hopkinson, "Salgado," p. 992. Unlike most other photojournalists, Salgado retains considerable control over how his images are presented in publications. When shooting in Kuwait in 1991, showing the aftereffects of the Gulf War on the region's oil industry, and the workers attempting to cap damaged wells, he used ten to twelve rolls of film per day. From those negatives he chose about six from each roll to print on contact sheets, and from those only forty-seven were selected and sent to the *New York Times Magazine* for possible publication. See Wald, "The Eye of the Photojournalist," p. 72. Control is even greater with respect to his book collections, for Salgado has his own agency, Amazonas Images in Paris, run by his partner Lélia Wanick Salgado, who oversees all aspects of printing and production.

46. See the two images captioned "Mali 1985" in "Famine in the Sahel 1984–85" at http://www.terra.com.br/sebastiaosalgado/.

47. Bloom, "Interview with Sebastião Salgado," p. 19.

48. William E. Connolly, *Identity\Difference: Democratic Negotiations of Political Paradox* (Ithaca, N.Y.: Cornell University Press, 1991 [reprint, Minneapolis: University of Minnesota Press, 2002]), pp. 154–57; William E. Connolly, *Why I Am Not a Secularist* (Minneapolis: University of Minnesota Press, 1999), p. 185ff. This focus on being is readily apparent in Salgado's series on children, in which the individual portraits of young refugees make a statement about what UNICEF has described as "the right of all children to *be*." See "Changing the World with Children: Photographs by Sebastião Salgado," http://www.unicef.org/salgado/. In his discussion with John Berger, Salgado spoke of these portraits as enabling the children to declare "I am here, I exist." See "The Spectre of Hope," *Arena*, BBC2, May 30, 2001. The full series of these portraits has been published as Sebastião Salgado, *The Children: Refugees and Migrants* (New York: Aperture, 2000).

49. "The Spectre of Hope." Some of Salgado's remarks from this documentary (including this quote) are recorded in "'A Tragedy the Size of the Planet,'" *Guardian* (G2), May 28, 2001, p. 10.

50. David Levi Strauss, "Epiphany of the Other," *Artforum* (February 1991): 99.

51. Quoted in Stallabrass, "Sebastião Salgado and Fine Art Journalism," pp. 143–44.

52. Quoted in David Schonauer, "The Sight of Despair," *American Photographer*, January–February 1990, p. 45. There is potentially a parallel here to the idea that even in the concentration camps of the Holocaust there was a moral life. See Tzetvan Todorov, *Facing the Extreme: Moral Life in the Concentration Camps* (London: Phoenix, 1999).

53. Harris, "Sebastião Salgado," p. 28.

54. Hamilton, "One Man's Struggle," p. 15. The comments were made with respect to Salgado's documenting of the Movement of Landless Peasants (MST) in Brazil. Shown in London under the auspices of Christian Aid, these images are published in Sebastião Salgado, *Terra: Struggle of the Landless* (London: Phaidon, 1997).

55. Shawcross and Hodgson, "Sebastião Salgado," p. 3.

56. Ibid, p. 4.

57. Ibid.

58. Hugo Slim, "Sharing a Universal Ethic: The Principle of Humanity in War," *International Journal of Human Rights* 2.4 (1988): 28–48.

59. Mark Duffield, *Global Governance and the New Wars: The Merging of Development and Security* (London: Zed Books, 2001), pp. 76–77.

60. Harris, "Sebastião Salgado," pp. 24 and 26.

61. Sebastião Salgado, *Migrations: Humanity in Transition* (New York: Aperture, 2000), p. 15.

62. Wald, "The Eye of the Photojournalist," p. 72; Susan E. Edwards, "Photography and the Representation of the Other: A Discussion Inspired by the Work of Sebastião Salgado," *Third Text* (Autumn 1991): 172; Cott, "Sebastião Salgado," p. 140.

63. Harris, "Sebastião Salgado," p. 26.

64. Stallabrass, "Sebastião Salgado and Fine Art Journalism," pp. 133–34.

65. Ritchin, "The Lyric Documentarian," p. 149.

66. The spread was in Shawcross and Hodgson, "Sebastião Salgado."

67. Edwards, "Photography and the Representation of the Other," p. 172.

68. Quoted in Wald, "The Eye of the Photojournalist," p. 58.

69. Ritchin, "The Lyric Documentarian," p. 149.

70. Galeano, "Salgado, 17 Times," p. 11.

71. Quoted in Ritchin, "The Lyric Documentarian," p. 147.

72. Miller, *Magnum*, p. 67.

73. Ibid., p. 198.

74. Bloom, "Interview with Sebastião Salgado," p. 12.

75. Ibid., p. 8.

76. Ibid., p. 12.

77. Ibid., p. 6.

78. Ritchin, "The Lyric Documentarian," p. 147.

79. Bloom, "Interview with Sebastião Salgado," p. 8.

80. Edwards, "Photography and the Representation of the Other," 160; Wald, "The Eye of the Photojournalist," p. 58; Innis, "The Photography of Sebastião Salgado."

81. Cott, "Sebastião Salgado," p. 138.

82. Wald, "The Eye of the Photojournalist," p. 58.

83. Ibid.; Cott, "Sebastião Salgado," p. 138.

84. Wald, "The Eye of the Photojournalist," p. 58.

85. Cott, "Sebastião Salgado," p. 138.

86. Ritchin, "The Lyric Documentarian," pp. 146–47. For an account, in the context of the conflict in El Salvador, of the tensions between parachute journalists and regional correspondents, see Mark Pedelty, *War Stories: The Culture of a Foreign Correspondent* (New York: Routledge, 1995).

87. Galeano, "Salgado, 17 Times," p. 11.

88. Edwards, "Photography and the Representation of the Other," p. 157.

89. For the first reading, see ibid., p. 160; for the second, see Watts and Boal, "Working-Class Heroes," p. 112.

90. For the first reading, see Ritchin, "The Lyric Documentarian," p. 147; for the second, see Strauss, "Epiphany of the Other," p. 99. For a discussion of the tensions between Buber and Levinas on the relationship to the other, see Daniel Warner, "Levinas, Buber and the Concept of Otherness in International Relations: A Reply to David Campbell," *Millennium: Journal of International Studies* 25 (spring 1996): pp. 111–28; and David Campbell, "The Politics of Radical Interdependence: A Rejoinder to Daniel Warner," *Millennium: Journal of International Studies* 25 (spring 1996): 129–41.

91. Strauss, "Epiphany of the Other," p. 96. For a discussion of the importance of ambiguity in the rhetorical power of what has been called the New Photojournalism—especially with regard to Susan Meiselas's images of Nicaragua—see Grundberg, *Crisis of the Real*, pp. 182 and 184. For the photographs in question, see Susan Meiselas, *Nicaragua June 1978–July 1979*, edited with Claire Rosenberg (London: Writers and Readers Publishing Cooperative, 1981).

92. Wald, "The Eye of the Photojournalist," p. 59.

93. Watts and Boal, "Working-Class Heroes," pp. 109–10.

94. Bloom, "Interview with Sebastião Salgado," p. 6.

95. Harris, "Sebastião Salgado," p. 24.

96. Cott, "Sebastião Salgado," p. 140; Wald, "The Eye of the Photojournalist," p. 72. For this political understanding of Salgado's ideology, see Watts and Boal, "Working-Class Heroes," p. 110.

97. Ritchin, "The Lyric Documentarian," p. 147. For a further exploration of the anonymous corporeality of most disaster representations, see Malkki, "Speechless Emissaries."

98. Galeano, "Salgado, 17 Times," p. 8.

99. Stallabrass, "Sebastião Salgado and Fine Art Journalism," p. 143.

100. Image captioned as "Ade, Chad, 1985," in "Famine in the Sahel 1984–85" at http://www.terra.com.br/sebastiaosalgado/

101. Schonauer, "The Sight of Despair," p. 40.

102. Benthall, *Disasters, Relief and the Media*, p. 178.

103. Ingrid Sischy, "Photography: Good Intentions," *New Yorker*, September 9, 1991, pp. 89–95.

104. Ibid., pp. 93 and 95.

105. Ibid., p. 93.

106. Ibid., p. 92.

107. Robert McFarlane, "Salgado Goes Deep as TV Flashes By," *Sydney Morning Herald*, June 10, 1995, p. 20A.

108. Sischy, "Photography," p. 92.

109. Image captioned "Mali, 1985" in "Famine in the Sahel 1984–85" at http://www.terra.com.br/sebastiaosalgado/.

110. Robin K. Andersen, "The Ideological Significance of News Photography: The Case of El Salvador," *Ideologies and Literature* 3.2 (fall 1988): 251.

111. Quoted in Kelleher, *The Feminization of Famine*, p. 3.

112. Stallabrass, "Sebastião Salgado and Fine Art Journalism," p. 143.

113. Sischy, "Photography," pp. 93 and 95.

114. Grundberg, *Crisis of the Real*, p. 175; emphasis added. For a thorough critique of *National Geographic*'s imagery, see Catherine A. Lutz and Jane L. Collins, *Reading National Geographic* (Chicago: University of Chicago Press, 1993).

115. Shawcross and Hodgson, "Sebastião Salgado," p. 3. Grundberg makes a similar point about Susan Meiselas's Nicaragua photographs, which he describes as "often intensely beautiful. *Nicaragua* becomes haunting precisely because of the precarious balance between the beauty of its pictures and the horror of what they depict" (*Crisis of the Real*, p. 181).

116. Salgado has been compared with Lewis Hine, but, according to Arthur C. Danto, whereas Hine's photos are valued more for their historical interest, Salgado's will not suffer the same fate. That is because Salgado's images, Danto argues (in response to Salgado's photographs of the workers at the Brazilian Serra Pelada gold mine), are "so abstracted from anything we know that you can't locate it in history. . . . You're astonished that anything like that could happen in the contemporary world. You don't have a frame to put around it, so you feel that you are looking at humanity in some universal way" (quoted in Wald, "The Eye of the Photojournalist," p. 59).

117. Arthur Kleinman and Joan Kleinman, "The Appeal of Experience; the Dismay of Images: Cultural Appropriations of Suffering in Our Times," *Daedalus* (January 1996): 3–9.

118. The story of Carter's photo and its legacy is discussed at length in Greg Marinovich and Joao Silva, *The Bang-Bang Club: Snapshots from a Hidden War* (London: William Heinemann, 2000).

119. David D. Perlmutter, *Photojournalism and Foreign Policy: Icons of Outrage in International Crises* (Westport, Conn.: Praeger, 1998), p. 28.

120. Tom Stoddart, Colin Jacobsen, and John Sweeny, "Moving Pictures," *Reportage* 4 (winter 1998): n.p.

121. Ibid.

CHAPTER FIVE

Sensationally Mediated Moralities
Innocence, Purity, and Danger

Moya Lloyd and Marysia Zalewski

Sensation: Young British Artists from the Saatchi Collection

Art is supposed to mean something; it is supposed to have an effect. The exhibition *Sensation: Young British Artists from the Saatchi Collection* clearly had an effect in keeping with its self-description. One of the authors of this chapter was sitting in a crowded train compartment on the journey home from a visit to London to view the *Sensation* exhibition. On the table, in full view, there was a copy of the catalog from the exhibition with its striking image of the tip of a tongue seemingly touching the tip of an iron (which one imagines is hot). When a train attendant asked if there was any rubbish (garbage) for collection, an elderly man said in an agitated voice, "yes—that book, that's rubbish!" pointing toward the *Sensation* catalog. He then muttered something about "you young people don't know anything these days" (he was *very* elderly), and then carried on reading his book while the other travelers exchanged bemused glances.

This brief anecdote starts to indicate some of the strength of feeling surrounding this exhibition that went on show in London in 1997 when it disturbed sensibilities with its array of "shocking" images by "young British artists." According to the marketing blurb for the show at the Brooklyn Museum in New York, *Sensation* was an attempt to define a generation of artists and their diverse artistic visions. The exhibition included approximately ninety paintings, sculptures, photographs, and installations by forty artists. Included among them was a sliced-up dead cow, a "blood head" (made with the artists' own blood), and a group of mannequin prepubescent children naked except for training shoes and with a "grotesque" variety of genitalia—male/female, intersex/transsex—attached to their faces, necks, and other parts of their bodies. The body and its cultural representations are reputedly the commonality within the artwork. This is represented through a number of themes including "contemporary and pop culture, identity politics, feminism, cultural diversity and racism, mortality, memory, class and social criticism."[1] Thus, on its own account (or at least the Royal Academy's), this exhibition was deemed to be of significant cultural importance.

In Britain it was Marcus Harvey's 3.9-meter-high painting of Myra Hindley that caused the most outrage. Hindley is notorious in Britain for being a child killer. She was convicted of the murders of two children and of being an accomplice in the murder of a third child.[2] The Harvey painting is constructed out of what *appear* to be dozens, even hundreds, of children's handprints.[3] For many the use of a child's handprint in the circumstances proved too much. Two men were arrested after throwing eggs and ink at the work. Much was written in the media expressing abhorrence about the use of Hindley's image as art. Hindley herself also condemned Harvey's artwork as "repugnant and repulsive."[4] When the exhibition was transported to the other side of the Atlantic to New York in 1999 it was Chris Ofili's painting of The Holy Virgin Mary, which included his trademark of elephant dung along with photographs of genitalia, that enraged.[5] Mayor Rudolph Giuliani threatened to withdraw $7 million of public funding if the Brooklyn Art Museum went ahead with the show. Giuliani called the exhibit "sick stuff," claiming: "you don't have a right to government subsidy for desecrating somebody else's religion."[6] On the day the exhibit opened in New York on October 2, 1999, about four hundred protesters from various Catholic organizations gathered around the museum praying and carrying placards that read "Why do you re-crucify me," "Paint Mary the way Jesus sees her," and "Is this the way to treat our Queen?."[7] The exhibition was scheduled to be shown at the National Gallery in Australia in June 2000, but the director of the gallery, Brian Kennedy, canceled it saying that "the issues raised so far have not been about the art; they have been political and too litigious, and I can't lead the gallery into that."[8]

Why all this shock and outrage? What do these responses mean? What can we draw from them? Is there something more (or less) going on than the classic disjunction between contemporary art and public sensibilities, politicians' desire for good publicity and votes alongside the need of the popular press to sell copy by printing "sensational" stories? In order to address these questions, we will discuss the two pieces that appeared to cause most of the controversy and shock: Harvey's portrait of Myra Hindley and Ofili's representation of the Virgin Mary. We have chosen to look at these two pieces in the context of the *Sensation* exhibition and this volume for two reasons. First, art is perceived as something that is global—all cultures "have art." This, of course, does not mean that all art is recognized as "art" either nationally or internationally. In the case of this exhibition, this was most starkly demonstrated through the resistant responses it generated. The second reason for our curiosity about these artworks concerns the transmission and representation of meaning. The usual forms of international exchange, such as media reports, foreign-policy documents, or international summits, are popularly perceived to be relatively transparent in terms of the transmission of meaning (given the premise of goodwill, logic, and rationality). Art, conversely, especially modern art, is generally understood in the public imagination to be in need of *explicit* interpretation and, moreover, is popularly believed to be largely irrelevant to the practices of international relations. By looking at these two pieces of art, we want to demonstrate that there are connections between artistic representations and how we think about the international. In order to demonstrate this we will concentrate on the representations of "femininity" in the images of *Myra* and *The Holy Virgin Mary*.

Femininity and the Question That Is Woman

> The phenomenon of Myra Hindley...the paintings, the songs, the hysteria that surrounds her crimes have made her a public force.[9]

> The "Moors Murders" are deeply embedded in the collective consciousness of our society and it is not an exaggeration to say that Hindley is popularly considered to be the embodiment of evil.[10]

One reason we want to ask about "femininity" and the "question of woman" is because "What is woman?" "Who are women?" "How are women supposed to be?" and "How do women become?" have been core questions within feminist theory since its inception. And when we look at these representations of Myra and Mary we are (im)mediately faced with two very different ideas about what a woman "can be" or "should be." Myra is taken to represent horror—she appears to manifest a paradigm of evil in the form of a woman who helped torture and murder children. It would be difficult to find anyone in Britain today—even those who were not born at the time of the "Moors murders" in the 1960s—who does not recognize this image of Myra Hindley and know (or think they know) what her crimes were.[11] The image chosen by Harvey, an image he describes as having a "kind of hideous attraction," is the police photograph taken of Myra after her arrest.[12] It shows a young woman with peroxide blond hair staring sullenly into the camera. It is the image that stood, and continues to stand, for Myra the child killer. We already "know" so much about this image in Britain as it immediately taps into a local structure of meaning that combines elements of horror and shock (at what happened) and incredulity (that a woman could be involved in the murder of innocent children).

The Virgin Mary, on the other hand, is taken to be the paradigm of feminine virtue and goodness. Although Ofili's depiction of her is not immediately visually recognizable, because the painting does not reproduce a familiar iconography of the Virgin, we would nevertheless be hard pressed to find anyone in the United States or Britain (or in many other places in the world) who did not know who the Virgin Mary is and what she is famous for. Moreover, as with the image of Myra, once we realize that this is a representation of Mary, we are immediately— or, rather, mediately—tied in to a series of discursive inscriptions or mediations already saturated with meaning. These inscriptions/mediations attempt to fix or close understandings of what Mary stands for. As we argue in the next section, one of the "problems" with Ofili's representation is precisely that it challenges how we are allowed to see Mary, making us see things that we do not want to see. Ofili's representation contests the boundaries of what art is and what it is for. It also compels us to rethink gender—particularly femininity—and its mediations. But what is it precisely that these works of art reveal to us about meaning and how it is mediated? What led critics to mobilize discourses of morality/ immorality around these twin images? What apparently inviolable barriers are they deemed to transgress?

Mary/Myra

While it may not be immediately obvious that *The Holy Virgin Mary* is a representation of Mary, the title works to performatively produce that effect.[13] This means that the title works to enact or produce that which it names. The title gives us Mary. Ofili cites, or rather re-cites, the term "Mary" in such a way as to almost magically invoke the history embedded in that name, and by doing so, he also invokes the understanding of the communities to whom Mary means something.[14] This naming not only positions Mary, it also positions us. Indeed, one might say that the artwork interpellates us into specific historical communities.[15] But what kind of history are we talking about here? Clearly, an important history and site of interpellation is that of Christianity. Mary is the mother of Christ. She sacrifices her only son for the good of humanity. She is that apparently most impossible of things, a "virgin mother," pure, innocent, chaste, and sacrificial.[16] Hers is an *internationally* recognized and recognizable narrative. But, of course, the chain of signification extends beyond this Catholic/Christian story. Mary stands metaphorically for all women—all mothers. She is the good mother who puts her children's needs before her own. It is she who is, in however deferred a fashion, appealed to in the image of mother Ireland, or throughout Latin America in the concept of *marianismo*. This is the worthy woman, the good woman, the *mother*. This is Mary the political woman. And, of course, the story would not be complete without the history of art and religious iconography. For many, the images of the Madonna—to give Mary her other name (and, of course, to invoke thereby other Madonnas, not least that most famed of pop stars)—that dominate the imagination are either those found in churches worldwide or those made famous during the Renaissance, that is to say, glorifications and idealizations of the maternal Mary.[17] Could a picture of Mary composed of dung and pieces of pornography constitute an equivalent glorification and idealization of her at the end of the twentieth century?[18] Critics are clear that it cannot.[19] Giuliani repeatedly castigated the work as "sick," "disgusting," and "anti-Catholic."[20] According to media reports at the time, he used his daily press briefings to "lambaste the show as sacrilegious ('throwing dung on important religious symbols')."[21] Cardinal John O'Connor, supporting the mayor of New York, observed, "I'm saddened by what appears to be an attack not only on our blessed mother...but...on religion itself, particularly Catholicism."[22] But the critics did not stop at the discourse of desecration and blasphemy. One also noted that the picture was "misanthropic."[23] But what then of Myra?

The image of Myra Hindley replicated in Marcus Harvey's painting has a particular resonance in Britain. What kinds of mediation are at work in relation to this cultural product? First, the painting of Myra is not a painting of her at all. It is a copy of the 1966 police photograph of Hindley. Thus, it is a painting of a photograph—and, importantly, a painting of the image that appeared in the newspapers of the time.[24] Indeed, looking at the painting, it appears to be a blown-up version of a newspaper reproduction of the police photograph. It is black and white, grainy, and the individual cells (pixels) of the newspaper picture are provided in the painting by repeated use of a child's handprint. *Myra* is a thoroughly mediated, dissimulated image. It is an image that plays deliberately upon mediation—or more accurately on mediatization—a simulated event à la Baudrillard, perhaps. One is immediately drawn to Baudrillard's observation about Mondrian: what Harvey has produced is an image of Myra that is more Myra than the original image of her.[25] This effect is secured, partially, by that aspect of the painting that most shocked many of those who saw (and did not see) it: the use of a child's handprints. It shocks because it *immediately* reminds us of the children who died and of the threat that the Moor's murderers posed to other "innocents." A Myra constituted by—or blotted out by?—the handprints of *children*.

But this immediacy is false; for it is only ever a *mediated* immediacy. The disgust provoked by the use of handprints in the painting is generated by the dissimulated (and not so dissimulated) historicity of the painting. This is no ordinary painting. It is a culmination of a narrative that links together in a complex chain of signification childhood, innocence, evil, loss, and the unnatural woman. One has only to wonder whether there would have been any adverse popular reaction to a painting of Mary composed of the handprints of children; for Myra quintessentially failed to be Mary: she did not sacrifice herself for children. Instead, Myra is that most "unnatural" of women, a child killer. Like the image of Mary discussed earlier, Harvey's representation of Myra interpellates us (or rather those of us who are British) into a particular community. It brings together two things we would really like to keep apart: the innocence of children and the depravity of adults.[26] As such it mobilizes a set of residual meanings that strive to control how Myra can be viewed. Interestingly, the *Sensation* catalog feeds this reading when it notes that "this already sinister image becomes all the more profane as one recognizes that the dotted paint marks are actually children's handprints."[27]

Where Mary is linked to purity, faith, and self-sacrifice, Myra is firmly located within a realm of criminality, deviance, and self-interest. Like Mary's image, Myra's has a symbolic function in the establishment of the categories of innocence and danger, purity and evil. It serves to define a key moment in the charting and production of British criminal history. This effect is achieved in part by the fact that almost every time Hindley is discussed in the media, the same police photograph is used. This image reminds us of what she is and what she represents. It is codified in such a way as to stand in for the notion of "evil" crimes, of the unnatural woman, much in the same way as the Bulger video works to define evil children.[28] It does more than this, however. If reactions in New York are any indication, it performatively evokes criminality and unnaturalness *wherever* it is deployed. Journalist Mark Bloch notes that "Likely to anger some critics is Marcus Harvey's painting *Myra*, a 13-foot rendering of a *British child-killer* created from children's handprints."[29] *Myra* is deemed to be an inappropriate piece of art. Although the use of handprints is significant here, the key issue is her status as a criminal. Art, it seems, according to the logic of the discourse of outrage mobilized by critics, should not glorify the criminal.[30] Art's role is to portray worthy subjects—Mary not Myra. It is one thing to reprint the police photograph of her in newspapers—it is quite another to cross the threshold into "art." It is at this point that the image of Myra begins to cause intense controversy.[31] Someone as morally ugly and repugnant as Myra Hindley cannot be a fit subject for artistic representation. Because it is seemingly not possible to forgive Hindley her crimes, it is not possible to have "innocent" representations of her image in an art gallery. She is not an acceptable sight for viewing. And, of course, the U.S. furor about the *Sensation* show—when not reiterating arguments from blasphemy—centered on the suitability of the exhibits for viewing by schoolchildren.[32]

Both *The Holy Virgin Mary* and *Myra* at once draw upon and mask a whole series of conventions, meanings, and mediations. They mobilize several sedimented histories. Once we know who we are looking at when we gaze at these works we are interpellated into historicized communities. But, of course, even in this context no meaning is ever truly and finally tied down. Just as every citation-depiction of Mary is always a recitation-redepiction, that recitation-redepiction is never only a straight unmediated citation-depiction. We may be directed through the weight of hegemonic interpretation to read these images in a particular way, but those readings are never closed. For the many critics of this painting, there were also those who took it at "face value" as art. In the case of *Myra*, we also have a citation-depiction that is always already a recitation-redepiction. Harvey's *Myra* is not a simple reproduction of the police photograph, however close a resemblance it bears to that photograph, but an artistic re-presentation of that image. And, as such, it too is potentially open to reinterpretation, to contestation, and to challenge.

So where does the preceding discussion leave us? Mediation, as presented, is far from an innocent activity or process. It does not serve to convey an accurate portrayal of reality. Mediation is neither impartial nor neutral. Rather, it generates particular realities and presents them as if they are normal and natural. It is a site where conceptions of what can count as morality, art, or culture and the international are formed, reformed, and performed. And when those conceptions are challenged, intense anxiety can result. Thus, when we are too obviously reminded of the connection between adult depravity and childlike innocence (as with Harvey's Myra) and of erotic desires and bodily excesses (as with Ofili's Mary), we are deeply disturbed. Significantly for our discussion, moreover, mediation is also the site at which conceptions of gender are "formed, reformed, and performed." It is not these artworks as discrete entities that interest us. It is their location within an overarching discourse of sensationally mediated gendered moralities that provokes thought: a discourse organized around innocence, purity, and danger; a discourse that establishes *women as a primary site of its articulation.* What, then, can an analysis of the artworks tell us about women, gender, and femininity?

Smearing

> There looms, within abjection, one of those violent, dark revolts of being, directed against a threat that seems to emanate from an exorbitant outside or inside, ejected beyond the scope of the possible, the tolerable, the thinkable. It lies there, quite close, but it cannot be assimilated. It beseeches, worries, and fascinates desire. . . . Apprehensive, desire turns aside; sickened, it rejects.[33]

The aspect of Ofili's painting that most offended viewers was the smearing of excrement on the image of Mary. Excrement suggests contamination. The pure defiled by the impure. Ofili has thought the unthinkable and connected the unconnectable. It is unthinkable that the mother of Christ should be associated with filth, with that which the body expels, with shit. But, of course, Ofili goes further. Mary is decorated/desecrated by fragmented pictures of genitalia. The Virgin is improperly sexualized and made earthly. Perhaps Mary has morphed into Myra. Myra, that most improper of women, not only a child killer but also a "loose" woman, the vulgar whore to Mary's virgin. The moral order has been disordered. A boundary has been transgressed. *The Holy Virgin Mary* is intolerable, sickening. It must be repudiated accordingly, rendered untouchable, alienated, made foreign.[34]

But there is something else going on. Myra excites us in a way that Mary cannot—or should not. Myra (despite our revulsion of her) remains a fascination. That kind of dyed blond hair of the 1960s carried with it an association of "smut," sex in the backseats of cars, and "fast" girls.[35] This expression of 1960s "fast femininity" dovetails well with our persistent incredulity but steadfast fascination with the "risqué femininity" that Myra personifies. She broke so many of the "proper" gender rules of the 1960s for "good girls" (dyed her hair brassy blond, had sex before she was married, and assisted in the torture and murder of children) even as she obeyed some of the rules of femininity as her man led her (on). But how easy is it for the "good" woman to become the "bad" woman, for Mary to become Myra? What does the (re)incarnation of Mary/Myra do?

Morphing

Despite the modernist obsession with individuality and sovereign subjectivity, what runs amok within modernity, or characterizes the modernist era, is a plethora of dualistic and multiplistic subjectivities. And what characterizes the moral, political, and social order is a drive to control and order those multiplicities into unilinear identities that are easy to read and identify, and even easier to maintain and control. But the artistic representations of the *Sensation* exhibit defy these attempts to circumscribe. They enact a blurring, bleeding, morphing, not only *within* each image, but also *between* them all.

Think of Myra. We cannot forget that she is a woman, though in the British mind-set she exists as a nonwoman, an antiwoman even. She is a bad woman as her behavior is incommensurable with the cultural expectations of womanhood. And yet, she continues to try to pass as a normal woman. But it is not just her defense of her womanness that disturbs through this artistic representation. It is also the relentless reminder of the interrelatedness between purity, innocence, and danger. This is brutally foisted upon us, in part, by the sheer size of Harvey's *Myra*. "The gigantic, particularly in art, is . . . unsettling. . . . it swallows us."[36] When we are unsettled, disheveled, we feel as if we are losing control, and control is essential to maintain order and sense, especially in the context of gender, innocence, and sex. So, women should not kill, especially children. But they do. And a child's world should be free from danger and depravity, and it is not. When allowed into public view, *Myra* disturbs all our certainties. She is dangerous to the life of innocents, to the system of law, to the integrity of moral and ethical borders.

There is, however, a fine line between morphed and singular identities. In an exhibition at the National Museum of Film, Photography and Television in Bradford, England, the curators chose to represent the power of the media by using the 1966 police photo of Myra Hindley. They also chose to display two other iconic images of twentieth-century womanhood on either side of Myra. On one side, there was the classic image of Marilyn Monroe with her white dress billowing up exposing her thighs. On the other side was Mother Teresa pictured holding a child. Monroe, of course, represents a paradigmatically heterosexually attractive woman— who "fortunately" died before her attractiveness began to wane with age. Therefore, on both counts, Marilyn Monroe deserved her place in the gender/sex order. Conversely, Mother Teresa was supposedly far removed from sexuality of any kind. But she also deserved her place in the gender/sex order as she sacrificed her life for others (God and children). What are these "clear" images telling us? And how do they make us feel?

And what of the morphed artistic image constructed by schoolgirl Hannah Brown? For her A-level art course work in 1997 (when the *Sensation* exhibition was shown in London), Hannah Brown painted a picture of herself that blended (or morphed) with the Myra image. She said, "When I considered the word evil, the image of Myra Hindley seemed to me to be its personification. I wanted to show how good and evil can merge and be present in all of us."[37] What does this morphed image do? How does it make us feel?

The first image is clearly intended to be less disturbing than the second. But perhaps neither image is sufficiently disturbing because we know what is supposed to be represented. It is obvious. In the first image,

Myra is counterposed against two women who "earned" their feminine status. This shows us starkly how bad Myra really is. The second image is more reflective as it starts to highlight that the good and the bad are not quite as distinct as we might like to think they are. Yet, with Myra and Mary, something else has occurred and we do not quite know what it is or why it instigates such adverse reactions. It does not seem enough simply to say that Myra is a child killer and her image should not be represented in this way, or that Mary is the mother of God and therefore should not be represented in this way. These explanations are not enough.

But perhaps a clue can be found in the following quote from critical philosopher Slavoj Žižek. Žižek writes: "[A] perfectly 'natural' and 'familiar' situation is denatured, becomes 'uncanny,' loaded with horror and threatening possibilities, as soon as we add to it a small supplementary feature, a detail that 'does not belong.'"38

In these artworks, the "detail that 'does not belong'"—the child's handprint or the animal excrement and pornographic cutouts—forces us, compels us, to know far too much. We can no longer ignore what we do not want to know. It is this compulsion to knowledge that distresses and horrifies us. So, what is it that we do not want to know but cannot ignore any longer?

The (Im)possibility of Woman, the (Im)possibility of Meaning

In the public imagination there is a vast difference between Mary and Myra. But they may in fact be very similar. Isn't it precisely their "sameness" that is exposed when contemplating these two images that shocks us?

Both these women suffer a similar "fate." Both are, in effect, cultural prisoners.39 They are both held in a place beyond that of "ordinary" mortals. Mary is permanently virginal, or, more accurately, nonsexual, despite the conception, gestation, and birth of a child. She is permanently held in the "revered" position of "Mother of God," with all the feminine selfless devotion, pain, and love that goes along with that. She is not allowed to change, not allowed to be anything other than what "we" want her to be, or as her son/God needed her to be. "Paint Mary the way *Jesus sees* her," one of the complaining captions by protesters in New York articulated it.

Myra is not allowed to change either. "We" (the British public?) need her to remain fixed too. As John Upton put it:

> The Moors murderers are one fixed bearing in a sea of relativist notions.
> Everyone knows what to think about Brady and Hindley: that they are
> bad. We derive a moral certainty from them which time has done nothing
> to wear away.... there is no better illustration of the extent to which we
> feel free to manipulate Hindley's image than the Marcus Harvey paint-
> ing exhibited as part of Sensation.... of arguable artistic merit the
> deeper significance [of the painting] lay in the fact that it demonstrated
> our eagerness to accept her decades-old mug-shot as pure art, detached
> from the current reality of her situation.[40]

Myra (at the time of writing) is still alive, and therefore there still exists
the possibility that she might be allowed to change. She can even show
that she has changed. After all, she has shown remorse for her crimes (if
belatedly). But, unlike Ian Brady, her co-accused and co-convicted partner in crime (who wishes never to be released, and indeed has asked to
be allowed to die), Myra has attempted to live something approaching a
satisfying life.[41] She obtained a degree, developed a faith in religion, and
wants to be released from prison. But for the British public, fueled by
tabloid energies, Myra can seemingly never be forgiven, however much
she tries to follow the rules of gender (working hard, being useful). She
appears to be both beyond these rules and to embody them.

And, as for Mary, can she ever become a "real" woman? Does the smearing of something so "impure" actually make her exciting, as exciting as
we find Myra, perhaps? Are these two images of femininity necessary to
support our need for certain and clear moral values expressed and transmitted through discourses of sexuality and gender? Is our "collective"
national and international insecurity secured by paralyzing these feminine beings?

Connections

> Perhaps Harvey's Myra can act as a metaphor for Sensation as a whole:
> superficially disturbing yet unproductively ambiguous, seemingly
> serious yet laden with all the intellectual and critical rigour of a
> miserably glib advertising campaign.[42]

From the perspective of art theory, art critic Suchin may well be right.
Perhaps Myra, as an example of modern British art, merely appropriates, recirculates, and repackages a familiar image of evil in very standard ways, much in the way that an advertising campaign appropriates,
recirculates, and repackages anything from classical music to film scripts
to "traditional" family life. But when we conjoin Myra with Mary in a

more explicitly political sense, an ambiguity emerges that is potentially more fecund. Our argument is that the uncertainty and discomfort instigated by these images of femininty and good and evil nurture the idea that perhaps Mary is Myra and Myra is Mary. We do not mean to say that as individuals these women were the same or acted in similar ways. Our point, rather, is one about the construction, manipulation, and articulation of identities within mediated discourses of (opposing?) moralities.

A classic tenet of feminist theory has been that "the personal is political." In the discipline of international relations, this has logically been transmuted into the idea of "the personal is international."[43] We started this essay with a personal anecdote, a story about an interaction between strangers on a train and an old man, apoplectic with rage at the idea that time, money, thought, and energy were being "wasted" on an unworthy art exhibition. He was not alone in his views. The agitation experienced internationally by the audaciousness of *Sensation* is, in our view, a manifestation of unease over the transgression of boundaries and a sense of distress at the merging of good and evil, cleanliness and filth. The old man was convinced that *Sensation* was garbage, rubbish only good for throwing away and destroying.

However, despite personal and international desires to purge evil and filth by drawing clear boundaries, these boundaries are fragile and arbitrary. Their work is to keep out all that is alien, undesirable, and foreign. Their aim is to exclude the inassimilable. But boundaries are persistently crossed, transgressed, and put under threat from that which is excluded. That which is excluded, the abject (Myra?), is precisely that which though outside (and constitutively outside at that) makes the inside (Mary?) function in the way it/she does. In the wake of the destruction of the World Trade Center, Mayor Giuliani was catapulted into the role of protector, controller, and moral guardian of the city of New York in order to ward off further threats to the city's moral and physical integrity. This reverential image of Giuliani is at odds with his previous reputation for being a "ruthless egomaniac...a world-class control freak,"[44] the man who attempted to police the moral boundaries of his city and, in a sense, failed. But, like Myra and Mary, the two-faced Giuliani reveals not the opposition between good and evil but the inseparability and interdependence of the moral and the immoral, the innocent and the guilty, the pure and the impure, the secure and the dangerous, the domestic/

national and the domestic/international. He is both that which threatens and protects, and that which damages and heals.

The two artworks that have formed the focal point of our discussion not only enable us to consider how the signification of what it is to be a woman operates in multiple registers, they have also compelled us to consider the construction of the international. The international is not simply a site for the iteration and reiteration of (moralistic) discourses of gender (collectively or individually). It is also a site that is formed through that kind of iteration and reiteration. The sign of the "international" is secured and contained only through the violence of abjection. Just as the images/signs of Myra and Mary bleed, blur, and morph into one another because of the constitutive instability of the strategy of containment, so too is the international always already threatened and compromised by that which it expels and purges. Myra and her abjected equivalents, individually and internationally, must be rejected in order for there to be order—moral, legal, international. But these abjected others will always haunt, menace, challenge, and return.

Notes

1. This is how the Brooklyn Museum site described the exhibition. (http://www.brooklynart.org/sensation/sens_more.html). See also the chapters in Royal Academy of Arts, *Sensation: Young British Artists from the Saatchi Collection* (London: Royal Academy of Arts in association with Thames Hudson, 1997).

2. J. M. Schone, "The Hardest Case of All: Myra Hindley, Life Sentences and the Rule of Law," *International Journal of the Sociology of Law* 28 (2000): 277. On May 6, 1966, Myra Hindley was convicted of committing two murders along with the other "Moors murderer," Ian Brady. Brady was also convicted of a third murder with Hindley as an "accessory after the fact." Both were sentenced to life imprisonment. In 1985, Brady confessed to another two murders committed at the same time as the earlier ones. At the time of writing, Brady is still serving his sentence, though he has been on hunger strike for the last three years as he wishes to die (he is being force-fed). Myra Hindley had campaigned for her release for many years, but she died—still a prisoner—in November 2002.

3. In fact, the mold of only one infant's hand was used. See Jennifer Friedlander, *Moving Pictures: Where the Police, the Press and the Art Image Meet* (Sheffield: Sheffield Hallam University Press, 1998), p. 9. Cultural theorist Friedlander notes that the constant misrepresentation of this may indicate more about the status of *Myra* as a "general cultural symbol" than its status as an actual work of art (p. 10). Thus, for instance, one description notes: "The exhibit includes a painting of . . . a serial child-killer whose face is formed with hundreds of children's handprints" (see Willow Lawson, "A Sensation-al Day: Art Exhibit Opens to Religious and Animal Rights Protests," at http://abcnews.go.com/sections/us/DailyNews/artflap991002.html),

continuing the mythology that hundreds of children have been deployed, somehow, in the making of the painting.

4. Friedlander, *Moving Pictures*, p. 28.

5. Significantly, a protester also defaced this image. This time the culprit was a seventy-two-year-old man who, when asked why he had done it, answered, "It's blasphemous" (Robert McFadden, "Art Attack—Pensioner Causes Sensation at New York Gallery by Defacing Ofili Painting," *Guardian*, December 18, 1999). (See also http://www.guardian.co.uk/Archive/Article/0,4273,3943037,00.html.)

6. "Sensation Sparks New York Storm," http://news.bbc.co.uk/hi/english/entertainment/newsid_4550000/455902.stml. See also "Court Tells Giuliani to Back Off in Feud over Art Show," http://www.latimes.com:80/cgi-bin/print.cgi. Deputy Mayor Joe Lhota also weighed in, declaring that a "government-owned facility" should not be used in an antireligious manner. See Geraldine Sealey, "Where Art and Politics Meet: The Conflict Is Nothing New," http://abcnews.go.com/sections/us/DailyNews/artpolitics991002.html.

7. Lawson, "A Sensation-al Day." There are echoes here of earlier protests against perceived anti-Catholic sentiments in Martin Scorsese's 1988 film *The Last Temptation of Christ*.

8. Will Woodward, "Australians Reject Untenable Sensation," *Guardian*, November 30, 1999. (See also http://www.guardian.co.uk/Archive/Article/0,4273,396503,00.html.) For additional coverage of the reaction in Australia, see Jason Nichols and Richard Phillips, "National Gallery of Australia Cancels *Sensation* Exhibition" at http://www.wsws.org/articles/1999/dec1999/sens-d29.shtml.

9. John Upton, "The Evil That Women Do," *Guardian*, October 17, 2000. See also www.guardian.co.uk/Archive/Article/0,4273,4077541,00.html.

10. Schone, "The Hardest Case of All," p. 273.

11. Ibid., p. 277. See also Friedlander, *Moving Pictures*, p. 7. Hindley was convicted of the murders of two children and of being an accomplice in the murder of a third child (Schone, "The Hardest Case of All," p. 277).

12. Harvey is quoted in Friedlander, *Moving Pictures*, p. 10.

13. Loosely speaking, Ofili's collage depicts a black madonna spotted in elephant dung and cutouts of genitalia. The yellow background to the collage is also littered with dung and cutouts. Looking at the image, the face is almost cartoon-like with its apparent caricaturing of black womanhood—large nose and mouth. At the same time, there is no sense of perspective. She does not appear to have a body under the flowing blue robe—or, if there is a body, it is disproportionately small in comparison to the head.

14. See Judith Butler, *Excitable Speech: A Politics of the Performative* (London and New York: Routledge, 1997), p. 49; also Jacques Derrida, "Signature Event Context," in Peggy Kamuf, ed., *Between the Blinds: A Derrida Reader* (Hemel Hempstead: Harvester Wheatsheaf, 1991), pp. 82–111.

15. Louis Althusser, "Ideology and Ideological State Apparatuses," in *Lenin and Philosophy and Other Essays* (New York: Monthly Review Press, 1971), pp. 127–86. Althusser's context is obviously different in that he argues that it is naming or "hailing" that interpellates us. We want to suggest that these artworks also "hail" us in different, often competing ways.

16. In the context of modern technology (such as in vitro fertilization, gamete intrafallopian transfer), "virgin" mothers are entirely possible. Additionally, artificial

(or more accurately nonsexual) insemination, or what we have come to call surrogate motherhood, has been practiced for generations. See Margrit Shildrick, *Leaky Bodies and Boundaries: Feminism, Postmodernism and (Bio)Ethics* (London: Routledge, 1997).

17. Typically, these idealizations are of Mary with the baby Jesus. The image is, as it were, an asexual image. During the Renaissance, however, there were exceptions to this. For instance, Piero della Francesca famously painted a pregnant—clearly fertile—Madonna, the *Madonna del Parto* (to be found at the chapel at Monterchi, Italy). For consideration of della Francesca's oeuvre, see Alessandro Angelini, *Piero della Francesca* (Florence: SCALA, Istituto Fotografico, 1985). In 1999, there was an outcry in Seattle over the "heavily bossomed and pregnant" *Picardo Venus* (a garden statue) that many found "too suggestive." One citizen commented that the Venus "glorifies fertility a little too much for kids," once more endorsing the idea that Mary cannot be seen to be womanly, with all the earthly connotations that may suggest (quotations from Dana Mack, "It isn't pretty...but Is It Art?" at http://www.csmonitor.com/durable/1999/11/09/p9s1.html).

18. Dana Mack contextualizes Ofili's work by observing that Ofili is a "Roman Catholic earnestly coming to terms with his faith, his African heritage, and a long Western tradition of representing the Madonna" ("It Isn't Pretty").

19. Interestingly, the *Sensation* catalog includes a comment about the ways in which Ofili's "multi-layered approach challenged the rules of good taste by a skillful combination of eclectic elements" (p. 29). Although this pertains to another artwork, it is an interesting insight into "taste" that could be extended to *The Holy Virgin Mary*.

20. See, for instance, "Brooklyn Museum Wages War: Files Suit, Vows Exhibit Will Start Saturday," http://more.abcnews.go.com/sections/us/DailyNews/bma-lawsuit990928.html; Tom Hays, "Judge Sides with Brooklyn Museum: Orders Funds Restored, Rebuffs Giuliani in Uproar over 'Sensation,'" http://www.msnbc.com:80/news/329989.asp?cp1=1; Melissa Russo, "Giuliani Angered by Art Ruling," http://www.msnbc.com/local/wnbc/531066.asp; Max J. Castro, "A 'Conservative' Giuliani—for a Very Good Reason," http://www.herald.com:80/content/wed/opinion/digdocs/024027.html; "NYC Ordered to Restore Funding for 'Sensation': Millions of Dollars at Issue," http://abcnews.go.com:80/sections/us/DailyNews/sensation991101.html. See also Fred Kaplan, "Court Orders N.Y. to Restore Museum Funds: Judge Says Mayor Violated Museum's Free Speech Rights," http://www.spokane.net:80/news-story-body.asp. For additional similar remarks, see Ellen Wulfhorst, "New York Mayor Loses Round in Art Museum Dispute," http://news.excite.com/mailstory/stories/r/991102/03/entertainment-art-museum.html, and Nick Clarke, "British Art Exhibition Faces Closure in New York," http://www.netlondon.com/news/1999-39/B983E40B990B1FD0802.html.

21. "Court Tells Giuliani to Back Off in Feud over Art Show."

22. Mark Bloch, "Art Exhibit Sparks Controversy, Ire: First Lady Joins the Fray over Museum's Funding," http://more.abcnews.go.com/section/us/DailyNews/BMA_giuliani990923.html. Many politicians joined the debate. For instance, George W. Bush commented that the "exhibit besmirches religion," and Hillary Clinton found it "objectionable," according to aides. See "Who Hates It Most? Politicians Continue Protests over Brooklyn Exhibit," http://abcnews.go.com/sections/politics/DailyNews/

brooklynmuseum991004.html. See also Wulfhorst, "New York Mayor Loses Round in Art Museum Dispute."

23. Debra J. Saunders, "A Heap of Art Grows in Brooklyn," http://www.sfgate.com:80/chronicle/archive/1999/11/02/ED44676.html.

24. Peter Suchin, "Sensation: Young British Artists from the Saatchi Collection, Royal Academy, London, September to December 1997," http://bak.spc.org/everything/e/hard/texts2/condensation.html. Art critic Suchin claims that much of the media reporting of the exhibition, and in particular of "Harvey's Myra," lacked any "intelligent discussion of its historical or cultural resonances." For example, despite the fact that *Myra* is a painting of a *photograph* of Hindley, commentators seem oblivious of any potential connections with the furor surrounding the impact of rampant photographing in relation to the death of the Princess of Wales in the same year as the launch of the *Sensation* exhibition. Suchin further mentions two other paintings that used photographs in connection with death: Warhol's *Most Wanted Men* and Richter's *18. Oktober 1977*, the latter based on police photographs of the Baader-Meinhof group's alleged collective suicide. There is, of course, something interesting going on in terms of what Friedlander calls the "different discursive economies" within which Myra's image circulates (*Moving Pictures*, p. 4), in this instance between the economies of the media-reproduced image and the artwork. As art critic John Molyneux observes, "insofar as this particular image of Hindley possesses iconic power in our culture it is the media's constant use of it . . . that created it," suggesting a certain hypocrisy on the part of the media in condemning Harvey's reproduction of this image. See his "State of the Art: A Review of the 'Sensation' exhibition at the Royal Academy of Arts, September–December 1997," *International Socialism*, issue 79 (July 1998); also at http://www.isj1text.fsnet.co.uk/pubs/isj79/molyneux.html.

25. As Baudrillard comments, "freed from the 'true' Mondrian, you are free to produce a Mondrian that is more Mondrian than Mondrian himself" (Jean Baudrillard, "Transpolitics, Transsexuality, Transaesthetics," in William Stearns and William Chaplouka, eds., *Jean Baudrillard: The Disappearance of Art and Politics* [New York: St. Martin's Press, 1992], p. 14).

26. Friedlander, *Moving Pictures*, p. 10.

27. Royal Academy of Arts, *Sensation: Young British Artists from the Saatchi Collection*, p. 198.

28. The "Bulger video" shows a toddler (James Bulger) being led by the hand by two older boys who shortly afterwards murdered him. This video has also been the subject of "artistic interpretation" by Jamie Wagg with his *History Painting: Shopping Mall* that he exhibited in 1994. It was generated from the surveillance camera image of James Bulger being led away by his murderers. See Friedlander, *Moving Pictures*, p. 3.

29. Bloch, "Art Exhibit Sparks Controversy, Ire."

30. Of course, art often does potentially glorify all manner of "deviant" identities. Examples might include the prostitutes in the work of Picasso and Lautrec and Goya's images of demons of war.

31. Friedlander, *Moving Pictures*, p. 4.

32. Hays, "Judge Sides with Brooklyn Museum"; Bloch, "Art Exhibit Sparks Controversy, Ire"; Russo, "Giuliani Angered by Art Ruling." The Brooklyn Museum's

own site notes state, "Because of the challenging aspects of some of the work, children under 16 must be accompanied by an adult" (http://www.brooklynart.org/sensation/sens_more.html).

33. Julia Kristeva, *Powers of Horror: An Essay on Abjection* (New York: Columbia University Press, 1984), p. 1.

34. And, intriguingly, to alienate it is to literally make it foreign: it is to acknowledge its Britishness. One placard carried by protesters outside the Brooklyn Museum read: "Is this the way to treat our Queen?" implying that the artwork, *The Holy Virgin Mary*, displays a xenophobic disrespect for the Queen of the Catholics.

35. Martin Maloney (lecturer and art critic) suggests that one motivation behind the exhibition is to expose a "particularly British mix of shabby sex and smutty jokes" ("Everyone a Winner! Selected British Art from the Saatchi Collection," in Royal Academy of Art, *Sensation*, p. 32).

36. Susan Stewart, quoted in Friedlander, *Moving Pictures*, p. 10.

37. "Schoolgirl's 'Me and Myra' Portrait," http://www.wightonline.co.uk/news/news_pages/oct97/11280.html.

38. Slavoj Žižek, *Looking Awry* (Cambridge: MIT Press, 1992), p. 88.

39. It might also be claimed that both are political prisoners. Certainly Hindley is frequently described as the latter. See, for instance, Friedlander, *Moving Pictures*, p. 11, and "Myra Hindley: Justice, the Law, the Judges and the Politicians: How Long Should Myra Hindley Stay in Prison?" (http://ourworld.compuserver.com/homepages/brianbarder/Hindley.html). For a consideration of the politics of sentencing, see Schone, "The Hardest Case of All."

40. Upton, "The Evil That Women Do."

41. The presiding judge (Justice Fenton Atkinson) at the trial of Brady and Hindley wrote to the then Home Secretary saying that Brady's influence had "deeply corrupted" Hindley and she should be "removed from his influence." In a later judicial review, Lord Chief Justice Thomas Bingham noted that "Brady was the initiator of these crimes and the actual killer; the applicant [Hindley] was cast as his willing accomplice, corrupted and dominated by him" (cited in Schone, "The Hardest Case of All," pp. 280–81). Brady was convicted of all three murders compared to Hindley's conviction for two.

42. Suchin, "Sensation."

43. Cynthia Enloe, *Bananas, Beaches and Bases: Making Feminist Sense of International Politics* (Berkeley: University of California Press, 1990), p. 195.

44. Ibid.

CHAPTER SIX

Site Improvements

Discovering Direct-Mail Retail as "B2C" Industrial Democracy

Timothy W. Luke

This analysis investigates a few qualities of culture and space in the transnational polity as they operate now in the twenty-first century. These concerns are important if we are to understand fully the reticulations of power and knowledge on a local, national, or global level through what Baudrillard has defined as "the system of objects." All of these terms, however, remain mutable in their meanings. And, they are constantly evolving every day in the systems at play in objects—capitalism, nationalism, technology, utility. At the same time, my goal is to begin assessing here the innumerable mediations creating many transnations behind the transnational. Although these developments have become overpowering, they are not entirely unprecedented.

A century ago in 1901, another cultural project was being articulated in the transnational space of European, and non-European but still Westernizing, imperialism as England, France, Germany, Italy, Spain, Portugal, Russia, and the Netherlands vied with each other as well as Japan, Ottoman Turkey, and the United States to create a globalized economy and society whose modernity rested upon the mediations of aristocratic myths, *haute bourgeoise* culture, and racial formulas of authority. Five decades ago in 1951, yet another cultural and spatial order was being cemented together by the mediating influences of ideological zone-regimes in which a Western liberal democratic capitalism, centered on NATO countries and the United States, faced off against an Eastern state-planned communism, tied to the Warsaw Pact countries and the Soviet Union. These two competing visions of modernity offered the world an allegedly individualist or collectivist notion of organizational efficiency, technological prowess, and personal consumption. Another visit to Earth in 1936—the midpoint of 1901 and 1951—would have found yet another project for reimagining culture and space transnationally in the fascist polities of Germany, Italy, and Spain, but all these popular representations of cultural identity, national place, and global power mostly have now crumbled into ruins after 1914, 1945, and 1989.

The world of 2001 is built upon those ruins, but the sites of its culture, space, and transnational polity all have their own new emergent properties—most of whose mediations are increasingly private, domestic, or personal. We need to explore how these sites and their improvement with things underpin the articulation of a new mode of power—culturally and spatially—in today's ill-defined projects of globalization. To do this, we must rethink how the USA once operated as a monotonic, fixed superpower for these decades, but now it has evolved, as an economy and society, in ways that have made it by comparison into a remarkably new kind of multicultural, flexible hyperpower.

First and foremost, during the space race and cold war, the USA accepted, along with nationality in territory, the new nodality of distributed authority and decentered power in networks, as a new axis for its civic life, enabling it to undercut older notions of ideological nationalism, patriotism, or fundamentalism with cultural scripts and packages from nowhere (or the networks) and everywhere (or the spaces bridged by networks). In this process, the monomorphic forms of national "hard power" in the United States, as the Arsenal of Democracy and Defender of the Four Freedoms in 1941, had fractalized by 2001 into the polymorphous expressions of American "soft power."[1] Hence, the winner of the space race to the Moon also has remade many spaces here on Earth. These remediations of space enabled forms of control flow through many nodalities that remediate ways of life, places of being, types of identity sourced from everywhere through Universal Paramount in Hollywood, Microsoft in Redmond, CNN in Atlanta, Citibank in Manhattan, Ford in Dearborn, Frito-Lay in Dallas, Disney in Orlando, or McDonald's in Chicago. Styles of dress, diet, design, and devotion from Europe, Asia, Africa, Australasia, and the Americas are continuously sucked into and switched through a dense tangle of global networks. These mediations now are tying together people and things at innumerable sites with commodities. Many of them have been, are, or will be regarded by some in the United States as "foreign," but once they enter the networks as signs or substance they also often become "American" content. Of course, other nodes with considerable content, scale, and authority route heavy traffic through Japan, France, Brazil, Germany, Taiwan, and Great Britain, but the key nodes of these networks rest in the USA. Hence, globalization in many ways is now a stealthy style of modernization and development, expressing the mostly nodalized Americanization of these commoditized transnations rather than a hard-core American nationalism rooted in one country.[2]

Ironically, the track record of American nationalism at spreading political democracy has been very mixed since 1945, especially when one looks outside of Western Europe. At the end of the day, the USA has been woefully unsuccessful in bringing much substantive democracy to the world—either during or after the cold war. Of course, this program for political democratization has brought formal democracy to many lands once ruled by communist apparatchiki, military strongmen, or landed oligarchs, but then what prevails in many formalized democracies is rule through undeveloped parties, parliaments, and policies under the administration of now "reformed" CP hacks, generals in suits, or wealthy agriculturalists. The vision of industrial democracy, however, which was openly propounded as "consumer democracy" during the ideological struggle with the USSR, has taken stronger hold through the magic of markets around the world. People might be barred from voting, and their votes every three, four, or five years might mean very little, but industrial democracy assures them that they can improve their lives daily at the market by voting with their money for what they see as progress, prosperity, or performance.[3]

So, while the hard slog for substantive democracy proceeds at its own halting pace, this globalized consumer democracy plays immediately to the perfectibility of people by advancing "development" at the most basic elemental level in people's everyday life-worlds. This formula for social control suggests that "better things will bring better living," and commercial culture at the local, national, and global levels of articulation moves consumers to vote with their pocketbooks in favor of this much more broadly democratized system of popular perfectibility.[4] As they say on the Net, this is "B2C" commerce, or the building of business-to-consumer trading relationships. Yet, the vendors of most goods and services, which are the source of new improvements sought by all, acquire cultural authority, first, by acting as the proponents of progress, and, second, by managing consumer demand for the goods and services that have been identified as being equivalent to a people's progressive perfection.[5] America's worldwide reimagination of consumer democracy with these aspirations to attain perfectibility for all, in turn, has created an essentially commercialized public space out of private needs.

"Getting the goods" in this environment becomes a political program for "ethical development," or the shaping of consumers' character around businesses' values and practices, not unlike those rhetorics pushed by progressive professionals in the USA during the twentieth century.[6] One advertising firm in Philadelphia summed up the essential ethos of B2C industrial democracy quite succinctly during 1914: "if we believe that people ought to keep on trying to live a little better and have a little more ambition, then we must believe that whatever shows people the way and rouses their ambition—to possess—and *produce* in order to possess—is a public service."[7]

Sites and Sources for Analysis

To illustrate how the mediations of B2C industrial democracy some-times work today, one can turn to many sources of evidence: television programs, major movies, department stores, highway billboards, monthly magazines, or Web content. One particularly rich source of these texts, however, can also be found in junk mail from niche retailers. Although many might disbelieve this assertion, the utopias of site improvement cannot be surpassed for many people after they read their latest catalogs from *The Sharper Image, Frontgate, Williams-Sonoma, Herrington, Crate & Barrel, L.L. Bean, Levenger, Hammacher Schlemmer, Cabela's, Land's End, Pottery Barn, Orvis, Eddie Bauer, Sur la Table, Talbots,* or *The Terri-tory Ahead.*

Of course, this evidence will have an idiosyncratic drift to it, because it is skewed in directions taken by the torrent of direct mail that pours into their homes. Culling through catalogs salvaged from neighbor-hood slick paper recycling bins or received at home for about four months, one can use these print capitalist documents to document how contemporary capitalism imprints itself in culture, space, and politics through an ethos of continuous improvement. Clearly, this is a constant communication that we cannot easily evade as we receive such mailings as representations of a newer, more perfect life, in which a normative regime of human perfectibility is tied to acquiring more, new, and better things. The systems of objects articulating globalization are seamless: local space holds the sites we must improve, and global culture grants guidance on what improvements are best in these spaces.

Each of these print capitalist enterprises, in turn, has a Web presence now, and one can enter their many respective utopian domains as easily today from Tokyo as Toledo, Delhi as Dallas, Bogotá as Boston, Lisbon as Louisville. Certainly, many more people in Toledo, Dallas, Boston, and Louisville have the income and leisure to improve their lives with goods drawn from these providers, but increasingly some others in the right neighborhoods of Tokyo, Delhi, Bogotá, and Lisbon also can conduct their lives in accord with such things.[8] And, more important, those without many things now in Tokyo and Toledo, Delhi and Dallas, Bogotá and Boston, Lisbon and Louisville all might imagine how their comparatively miserable places might be improved and their identities enhanced—in accord with the system of objects—by getting almost anything from these prestigious sources of perfection. No one at any of these sites forces them to become "Americanized," if this even is Americanization, because they typically will desire these goods as one key among many for unlocking the goods for what the transnations behind global mass culture project as their human perfectibility.[9]

These texts are suggestive, because they are so raw about the project of remediating B2C industrial democracy as personal "site improvement." Whether it is the great outdoors with *Cabela's* or *L. L. Bean,* the home with *Williams-Sonoma* or *Pottery Barn,* the office with *Levenger* or *Store Everything,* or the car with *International Auto Enthusiast* or *Herrington,* their common conceit, as *Lifestyle Fascination* asserts, is that they bring "America's most innovative products" to market. Still, each wish or purchase made in their pages actually produces the most innovative aspects of what many would desire, and/or deride, as Americanization. In a world cast around hard power, "America's most innovative products" would have once meant the most innovative products produced in America by Americans. Today it only means the most innovative products produced everywhere for America, and those who consume their culture and identity like Americans, but now available for sale at "www.shoplifestyle.com." Thus, in keeping with the original implications of "fascination" from the Latin *fascinare,* or to hold in spell, captivate, or possess, the goods and services available from *Lifestyle*

Fascination, and all of these other slick catalogs for lifestyle management, create captivating lifestyles whose commodified spell possesses their users in commercialized quests for personal perfection. It is from these normative injunctions to find perfection in things that one finds the habitus of site improvements. As a structured and structuring structure, these rules rest upon "the capacity of produce classifiable practices and products (taste)" upon which "the represented social world, i.e., the space of life-styles [habitus] is constituted."[10]

The accumulation of things under the B2C practices for making site improvements discloses "the processes whereby people relate to them and with the systems of human behavior and relationships that result therefrom."[11] In many ways, then, this analysis only begins to probe the habitus of social control, political organization, and economic order underpinning the transnational polity. The system of habituation at stake here surfaces in many places, but I want to probe it on very elemental levels where it captures and confines the conduct of everyday conduct at sites located in home, work, or leisure. Although these ephemera may appear to be trivial texts for those who believe our ideas and goals only can come from the philosophical works of Descartes, Hume, or Kant, it seems more likely that many more people, if they read at all, turn to Eddie Bauer, L. L. Bean, or Williams-Sonoma for their ideas of, and goals for, the good life.[12]

The legitimacy of each national polity now basically rests upon delivering these goods at a local, national, and global level. Intellectuals might chatter on about a spiritual perfection tied to spectral goods, such as liberty, equality, or justice, but most voters seek material satisfaction as consumers. So an identity linked to getting new DVD machines, stainless outdoor grills, exotic Eurostyle appliances, or cool car stuff is the "Progress" that most firmly legitimates the working of a transnational polity today.

Peoples and places who do not get these goods to improve themselves and their sites immediately acquire other less favorable identities in the world system. More favored sites, and the things available for purchase and installation in them, also are popularized throughout the world in TV sitcoms, Hollywood blockbusters, and the print media. Every episode of *Friends,* the *Home Alone* movies, or *USA Today* dailies, for example, mediates popular cultural representations internationally of how modern life in the twenty-first century ought to be lived by

focusing on domestic and work spaces where people are shown perfecting their lives by improving these private places with new things.
The total abstraction of markets returns in the abstract totality of the
market for things. Perfectibility is the ultimate means of projecting
power and order cathexis. In this assemblage of things, "everything has
to intercommunicate, everything has to be functional—no more secrets, no more mysteries, everything is organized, therefore everything is
clear."[13] Thus, global corporations, like General Electric, can boast that
their business is "bringing good things to life," which positions the living
in networks of people and things that convey goodness in/to life, and
turns international business into those enterprises tied to bringing such
good things to market.

Retail as Realpolitik

Direct marketing of consumer goods is a ceaseless war of position conducted through systems of objects by contemporary global business in
support of an emergent transnational polity. There are many sources of
this war, but the key sites that its aggressive B2C campaigns besiege are
the home, the outdoors, the office, and the car. Each one of these sites
can be made the focus of various improvements to perfect the individual and society by embellishing features of the sites. As individuals seek
perfection at their personal sites by the satisfying of their needs in the
economic system, Baudrillard maintains that "it is the economic system
that induces the individual function and parallel functionality of objects and needs."[14]

The Home

Everyone's domestic spaces are the penultimate site for improvement in
the networks of contemporary globalization. Whether one lives in the
flashy suburbs of southern California or the seething favelas of São Paulo,
the household is where the global consumer society envisions the good
life coming to reality from transnational commerce's goods and services.
In the United States, *Frontgate* asserts that it is "outfitting America's
finest homes," but it also thereby packages "America's finest home outfits"
for anyone else who would buy *Frontgate* products—"for everyday living on a grand scale."[15]

From Luxury Bath, Personal Care, Kitchen Accessories Gourmet
Kitchen to Luxury Shower, Home Office, Outdoor Enchantments, Home

Convenience, *Frontgate* offers a panoply of high-status, high-tech, and high-end goods to improve each one of these microsites in everyday life. Taking a shower can be cleaning one's body with a spray of water, but *Frontgate*'s Luxury Shower things transform this corner of the bathroom into something "more than a shower, this is an experience."[16] As an experience, a German-engineered "ultimate shower system from Hansgrohe," which, of course, resonates with many professional-technical workers' "ultimate driving experience" in their BMWs, offers daily contact with perfection. And, of course, those seeking such perfect showering experiences will need "authentic English Baskets" in brass or chrome to give "soaps and sponges a place of their own."[17]

Accumulating things to perfect one's life, and then finding more perfect things to gain more organization and efficiency, is the watchword of Frontgate. Page after page promises an ongoing modernization campaign to improve one's sites of life. The perfect things one acquires to perfect the self all have their own spatial improvements, which can advance global consumer culture. Each quadrant of the life-world, then, needs new things to give those things special places of their own, end bath clutter, store fine jewelry, restore order in the laundry, organize mail, eliminate odds-and-ends clutter, personalize your home, get professional results at great value, keep walkways clean and safe, find perfect solutions to garden tool clutter, bring the efficiency of a European bath to your home, provide ample storage, and so on. Thus, any ensemble of attractive objects simply serves "to reintroduce any conceivable element, whatever subjective associations it may carry, into the logic of the system."[18]

What *Frontgate* presents most aggressively as its site improvements are the imperatives of clutter containment. An industrial ecology tied to Francis Fukuyama's blessed state of "accumulation with end" needs its own transcendent ends for managing these new waves of life-perfecting accumulation.[19] Creating more social order and personal improvement with things, then, requires ever-vigilant personal guardianship over these things to enforce order, efficiency, and safety. Such things will transmit their improvements to people and other things, enhancing the placement of things in accord with these normatively charged assessments of personal space.

Frontgate's site improvements are paralleled by many other providers of cultural expression and spatial enhancement. *L. L. Bean Home, Eddie*

Bauer Home, Williams-Sonoma, Herrington, The Sharper Image, Hammacher Schlemmer, Pottery Barn, or *Crate & Barrel* all can serve as sources of key site improvements. *Crate & Barrel* and *Sur la Table* offer elements of urban panache in chi-chi glassware, Eurodesign cookware, and Italian widgets. The edgy urban look can be accessed at *The Sharper Image* and *Hammacher Schlemmer,* while "the country" is on sale at *L. L. Bean* and *Eddie Bauer.* Beyond these specific product semantics, the goods and services being offered by direct-mail retailing articulate a common vision of culture and space. To attain perfection, one only needs to improve one's home, office, auto, and outdoor sites with newer, better things, which are, first, represented by retailers, and then, second, acquired by consumers, as representatives of abundance, progress, order, efficiency, or good taste.

Therefore, consumers seek a systematized sense of perfectibility in reading these representations into their lives, and then accepting with their purchases the representatives of perfection brought to them as Greek rugs, New Zealand sweaters, Italian coffeemakers, German showerheads, English flatware, French pans, or Hungarian stemware. Private space is what counts, and perfecting those sites with more, better, finer things brings greater human perfectibility. Such dicta, then, move consumers with the credit or cash to import ensembles of leather club chairs cued to art deco Paris, systems of wood furniture styled off of Mission Period California, office setups pitched out of Milano chic, and 4x4 truck accessories tied to clearing kangaroos in Australia's outback.

To become better as a person, one burrows further into more classic and classy things, and thereby goes farther toward improving one's ever-perfectible sites. Every catalog photograph stages a normative moment of almost perfect satisfaction. Some—like *Pottery Barn* or *Williams-Sonoma*—stage interior scenes without any people, like exotic outdoor nature photographs, giving consumers an unsullied vista of virgin leather, roaring fires, lit candles, untracked rugs, cozy couches all standing forth as representatives of a high-end lifestyle. With this chair, your space becomes perfected. With this bed, you sleep most restfully. With this pan, you attain professional performance. Space is a domain of frozen action with still artifacts wanting to impart their improvements to the perfection-seeking buyer. Other outlets—like *The Sharper Image* or *Frontgate*—reveal intense obscenes of towel-swathed blondes attaining ecstasy in the shower, by the bathtub, in a closet, or on the bed as they assure readers of a shower seat's reliability, a bath sheet's softness, a closet organizer's efficiency, or a down comforter's warmth. Things are still representatives of perfection, but the human models are their emissaries of excellence to give an even clearer sighting of how human beings improve their sites with these things."

The Outdoors

For some, spaces outside of the home could be difficult sites to improve, but niche retailers have many things on sale to steer the conduct of conduct in these locales as sport, leisure, and homemaking. Flicking through *L. L. Bean's* or *Eddie Bauer's* catalogs, one gets the Great Outdoors as a boutique lifestyle, which either brings the suburbs out to the woods or the woods into suburbia. *L. L. Bean's* and *Eddie Bauer's* gear for suburbanites' weekend outdoor enthusiasms, however, are totally eclipsed in the gear available from *Cabela's.*

Here the perfection of better big-game hunting, sport fishing, or cross-country orienteering is given form with charcoal-lined camo suits, expensive fishing waders, and tough hiking boots as well as powerful compound bows, ATV accessories, and survival tools. Its "Master Catalogue" sells technologies of power to its customers, who clearly want the best boots, camo suits, ammunition, tree stands, tents, rifle telescopes, camp stoves, and gutting knives that money can buy for the expeditions afield.

Sporty's, on the other hand, presents goods for other sorts of outdoor enthusiasms, ranging from power buffers for one's classic Corvette, power washers for one's three-car garage driveway, or power food cooler/warmer for one's SUV to a GPS system for the motor yacht, super high-end stainless patio ranges, or folding garden carts. The endless disorder of the lawn, garden, campsite, or beach is promised permanent solutions with *Sporty's* goods. Again, uncluttering with ease, efficiency, and excellence is what counts, so the highest quality, most accuracy, greatest strength, fullest flexibility, and toughest materials are what *Sporty's* touts. Here, the company says, superior performance counts: "As the undisputed leader in product testing, *Sporty's* has time and time again made the products we carry prove themselves.... Why such extremes? Because we want everyone who buys from *Sporty's* to know they are getting the best of what's around."[20] One, then, rests fully assured that these outstanding goods will improve one's outdoors sites, and each good is a representative of field-tested performance.

The Office

Work spaces are the center of most people's waking hours. Hence, it is no surprise that the direct-mail retail industry targets these sites with numerous artifacts to perfect those places. One clearly wants to appear to be progressing toward perfection at work every day, so office things typically are heavily encoded with perfectibility performance.

Levenger sees the office as a space needing customization and class. Work appliances, such as Palm Pilots or laptops, need wood veneer facings or high-class leather accessory cases. Finding comfort, style, and quality are the requisite goals of office-improving buyers, and *Levenger's* supplies of Aeron chairs, Danish Euro desks, and Watermen pens are pitched perfectly at these markets. So fine woods, European craftsmanship, and supple leathers are the signs of superlative service that *Levenger* trades upon to vend its "tools for serious readers."

The Sharper Image's office improvements promise a sleek, high-tech set of solutions to the average consumer who hopes to attain existential perfection with personal gadgets and neat toys. Whether it is an Electronic Driving Range, Interactive Talking Globe, Ionic Air Purifier, Electronic Memo Recorder, Executive DC Stereo System, or Leather Rolling Computer Briefcase, this outlet aims at the corporate consumer eager for image sharpening through the accumulation of electronics-intensive, platinum-colored, design-expressive goods. Here things reveal their buyers as having "the right stuff," or, as Richard Thalheimer, *Sharper Image's* founder, asserts about his company's goods as gifts, these things are material representations of quality that are "fun. Imaginative. Surprising. Useful. Heartfelt. Memorable."[21]

The Car

Another critical space that centers many individuals' everyday life is the automobile, as it carries people in mobile private spaces on public roads from their personal households to corporate workplaces. Travel is taxing, especially the daily commute to and from work. Consequently, the good life can be continuously reimagined around many other fine things for the car, driver, or garage. As *International Auto Sport* suggests, one's automotive vehicle is at the center of "life and leisure," so it provides those things needed "to get the most utility—and enjoyment—out of your vehicle."[22]

As the connective medium between house and office, home and the outdoors, or familiar route and uncommon road trip, autos are a site that requires many different kinds of improvement. Clutter containment, continuous cleaning, and customized convenience, in particular, are all outcomes that the system of objects stresses for the car. Cargo liners for SUVs, special waxing tools, and hands-free cell phones are valorized as things to perfect the driving experience to and from one's equally customized household and office. Tools that fit into each site are shown interoperating in all sites to support a perfectible existence on the road and off.

Plainly, the automobile is a strange attractor—an office offshoot and mobile homespace, moving rapidly through the Great Outdoors from home to leisure and/or labor. Thus, the car easily mediates the orders of site improvements. As Baudrillard claims, the automotive cannot be ignored as a major mediation of the transnational polity's culture and space. Cars provide "the rendering abstract of any practical goal in the interests of speed and prestige, formal connotation, technical connotation, forced differentiation, emotional cathexis, and projection in phantasy. Here more easily than anywhere else we may discern the collusion between the subjective system of needs and the objective system of production."[23]

Globalization/Americanization

The anationalized substance of transnationalizing American nodality also is revealed quite openly in these direct B2C retailing texts. *Levenger* touts its "flagship pen," which is "a top-of-line writing instrument—our finest pen, combining the best of German and Italian craftsmanship," and "luxury for less—the Spanish secret" that comes from "leather goods from Spain that demonstrate world-class craftsmanship and reasonable prices, too."[24] *Williams-Sonoma,* by the same token, prides itself in bringing "something home cooks in Europe have done for generations."[25] Whether it is Hungarian glassware, Italian flatware, French stoveware, or Indian table linens, this operation reformats "America" for the world as not what the USA makes, but what Americans want—old favorites, choice of commercial kitchens, modern versions, just like those in bakeries, modeled after fine restaurants, professional quality—extruded through the mythos of the greater San Francisco Bay region. And, most shamelessly, *The Territory Ahead* of Santa Barbara, California, touts its Matanuska Alaska shirts (imported), Bush Pilot bomber jackets (imported), Yukon leather dusters (imported), Mesa Verde shirts (imported), Arroyo Seco pullovers (imported), and Lakota horsehair belts (imported) as ensemble players in its rugged "U.S.-made" lifestyle, only now played out in scenic Alaska, Canada, Costa Rica, or New Zealand.[26] As "clothes for the journey," exotic places abroad underpin a status-besotted identity in the USA for redistribution worldwide as "globalization." The system of objects generates its power and order out of denationalizing space and decentering culture. Things from somewhere are taken into global networks for sale almost anywhere that increasingly re-create everywhere as sites of improvement that turn into nowhere in the endless accumulation of perfect wares—visions of place and identity such as these are "made in the USA," but in this era of nodal authority it is not clear they really are "made by the USA," because such sites and improvements emerge from simply global networks for local consumption for anyone who can buy into them, which, in practice, mostly means they are "made for the USA."

One remarkable sign of nodal soft power's adaptable flexibility can be found in another niche catalog, specializing in marketing the ideological flotsam and military jetsam of the former Soviet Union, *Sovietski Collection*. Billing itself as a specialist in "treasures from a by-gone era," the *Sovietski Collection* offers strange curios and accouterments to spiff up the home, office, and auto. The Fall Preview 2000 catalog, for example, appeals to the *Eddie Bauer, Cabela's*, or *L. L. Bean* crowd with an outdoors still-life cover photo of a Red Army gas lantern, Soviet Air Force machete, East German binoculars, and Red Army officer's compass; and, on the inside, buyers can have Czech porcelains, Orthodox icons, matryosha dolls; discriminating consumers can buy busts of Yuri Gagarin, Stasi handcuffs, Spetznaz entrenching tools, and MiG fighter-pilot jackets.[27] What were once the essential tools or vital signs of the Evil Empire are reduced to conversation pieces, cheap sporting goods, and exotic oddities by the networks of global consumerism whose authority has become so great that the last bastion of hard-core national power crumbled before its B2C models for personal perfection through private purchases.

Plainly, things for/of improvement come from all over the world, but they often are only outsourced bits of transnational produce built for or by firms headquartered in the USA. These same firms, then, recruit management and labor, raise capital and support, buy goods and services from all over the world, but they switch these transactions through their root nodes in the USA. Similarly, the lifestyles and desires they valorize, and then vend, are pieced together from practices and products from all over the world, but they are reformatted to fit into the households, offices, and autos of populations found first or foremost in the USA. As a result, people in the USA arrange their existence around the acquisition of such things, and then once they become possessed by such possessions, new types of conduct can be reconducted through the networks as mediated international commoditizations of Americanization, globalization, modernization.

Giving free play to these conductions of conduct increasingly denationalizes, deregionalizes, or delocalizes innumerable sites with the improvements conducted by such goods and services. Nationally embedded, regionally emplaced, or locally enmeshed things are believed to be malconductive circuits of tradition, backwardness, or stylishlessness as such in the traffic of the network. Sites only improve, then, by reconstructing everyday life, and the conduct of people's conduct in everyday living, around many new artifacts, which are the tiny links of the remediating internationals behind the transnations in many global commodity chains. Places are perfected with new things, identity is generated out of new conduct conducted by such things, and culture shifts toward new collective understandings drawn from other acts and artifacts made manifest in world markets rather than local traditions. As Baudrillard asserts, "the way objects are used in everyday life implies an almost authoritarian set of assumptions about the world," and each commodified objective thing suggests "a world without effort, an abstract and completely mobile energy, and the total efficacy of sign-gestures."[28]

Conclusion

Once these B2C representations of the good life are bought whole hog by people seeking perfectibility from things, the things also operate as representatives of the networks that imagine people and things gaining a better life from such representations. As the perfecting of places turns into a global strategy for perfecting people with tactics tied to enhanced artifacts and perfect possessions, the artifacts work in a sense as "smartifacts," engaging their embedded intelligence on how to conduct one's conduct by impelling their owners to emulate the smartness conveyed by using these objects. Thus, "symbolic values, and along with them use values, are being supplanted by organizational values," and, thus, artifacts increasingly no longer mediate relationships that are "instinctive or psychological but, rather, of a tactical kind."[29] The transnational polity of "the West," in turn, pushes itself and "the Rest" toward the strange projects of perfectibility through a self-reinforcing cycle of producers, who build and sell improved sites, interoperating with consumers, who buy and accumulate site improvements. All of the consumer goods pushed for so long by direct-mail retailers in the USA also now suffuse late-night TV in Egypt, Mexico, Finland, and Australia, as transnational firms enroll new initiates into their networks of power. Now on a worldwide scale, things constitute new places, commodities project new identities, and networks recontour old localities around their new globalities.

The foundationalist demands of older ethical, moral, or spiritual projects for human perfection in various nations continue to be contested successfully in the name of otherness, leaving a free space for alternative visions of perfectibility to come into play from the mediating internationals linking the transnations. Perfecting people and places by enhancing their infrastructures, getting them possessions, or upgrading their artifacts, however, is now ideally suited to the soft powers exerted through nodal forms of authority. Bringing good things to life might build good things, expand fine markets, and make life better in the transnations by seeking the perfectibility of individuals through the perfection of things. Possessions possess persons; and, once possessed, these persons often remediate the world-class perfection now being valued internationally.[30] Consequently, soft power flows into the postmodern spaces it can capture with diversity and openness, while more modern systems struggle to define the best uniformities and closures for moral fulfillment.

American nodality in these corporate-controlled articulations now is a diffuse background condition in the contemporary world system. Like the strontium, cesium, or uranium isotopes spewed forth by the cold war's nuclear bomb tests, "America is everywhere." Yet, its isotopes are no longer necessarily those of a nationalist United States of America full of Puritan fire, republican ardor, or industrial supremacy; instead, Americanization is a nodal condition connecting clusters of cultural/

economic/technical isotopes—Boeing jets, Starbucks coffee, Microsoft computer codes, McDonald's restaurants, United flights, BP Amoco gas stations, Citibank ATMs, GE capital, AOL Time Warner programs—in worldwide webs of shared acts and artifacts that are today's real "world trade center." The commercial culture and identity that such nodalized soft power imparts to the world as "globalization," however, often have proven as sacrilegious or outrageous in Tulsa as they have in Teheran, so localities in the United States of America can suffer as grievously from these modes of Americanization as do the United Arab Emirates. To oppose the mediations of these transnations around the world, one probably must assault symbols. Consequently, it makes perfect sense to bomb the World Trade Center in order to resist the international mediations of world trade centers. Still, hyperpower, as a war machine, mostly rests upon one nation in this transnational polity, which CNN, B-2 bomber strikes, and U.S. Marine Corps landings always are ready to enforce from afar, overhead, and in the dirt.

However, this hyperpower depends, most importantly, on its transnational softer sides, and they are out on display every day in the desires for new goods and services being ginned up in the B2C world marketplace. Although many states may have big geopolitical bones to pick with Washington, almost every people find many of their most ardent personal desires discovered, tested, and shipped to them from Seattle, Los Angeles, Chicago, or New York. And, in these confounding tangles of influence, it is not surprising that neither the national significance of small-town America can be assured nor the patriotic identity of average American citizens guaranteed.

The most disturbing qualities of this transnational polity, therefore, are found in its culture of inequality, which truly imagines that better living can be attained through better things to improve human beings. Rather than defining attainable projects for everyone's collective good, the public's welfare is accepted as the arithmetic aggregates of countless little consumer choices. Of the world's 6 billion human inhabitants, nearly a billion live on a dollar or less of income a day. Their lives will never improve by turning down these tracks of existence because they do not have the incomes to accumulate more perfect things. When one midrange briefcase, espresso maker, or designer lamp at *Levenger, Williams-Sonoma,* and *Pottery Barn* costs more than an average Afghan's, Haitian's, or Chadian's annual income, how can such artifacts perfect their lives? This reality is the dark and dirty secret of consumer democracy's failure for many of our contemporaries. Of course, one could argue that this is why American Tobacco, Coca-Cola, or Universal Pictures now conduct so much of their business abroad. Everyone improves their sites as best they can, so a smoke, a Coke, and a flick are, as they were in the USA a century ago, the first steps toward a better life for these impoverished peoples in the global economy.

Rather than perfecting people by perfecting their places, the culture of consumption mostly puts people in their places through the psychodemography of product producers, marketing agencies, and service vendors that have constructed those places for them. These networks of people and things are normative systems meant, on one level, to order societies based on corporate-controlled consumption, and arrayed, on another level, in ways that reticulate the nodal authority of North American trendsetters, sign-generators, and capacity-utilizers. Through these collectives of action, 25 percent of the world's material resources go into improving sites for 5 percent of the world's population. Given the alternatives of being with the other 95 percent of the world scrambling to enjoy the remaining 75 percent of its resources, most Americans accept the places that the culture of consumption assigns to them, finding it a marvelous identity for working toward personal and social perfectibility.

Notes

An earlier version of this chapter was presented at the Culture and Space in the Transnational Polity Conference, Florida International University, February 2001.

1. See Joseph Nye, *Bound to Lead: The Changing Nature of American Power* (New York: Basic Books, 1990).

2. See Timothy W. Luke, *Capitalism, Democracy, and Ecology: Departing from Marx* (Urbana: University of Illinois Press, 1999).

3. For more on industrial democracy, see Alan Wolfe, *The Limits of Legitimacy* (New York: Basic Books, 1977).

4. See William Leach, *Land of Desire: Merchants, Power, and the Rise of a New American Culture* (New York: Pantheon, 1993).

5. Jean Baudrillard, *For a Critique of the Political Economy of the Sign* (St. Louis: Telos Press, 1981).

6. Pamela Walker Laird, *Advertising Progress: American Business and the Rise of Consumer Marketing* (Baltimore: Johns Hopkins University Press, 1998).

7. Curtis Publishing Company, *Obiter Dicta* (Philadelphia: Curtis Publishing, 1914), p. 4.

8. See Hans-Peter Martin and Harald Schumann, *The Global Trap: Globalization and the Assault on Democracy and Prosperity* (London: Zed Press, 1997).

9. See Arjun Appadurai, *Modernity at Large: Cultural Dimensions of Globalization* (Minneapolis: University of Minnesota Press, 1996).

10. Pierre Bourdieu, *Distinction: A Social Critique of the Judgment of Taste* (Cambridge: Harvard University Press, 1984), p. 170.

11. Jean Baudrillard, *The System of Objects* (London: Verso, 1996), p. 81.

12. Ibid., p. 29.

13. Baudrillard, *For a Critique*, p. 183.

14. Ibid.

15. *Frontgate* (early spring 2001), p. 3.

16. Ibid., p. 13.

17. Ibid., p. 12.

18. Baudrillard, *System of Objects*, p. 40.

19. Francis Fukuyama, *The Last Man and the End of History* (New York: Basic Books, 1992), p. 11.

20. *Sporty's* (January–April 2001), p. 3.

21. *The Sharper Image* (Holiday 2000), p. 2.

22. *International Auto Sport* (winter 2001), p. 2.

23. Baudrillard, *System of Objects*, p. 65.

24. *Levenger* (Christmas 2000), pp. 9, 8.

25. *Williams-Sonoma* (February 2001), p. 2.

26. *Territory Ahead* (spring 2001), pp. 3–37.

27. *Sovietski Collection* (Fall Preview 2000), pp. 1–18.

28. Baudrillard, *System of Objects*, p. 58.

29. Ibid., p. 21.

30. Timothy W. Luke, "Liberal Society and Cyborg Subjectivity: The Politics of Environments, Bodies, and Nature," *Alternatives: A Journal of World Policy* 21 (1996): 1–30.

Part III
Mediation, Cultural Governance, and the Political

CHAPTER SEVEN

Culture, Governance, and Global Biopolitics

Michael Dillon

There are no international relations without representation. As in science, in international politics representation is a mangle of mediatory practices.[1] Global governance refers to a particular collection of such practices. These came to prominence in the last twenty years of the twentieth century. They comprise complex technical means of managing populations. To be precise, global governance is a Foucauldian system of power/knowledge that depends on the strategic orchestration of the self-regulating freedoms of populations, the relations between whose subjects form complex and dynamic networks of power. These networks operate through the strategic manipulation of different generative principles of formation—profit, scarcity, security, and so on. Orchestrating domains of self-regulating freedom also requires detailed knowledge of populations and the terrains that they inhabit. The object of power here is the exercise of power over life, rather than power over death. Global governance is therefore a domain of "bio" rather than "geo" politics. The purpose of this chapter is to explore how culture is necessarily drawn into the orbit of governmental power and some of the purposes it serves there.

The Paradox of Culture and Governance

For a variety of reasons, some of which are discussed here, the 1990s witnessed the transformation of global development into a form of global biopolitics whose concern was to reconstitute the global poor and specify new population welfare goals in respect of their development.

Development issues quickly became allied also to changing discourses of security. On the one hand, cold-war security discourses had lost their very raison d'être. On the other hand, global conflicts quickly became interethnic and internecine conflicts among the world's poorest peoples. Nothing advances the priority of a policy domain more than to be associated with a discourse of security. Neither, however, could you reconstitute the global poor and figure out how to improve their lot without also addressing the issue of violent conflict. More to the point, international and nongovernmental agencies, as well even as some national institutions, devoted to the global poor had once defined themselves in contradistinction to the geopolitical ideological conflict between the Soviets and the West, specifically the United States. With the disappearance of that geopolitical cartography of allegiances and neutralities, such agencies found themselves in very unfamiliar territory. One consequence was that they found that they could no longer easily define themselves neutrally in the ways that they once did. In conflicts that were themselves internecine, neutrality often became an unsustainable position, let alone a moot concept. Deeply involved in intervention strategies that were not simply designed to win geopolitical allies but to transform societies wholesale, neutrality was additionally difficult to maintain because bringing succor to populations increasingly meant becoming embroiled in widely contested plans to improve their long-term conditions of survivability and economic viability in a capitalist economy gone global.

Networks of self-regulating freedom rapidly became the device by which all manner of related international issues therefore came to be addressed, including most notably those of peace, security, and human rights. As a new and radically more complex international order emerged in which conflict went civil and liberal forms of power achieved international hegemony, so the preoccupation with good governance began to effect a novel intersection between security and development politics. Until at least September 11, 2001, war became policing for liberal powers closely allied also to regimes of governance that related poverty, rights, and conflict very closely. Thus questions of development became intimately related to questions of security as development analysts and agencies brought the impoverishing effects of civil wars into their development equations concerning civil societies. Conversely, questions of security became intimately allied with questions of economic development and the cultures of civil societies as security analysts and agencies brought impoverishment into their security equations. The outcome was what Mark Duffield called a development-security complex.[2] Addressing war and development through biopolitical forms of analysis and power, precisely because biopower works through the orchestration of the kind of self-regulating freedoms said to constitute a culture, rapidly drew culture into the emerging terrain of global biopolitics.

However you define culture, then, you cannot change the ways of life of entire populations unless you transform their symbolic structures, their signifying practices, and the way that things are valued among them. In short, there can be no biopolitics without an accompanying form of cultural politics, or at least without constituting culture itself as a vital terrain of governmental intervention. There is nothing especially scandalous or even novel about suborning culture for political purposes. Nation builders do it all the time. It can be a very bloody business, often laying down stores of violent conflict for the future; it may also support a successful process of political stabilization.

Nothing especially difficult or scandalous, that is to say, unless you subscribe to the view that culture stands for domains of life independent of, to be secured from, and valuable irrespective of the interventions of power. The great paradox of liberal governance is that it does in effect subscribe to precisely this view. However you define culture, for liberal governance it is the domain of self-regulating freedoms whose self-organization is the technical instrument of power at a distance that makes liberal governance such a positive and effective operation of power. While ineluctably drawn into the orbit of governance, cultural governance thus exhibits all the paradoxes of liberal governance. No governance without culture. No culture without governance. You cannot have a technical management of social forms through the operation of self-regulating freedoms without the culture of self-regulating freedom itself. Here culture loses whatever innocence it has, or claims in respect of governance, and becomes enmeshed in the web of biopower itself. Whatever culture might be said to be, power/knowledge has to say what it is and what it has normally to be taken to be. Governance is therefore distinguished by this epistemological sleight of hand in which it posits autonomy to processes in which it is nonetheless deeply implicated through an epistemologized form of government at a distance. This trick seems most pronounced in respect of culture.

But the sleight of hand is no impediment to governmental processes. Treating life processes as exterior to the procedures by which they are observed and enumerated so as to discover the laws of their morphogenesis is, of course, common to modern life. With culture it is merely extended to its widest extent. Thus extended, it nonetheless tends to become attenuated to the point of becoming see-through. It is not merely by means of its very lack of definition that culture both invites and defeats secure epistemological grasp. Whatever else it is, culture is a mode of being-in-relation that is peculiar also because it is performative rather than epistemic in relation to the very relating that it names, itself serving to bring that relating into being. Not only somehow integrally related to the very enactment of forms of life, culture is distinguished by the very ways in which it assimilates and enacts whatever it is said to be. That performativity further serves to erode the very distinction between putatively independent life processes and that detailed observation and re-presentation of them that is so critical to the (epistemic) governance of self-regulating freedom.

An obvious difficulty thus arises in the contradiction of seeking to effect governance of something that is nonetheless said in principle to be best able to govern itself. The contradiction is, however, freely admitted as a paradox. Negotiating it furnishes reflexive governance with its very agendas of power/knowledge. New, more refined and more accountable, ways must continuously be fashioned for an exercise of freedom that is continuously subjected to remedial programs of improvement despite its putative autonomy. The contradiction would be no more than an academic observation if it were not for the fact that culture in cultural governance does more than merely exhibit the paradox of positing autonomous life processes for the very purposes of intervening effectively in them with the express object of making them more amenable to various technical rationalities. For liberal governance is itself by no means neutral in relation to the everyday life processes of populations and it requires ways of discriminating between the deserving, the less deserving, and the undeserving or downright intractable. It constitutes a moral economy as it proclaims the autonomy of economy, for example, and it fiercely discriminates between the deserving and the adept practitioners of the self-regulating freedom that it cultivates even as it operates through them. Culture also becomes the locale, then, for those signifying practices that define whether or not you are engaged in the exercise of self-regulating freedom in the approved manner and whether or not, if failing at these complex practices, you nonetheless also constitute a deserving case for aid and assistance designed to improve you.

Thus, biopolitics is not indiscriminate. If it were, then the power associated with it would not merit the term *power/knowledge*. Its very practices of discrimination, of differentiation and formation, are its very modalities of power. Intervening in domains said to be independent of power relations is not mere contradiction or paradox. It is integral to the operation of the kind of power that biopower is. Not just paradoxical, cultural governance concerns the identification of eligibilities that themselves help determine the life chances and prospects of populations in respect of both long-term development and short-term emergency assistance and succor. If culture is a text, to use a popular if infuriating metaphor for some, then it is certainly read in ways that define who counts and who does not, how they should count, and how much they should count. Evaluating cultural sensibility and eligibility is as much a part of the biopolitics of global liberal governance as the specification of subsistence levels, the setting of growth targets, the construction of markets, the study of incidence of diseases and its correlation with other key features and practices of populations, and so on.

Biopolitics is thus a very discrete form of humanitarianism that requires measures of cultural governance in order to specify improving and improvable life processes. "X" is improvable; "Y" is not. Certain populations are adaptable in certain ways; others not. Hence power over life pursues policies for the improvement of life through discriminating between those most eligible to effect such improvements. That cultural knowledge is itself part of the power/knowledge of biopolitics. Culture, however it is specified, becomes important for global liberal governance because it promises to make the eligible legible, thus strengthening its practice of political conditionality. It helps map the terrain of the corrigible, not simply by differentiating the corrigible from the incorrigible but also by assaying degrees of corrigibility as such. Experimentally, while it fixes, it does not fix in perpetuity the material life processes that it takes as its data. It is, instead, critically reflexive in respect of what it can discover about the very (in)corrigibilities of that material for the manifold purposes of refashioning it.

Biopolitically, then, improving requires proving oneself capable of approved and approval conduct. Because it does not merely assimilate and appropriate cultural practices as if it stood outside of en-culturation, biopolitical governance is also, of course, itself a cultural practice. All this became evident in the biopolitics of global development from the late 1980s onwards.

Culture, Development, and Governance

The discursive conditions of emergence of global governance were many and complex. The biopolitics of governance also has a long tradition of development in the historical development of modern forms of power. Two of the more contemporary reasons why governance became a feature of global power relations were, however, the dissolution of cold-war politics and the failure of the 1980s' economic structural adjustment programs for world development. The collapse of the Soviet empire created a vacuum in geopolitics that allowed power over life an opportunity in global politics to displace the priority that had been accorded to power over death in the ideological confrontation that followed the Second World War. Specifically, better means of managing the life processes of the global poor, itself an aspect of the emergence of wider global population management in the extension of the self-regulating freedoms of global capital economics, were sought in the process of effecting a wide-ranging reform of global development policies.

It was no coincidence that the World Bank was first responsible for putting the term *governance* into use at the global level through a series of influential reports issued between 1989 and 1994. In 1991 the World Bank Board of Governors approved the staff paper on governance and development based on the concerns already raised in the book *Sub-Saharan Africa: From Crisis to Sustainable Growth* (1989), where the problem was identified as "crisis of governance."[3] The publication of the Bank's *World Development Report 1990: Poverty* was followed by *Governance and Development* claiming that good governance creates strong and equitable development and complements sound economic policies.[4] Defining governance as the management of the development process allowed the Bank to circumvent its Articles of Agreement forbidding political considerations in the bank's operation.

Neither was it coincidental that the definition of governance, as "the manner in which power is exercised in the management of a country's economic and social resources for development,"[5] was quickly to be shared with the Commission on Global Governance that was founded in 1995: "[governance] is the sum of the many ways individuals and institutions, public and private, manage their own affairs."[6] The United Nations Development Program (UNDP) also went on to recommend stronger governance to preserve markets and ensure that globalization "works for the people." Governance at all levels has now become the defining motif of the World Bank's 2000 poverty reduction strategy.[7] Thus, international institutions from the United Nations through to the International Monetary Fund (IMF) all became intensely involved in prioritizing the social and cultural conditions necessary to achieve changing development goals throughout the 1990s. In 1995, the Copenhagen Declaration on Social Development, for example, committed world leaders to eradicating poverty and to integrating social goals in structural adjustment programs.[8] In 1996, the Organization for Economic Cooperation and Development (OECD) also established worldwide socioeconomic goals, explicitly linking these with a demand for new cultural policies as well. By 2012, it aimed to achieve universal primary education in all countries, significant progress toward gender equality, two-thirds reduction in infant and child mortality, three-quarter reduction in maternal mortality ratios, provide access for all who need reproductive health services, and establish national strategies for sustainable development. By 2015, it aimed to reduce extreme poverty by half. In 2000 these goals were adopted by the IMF, the OECD, the United Nations, and the World Bank. The IMF's Enhanced Structural Facility (ESF) program was changed to the Poverty Reduction and Growth Facility (PRGF) to emphasize its sociocultural rather than exclusively economic content.[9] The trend toward incorporating the sociocultural into the economic was widely endorsed by the United Nations throughout the second part of the decade, with the secretary-general urging that private corporations and international development institutions adopt a global compact. This is not to say that the strategies were uniform. Of course they were not. What began as an emphasis on the individual pauper and on political conditionalities ended up by the late 1990s as an emphasis on collective social transformation and partnership between local and global institutions in pursuing holistic approaches to sociocultural and economic development.

As Christine Rojas notes, "Washington's technocracy [first] undertook the mission of reforming the economy of the Third World by purchasing aid for reform and introducing conditionality as the instrument of restraint."[10] Such conditionality began in the 1970s, in part facilitated by the disappearance of industrialized countries from the IMF's list of regular clients.[11] It became widespread during the 1980s with the adoption of the so-called Washington Consensus and the adoption by the World Bank of a policy of structural adjustment lending. With the adoption of the Washington Consensus conditionalities both widened and deepened. The average number of criteria for conditionality rose from about 6 in the 1970s to 10 in the 1980s. In the Bank's case the average number of conditions rose from 32 in 1980–83 to 56 by the end of the decade. Between 1997 and 1999, the average number of criteria for conditionality was 26. Furthermore, the burden of conditionality was not distributed equally for all regions: the average number of conditionalities is 114 in Africa, 84 in Asia, 93 in Central Asia and Eastern Europe, and 78 in Latin America.[12] Africa, the poorest continent, thus became the most subject to conditionalities, and in general they applied "most stringently to the smallest, poorest, and most aid-dependent countries."[13] For a wide variety of reasons, the development industry concluded by the late 1990s that conditionality had failed and needed to be replaced by other means of governing the global poor via aid and development policies.[14] The outcome was an intensification of interest in cultural governance rather than less, and global poverty began to attain the status of a global security risk. A new governmental approach began to emerge well represented by a former vice president of the World Bank, Joseph Stiglitz, who endorsed wholesale societal transformation:

> Development represents a *transformation* of society, a movement from traditional relations, traditional ways of thinking, traditional ways of dealing with health and education, traditional methods of production, to more "modern" ways. For instance, a characteristic of traditional societies is the acceptance of the world as it is; the modern perspective recognizes change, it recognizes that we, as individuals and societies, can take actions that, for instance, reduce infant mortality, extend life spans, and increase productivity. Key to these changes is the movement to "scientific" ways of thinking, identifying critical variables that affect outcomes, attempting to make inferences based on available data, recognizing what we know and what we do not know.[15]

Reconstituting the global poor as an object of intense epistemic concern, with the purpose of determining the social and cultural features that would both help improve their material conditions and make them eligible for aid and development support, was intimately associated with encouraging the governance of the self-regulating freedoms of nongovernmental aid agencies as well. These agencies became involved in governance in two ways. First, they were proponents of more intense governmental policies for development. They themselves, however, also came under pressure to exhibit the same good governance practices of transparency, accountability, and enterprise-based management practices that their clients were required to display. What was good for the developing was good for the developers as well.

Nongovernmental organizations (NGOs) thus first proselytized on behalf of governance for and of the global poor. Oxfam claimed in 1995, for example, that "new forms of conditionality could help to bring about positive policy reforms. . . . Governments and donors could, in principle, agree to incremental steps for raising investment in primary health care, basic education, and the provision of water and sanitation."[16] Later, they themselves were drawn ineluctably into the closer governmental policing of their own self-regulating freedoms. And the more they did so, the more they tended to suffer significant disorientation in respect of their core missions and self-definitions, because these had once been defined humanitarianly in contradistinction to political conditionality of any sort. Independence from political power was part of their self-definition. But within the intricacies of governmental power such differentiation became increasingly fraught, if not wholly problematic.

One good example is the Sphere Project established by the Steering Committee for Humanitarian Response (SCHR) in 1997. SCHR is an alliance of organizations for voluntary action. It was created both to improve coordination and cooperation among humanitarian agencies and to effect and disseminate good practice, but also to respond effectively to the need to work smoothly with governmental and international agencies that themselves began to demand higher standards of self-governance on behalf of NGOs. Sphere thus also operates effectively as an informal means of accreditation, helping, for example, to provide grounds for drawing distinctions between agencies that are regarded as responsible and those whose operations and standards of self-regulation cause confusion or difficulty for better-regulated voluntary agencies, especially in respect of working with state and international organizations from whom NGOs get most of their jobs, resources, access to the poor, and sometimes also protection from the violent.

In addition to training programs, and in response to a perceived need to "improve both the effectiveness of their assistance and accountability to their stakeholders," the Sphere Project has adopted a "Humanitarian Charter and Minimum Standards in Disaster Response."[17] Primarily aimed at humanitarian agency staff, this document is directed also at "disaster affected populations and other stake holders including coordinating bodies, local authorities, institutional donors, individual donors, scholars and journalists." It was explicitly adopted as a means "by which agencies can define the extent and limit of their assistance, and firmly allocate the primary responsibility for prevention and mitigation of conflict and calamity to political actors." This last point is especially interesting. Dividing practices such as these involves NGOs in a considerable degree of negotiated and contested intimacy with national and international political organizations in the constitution of their very own cultural and civil spheres.

Cultural Policies for Development

Development and culture are protean concepts. Just as the very idea of development stretches back historically into the nineteenth century and more conceptually into the deep ontological and epistemological subventions of modernity, so also the connection with culture has been an abiding one.[18] In his study of French colonialism, Paul Rabinow shows how its norms and forms included fields of knowledge (hygienic, statistical, geographic), social technologies of pacification (welfare and planning), and the creation of new forms of space (towns, laboratories, architecture).[19] Development has always been conceived as a cultural condition, and as a cultural condition it has been linked historically to the absence of development (the primitive and uncivilized), as well as to the alternatives to development.[20] As Jonathan Crush notes, the "texts of development have always been avowedly strategic and tactical—promoting, licensing and justifying certain interventions and practices, delegitimizing some and excluding others."[21] So also have been those of culture. Michael Watts observes that the grounds on which the normalizing efforts of biopower/knowledge have been made are "typically the welfare of populations, and the relations of individuals (for example the poor) to society."[22] Rabinow too has explored welfare as the third leg of modernity.[23]

An important contribution to this process has been made through UNESCO, which explicitly identifies culture as a life process that is both a means to and an end of development.[24] Specifically, this began with attempting to operationalize the recommendation of the World Commission on Culture and Development,[25] whose report *Our Creative Cultural Diversity* called for the effective linking of culture and development.[26] It did so, for example, through adoption of an "Action Plan on Cultural Policies for Development" at its Stockholm Conference of April 1998. This was also backed by a new program on cultural policies for development being prepared for 2000–2001.[27] Here, it is acknowledged that "Cultural freedom is rather special: it is not quite like other forms of freedom. . . . Cultural freedom is a collective freedom [which] properly interpreted is the condition for individual freedom to flourish." (Note the "properly interpreted" phrasing.) In short, culture is identified not simply as an important life process, but as one that is integral to the very operation of self-regulating individual freedom.

Chapter 9 of *Our Creative Diversity* also identifies the need for and the lack of "reliable comparative data" on culture. It laments the fact that although "work in areas such as cultural participation and consumption has been considerable in some countries, it does not inform the linkages between cultural policy and development." Culture is then linked as a critical life process to other life processes that have themselves already been identified as vital domains of governmental self-regulation: "Cultural policy, as one of the main components of endogenous and sustainable development policy, should be implemented in co-ordination with policy in other social areas on the basis of an integrated approach. Any policy for development must be profoundly sensitive to culture itself." The key conclusions stressed the importance of the link between sustainable development and "the flourishing of culture." While recruiting culture into the realm of governance, limits to the governance of culture set by its own independent value and character were also acknowledged:

> It is therefore important both to acknowledge the far-reaching instrumental function of culture in development, and at the same time to recognise that this cannot be all there is to culture in judgements of development. There is, in addition, the role of culture as a desirable end in itself. This dual role of culture applies not only in the context of the promotion of economic growth, but also in relation to other objectives, such as sustaining the physical environment, preserving family values, protecting civil institutions in a society, and so on.

Given the wide remit accorded to culture and its defiance of close definition, it is not surprising that culture now comes recommended as an integral part of the solution to so many global problematics in addition to development. Flourishing cultures of the right sort are then both means and ends, instrumental to, but also the object of, development. This sets up a logic that calls for the need to codify and normalize the terrain of "culture" so that it can provide the protocols and norms required of the self-regulatory freedom by which it operates. The impulse was well expressed in the background papers to the UNESCO document.[28] The following example from the Council of Europe's contribution to the governmentalizing of culture shows how widely this logic has been disseminated. Issued in response to *Our Creative Diversity* published by the World Commission on Culture and Development,[29] the Executive Summary of the Council's Report accepted that "both governments and the cultural sector face an uncomfortable paradox if a higher priority is accorded to culture. Looking for an effective instrument of policy, governments may try to control or manage it. In the search for resources, the cultural sector may consent to justifications of support on non-cultural grounds."[30] This paradox directly poses the dilemma that constantly arises between governing too little and governing too much. The report gave explicit and precise expression to it:

> Experience suggests that the utilitarian exploitation of culture will only succeed if, at the level of individual creativity, it is allowed to function outside state control. Freedom of expression is a crucial principle and cultural policies should establish a general framework within which individuals and institutions can work rather than intervene closely in what they do or say. But more than that there is a need for a consistent theory of cultural policy which accepts that culture has its instrumental uses, but also to recognise the limits to which this can be applied without endangering it.[31]

Culture, Governance, and Deserving Subjects

It is remarkable, for practitioners of governance, how incompetent people can be at the exercise of self-regulating freedom. Some just don't get it, can't get it, or seem willfully opposed to having it.[32] The reason is simple. Self-regulating freedom is a discipline. Not natural in any reified sense, it is an acquired expertise the talent and the taste for which seem to be unequally distributed within as well as between societies—not least because there are, of course, competing accounts of freedom and many other diverse forms of cultural existence in which different kinds of freedom take place. It is conceivable, at least to those not thoroughly captured by the account of freedom circulating within governmental capillaries of power, that such formations may operate according to quite different principles of formation than those at work in governance.

However "natural" it is said to be, governmental subjectivity, recalling Kantian conceptions of enlightenment, is nonetheless always very much a function of processes of maturation. Thus, Bentham's principle of "less eligibility" always informs governance's account of the self-regulating, self-improving subject. In that way, liberal political philosophy's moral cartography of natural equality is redrawn as the detail of governmental practices differentiates between the eligible, the deserving, the domesticated, and the unsafe.[33] Not all, it turns out, can, will, or do bear the responsibilities of self-regulating freedoms of governance. Responsible autonomy is the hard labor that governance requires of its subjects and some just don't have what it takes. Others just won't learn. For both of these categories, liberal governance has often prescribed quite despotic and brutal forms of care, correction, and containment.[34] Seeking to realize the good of society as a whole through this "professionalization of human beings" requires cultural induction of the undersocialized or even antisocial bodies of the poor, the deviant, the unhealthy, and the minor into governance's detailed mechanisms of self-regulating freedom.[35]

Global governance is therefore as ambivalent about the freedom through which it operates as it is about the power of government as such. The reason is twofold. Practices of government recognize that it is possible, first, to be free in the wrong ways and, second, to govern too much.[36] Thus, while governing through self-regulating freedom, governance nonetheless harbors deep suspicions about both freedom and government. Each acquires its specificity through changing traditions, institutions, and practices. Governance is distinguished by the continuous ways in which it continuously interrogates its own governing impulses and seeks to contain these by reference to life processes that are assumed to have a large measure of independence from the procedures of governance itself.[37] The freedoms of governance are, however, ones in which novel class distinctions must also be drawn between those able and willing to exercise the burdens and exploit the opportunities offered by its self-regulating subjectivities and those who are not.[38] Given that the rationale of governance is the improved self-regulation of whatever processes it addresses, self-improvement—specifically normatively sanctioned self-improvement—cannot simply be a desirable goal for governance. It is a positive social—indeed, moral and political—obligation.

There is no improvement, however, without fallibility. As the very condition of possibility and operability for liberal governance, fallibility drives its remorselessly remedial impulse: its audits, codes of conduct, rising standards, improved performance, and further audit. Where normatively sanctioned self-improvement is resisted, where individuals and populations for whatever reason do not, will not, or cannot measure up to its standards of subjectivity and its performance criteria, governance is compelled to differentiate between populations and subjects alike on the basis of those who avail themselves of the opportunity for self-improvement and those who do not. Cultural markers help make these legible.

Thus, and in classic governance fashion, at the heart of development strategies instituted in the 1990s were practices that the World Bank insisted would allow "ordinary people . . . to take charge of their lives."[39] Self-reliance meant institutions and practices for enhancing entrepreneurial, managerial, and technical capabilities.[40] Watts notes that the outcome of this development of development was a "convergence around social institutions, not least the fascination with non-governmental organisations, citizenship and human rights, . . . the re-emergence of civil society, new configurations of state, markets and civil organisation unencumbered by outmoded or ideological notions of central planning or unhindered free markets." He concluded that "what is so striking in this confluence of analytics is the centrality of civil society; markets have to be socially embedded, economic dynamism demands social capital, economies are built around trust, obligation and accountability."[41] More generally, D. L. Sheth concludes that the market triumphalism of the 1980s began to produce a "new mode" of doing politics.[42] Composed of new sorts of fragmented subjects and a bottom-up horizontal vectoring, the outcome was to be a redefinition of political and economic democracy. As Watts noted, governance embraced "orthodox" and "alternative" protagonists in the development debate: "Both the new development economics of the 1990s and the anti-development paradigm stake claims for alternative strategies. Furthermore they speak in the same register in reasserting the role of civil society and in questioning the form, function and character of the development state."[43] It was not simply poverty alone that was the object of policy attack, but "poverty intensified at the level of social danger where the object is the suppression of *different forms of conduct,* namely those which are not amenable to the project of socialization which is being elaborated."[44] Elevated to the level of a social danger, it not only became possible to claim more governance of poverty (because poverty was then allied to the very foundations of peace and social order), but also to introduce other discriminating practices when it came to figuring out who was "deserving" of governance.

In thus creating a novel cartography of power, governance generates a different topography for politics. It is one that exceeds the usual confines of politics understood in terms of the activities of the state or of the government and, in liberal societies, of the representative procedures associated with them. This is not mere administration or depoliticization. As Jonathan Crush has noted, "development, for all its power to speak and to control the terms of speaking, has never been impervious to challenge and resistance, nor, in response, to reformulation and change.... Without the possibility of reaction and resistance there is no place for the agents and victims of development to exert their explicit and implicit influence on the ways in which it is constructed, thought, planned and implemented."[45] Politics is resituated and acquires new tropes. Complex fields of strategic calculation are thereby opened up for all kinds of individual and collective subjects through the introduction of governance and novel politics of development emerging within the developing as well as the developed world.

Conclusion

Any claim to know what is best for poor people, to know what it takes to escape poverty and what needs must be met in order to be fully human, is not only a claim to power but also a specification of the moral and cultural regulation to which the global poor have to be subject in order to merit the development of governance. These "additional virtues" are cultural and civic. The recruitment of culture as a terrain of governmental self-regulation follows ineluctably from the kind of power that biopower is. As a corrective to the arguments of those who, like Manuel Castells, have devoted a considerable effort to analyzing the dynamics of network societies of liberal governance, the power of the globally rich and powerful depends on the strategization of the world's poor via their recruitment into the complex relational networks of global liberal governance as much as it does on their exclusion and abjection.[46]

Traditionally, culture was allotted a relatively inferior and residual status in policy and political matters. In contrast to economic and political as well as sociological processes, for example (and their allied disciplinary subjects, including international relations as a branch of political science), culture was thought to deal with the ephemeral and nonserious. While the disciplines of politics, economics, and sociology laid claim to the interpretation and scientific study of real-world material processes, pursuing the ambition of acquiring "hard knowledge" of enduring facts and values for the purpose of policy relevant research and socially relevant prescriptions, culture seemed steeped in the superficial, transient, superstructural, and impermanent. Culture's territory was that of signs, metaphors, figures, images, unruly languages, beliefs, phases, fashions, and ephemera. With cultural governance, culture is generally recognized now to be constitutive of the political, the economic, and the social. Thus, it is given greater epistemic, as well as policy, relevance within the changing technologies of global liberal governance.

Foucault drew analytical attention long ago to the very "artifactual" production of the state–civil society distinction. Graham Burchell neatly glossed Foucault when he noted that civil society should be viewed neither as an aboriginal reality—a natural given standing in opposition to the timeless essential nature of the state—nor as an ideological construct, something simply fabricated by the state. Rather, he said, civil society should be regarded as "the correlate of a particular technology of government." He continued: "The distinction between civil society and the state is a form of 'schematism' for the exercise of political power. Foucault describes civil society as in a sense a transactional reality existing at the mutable interface of political power and everything which permanently outstrips its reach."[47] The mechanisms of liberal governance, Foucault argued, do not therefore depend on the manufacture of some generalized form of consent through the cultural mechanisms of ideological articulation and hegemonic production via which the ideologies and beliefs of subordinate classes are aligned with those of the ruling bloc. Culture works less in the service of the power of a preconceived agent or bloc than as the specific and diverse modality of a pluralizing set of continuously self-modifying strategies of power: those of liberal governance. Far from mediating the relations between civil society and the state in a Gramscian way so as to align the different levels of social formation ideologically, culture emerges here as one of the pluralized and dispersed fields of governmental power characteristic of global liberal governance.

A new field of self-regulating freedom is in the process of formation with the advent of cultural governance. That development has been taking place globally in alliance with the changing strategies of development on which I have concentrated. It has, of course, been taking place locally as well within liberal states. This induces a considerable degree of skepticism about the state–civil society distinction, specifically about the critical uses to which it is increasingly put in the extension of the notion of global civil society. Culture appears instead here as a *correlate* of a specific form of political technology or political rationality, that of liberal governance. Setting cultural subjects free in ways that will ensure the operation of cultural processes that, in their specificities and norms, themselves become the discovery of expertise and knowledge is itself no natural thing but a vast labor. In addition to the epistemic labor of knowledge production and policy formulation, it also includes vast programs of institution building, inventive practices of mediation, community reconstruction, detailed codes of practice, education, socialization, and cultural regulation. Being free as a subject of autonomous life processes is a demanding affair. Committed to this labor, governance cannot leave it to the license of any actors anywhere, anyhow. Its freedom is no longer quite the natural attribute of Adam Smith's *homo oeconomicus* but more the Hayekian artifact of liberal civilization.[48] It has thus to be secured. This securing constitutes the detailed and extensive work of the capillary processes by which technologies of governance operate so as to construct a complex and dynamic strategic field of securitization. This strategic field furnishes an additional incentive toward fashioning a development-security complex in which culture is a correlate of rather than an escape from power.

Notes

1. The phrase is taken from the title and thesis of Andrew Pickering's *The Mangle of Practices: Time, Agency and Science* (Chicago: University of Chicago Press, 1995).

2. Mark Duffield, *Global Governance and the New Wars: The Merging of Development and Security* (London: Zed Books, 2001).

3. World Bank, *Governance: The World Bank's Experience* (Washington, D.C.: World Bank, 1994), p. vii; World Bank, *Sub-Saharan Africa: From Crisis to Sustainable Growth* (Washington, D.C.: World Bank, 1989).

4. World Bank, *World Development Report 1990: Poverty* (Oxford: Oxford University Press, 1990); World Bank, *Governance and Development* (Washington, D.C.: World Bank, 1992).

5. World Bank, *Governance: The World Bank's Experience* (1994), p. 16.

6. Report of the Commission on Global Governance, *Our Global Neighbourhood* (Oxford: Oxford University Press, 1995), p. 2.

7. World Bank, "Governance," available at www.worldbank.org/htmal/gc/governance/governance.htm.

8. World Summit for Social Development, "The Copenhagen Declaration and Program Action," March 6–12, 1995.

9. Sanjeeve Gupta, Louis Dicks-Mireaux, Ritha Khemani, Calvin McDonald, and Marijn Verhoeven, *Social Issues in IMF-Supported Programs* (Washington, D.C.: International Monetary Fund, 2000).

10. Christine Rojas, "Governing through the Social: The Role of International Financial Institutions in the Third World," paper presented to the International Studies Association, Chicago, 2001, p. 9. Rojas also notes that, according to Paul Collier, the core principle of conditionality is that "aid buys reforms." See Paul Collier, "The Failure of Conditionality," in Catherine Gwin and Joan M. Nelson, eds., *Perspectives on Aid and Development* (Washington, D.C.: Overseas Development Council, 1997), p. 56.

11. Devesh Kapur and Richar Webb, "Governance-Related Conditionalities of International Financial Institutions" (Harvard: G-24 Discussion Paper Series, UNCTAD, International Center for Development, August 2000), p. 2.

12. Rojas, "Governing through the Social," p. 9.

13. Gerry Helleiner, "External Conditionality, Local Ownership, and Development," in Jim Freedman, ed., *Transforming Development: Foreign Aid for a Changing World* (Toronto: University of Toronto Press, 2000), p. 96.

14. Collier, "The Failure of Conditionality," p. 51.

15. Joseph Stiglitz, "Towards a New Paradigm for Development: Strategies, Policies, and Processes," lecture given as the 1998 Prebisch Lecture at UNCTAD, Geneva, October 19, 1998, p. 3.

16. Oxfam, *The Oxfam Poverty Report* (London: Oxfam Publications, 1995); quoted in Ravi Kanbur, "Aid Conditionality and Debt in Africa," in Finn Tarp, ed., *Foreign Aid and Development: Lessons Learnt and Directions for the Future* (London: Routledge: 2000), p. 4.

17. http://www.sphereproject.org.html.

18. See Kate Manzo, *Domination, Resistance and Social Change: The Local Effect of Global Power* (New York: Praeger, 1992).

19. Paul Rabinow, *French Modern* (Boston: MIT Press, 1990).

20. Michael Watts, "The Crisis of Development," in Jonathan Crush, ed., *Power of Development* (London: Routledge, 1995).

21. Crush, *Power of Development*, p. 5.

22. Watts, "The Crisis of Development," p. 48.

23. Rabinow, *French Modern.*

24. Tony Bennett and Colin Mercer, "Preparatory Paper IV: Improving Research and International Cooperation for Cultural Policy"; Sally Norman, "Preparatory Paper IX: Culture and the New Media Technologies"; and Jerome Huet, "Preparatory Paper X: What Culture in Cyberspace. And What Intellectual Property Rights for 'Cyberculture'?" all in *Stockholm Intergovernmental Conference on Cultural Policies of Development* (UNESCO, 1998). All documents available at http://sweden.org/conference/papers.

25. See http://www.unesco.org/culture_and_development/wccd/wccd.html.

26. UNESCO Publishing; also available at http://www.unesco.org/culture_and_development/ocd/ocd.html.

27. Ibid. Subsequent references in the text are to this document.

28. Ibid.

29. Javier Pérez de Cuéllar, *Our Creative Diversity: The Report of the World Commission* (Paris: UNESCO Publications, 1997).

30. Council of Europe, *In From the Margins: A Contribution to the Debate on Culture and Development in Europe* (Strasbourg: Council of Europe Publishing, 1997), p. 10.

31. Ibid.

32. Barbara Cruickshank, *The Will to Empower* (Ithaca, N.Y.: Cornell University Press, 1999).

33. Ibid.

34. Mitchell Dean, *The Constitution of Poverty: Towards a Genealogy of Liberal Governance* (London: Routledge, 1991); Mitchell Dean, *Governmentality: Power and Rule in Modern Society* (London: Routledge, 1999); see also Cruickshank, *The Will to Empower.*

35. Cruickshank, *The Will to Empower.*

36. Nikolas Rose, *Powers of Freedom* (Cambridge: Cambridge University Press, 1999); and Dean, *Governmentality.*

37. See ibid.

38. Cruickshank, *The Will to Empower;* Dean, *Governmentality;* Rose, *Powers of Freedom.*

39. World Bank, *Sub-Saharan Africa,* p. 4.

40. Ibid., pp. 122 and 186.

41. Watts, "The Crisis of Development," p. 58.

42. D. L. Sheth, "Alternative Development as Political Practice," *Alternatives* 12.2 (1987): 155–71.

43. Watts, "The Crisis of Development," p. 59.

44. Giovana Procacci, "Social Economy and the Government of Poverty," in Graham Burchell, Colin Gordon, and Peter Miller, eds., *The Foucault Effect: Studies in Governmentality* (Chicago: University of Chicago Press, 1991), p. 158.

45. Crush, *Power of Development,* p. 8.

46. Manuel Castells, *The Rise of Network Society,* 3 vols. (Oxford: Blackwell, 1996).

47. Burchell, Gordon, and Miller, *The Foucault Effect,* p. 141.

48. Dean, *Governmentality,* p. 156.

CHAPTER EIGHT

Spinning the World

Spin Doctors, Mediation, and Foreign Policy

Robin Brown

A recent television documentary showed the Russian ambassador to the Court of St. James inside 10 Downing Street preparing the visit of President Putin. His preparation did not consist of negotiating geopolitical realities with Tony Blair but discussing camera angles with the prime minister's official spokesman, his chief spin doctor, Alastair Campbell. The *diplomatic* mediator was attempting to influence the *televisual* mediation. A little later in the film we see the visit in progress. When Blair and Putin are out of the public gaze, their chief topic of discussion is how they will perform their press conference.[1] Of course, a documentary about the work of Alastair Campbell is not the place to find an authoritative account of British–Russian relations, but it does suggest one truth of contemporary political life: political effects of international events lie more in the pictures produced than in the agreements reached.

For many, the spin doctor represents the epitome of late modernity, but I want to argue that the spin doctor raises more fundamental and permanent questions about the nature of the international realm. All politics is a mediated activity: the political world of the Athenian citizen was created by the rhetoric of the agora just as television news creates the political world of contemporary citizens. However, changes in practices of mediation in society at large are reflected in the practice of political communication. Changing forms of mediation change the nature of the political object and the form of the political subject. What constitutes the international is changed by shifting practices of mediation. If classical diplomacy is mediation by letter and emissary conducted in secret, contemporary diplomacy is mediation via television and Internet. The rise of spin represents a realization that a transparent world requires different strategies than an opaque one. Spin is the rhetoric of an information age.

In a world where electronic networks of communication penetrate ever more deeply into the realms of everyday life and diplomacy, much of diplomacy is simply concerned with the management of the consequences of this mediation. If international relations is experienced as a set of television pictures or words in a newspaper, then shaping those pictures and stories must become a source of power and influence. Once we begin to think in these terms, international relations stops being a set of real events occurring out in the world and begins to look like something that exists only in the news media. Mediation does not simply transmit or even transform the event but constitutes it. This might be seen as evidence of the final disappearance of the real into the hyperreal, as Baudrillard would argue.[2] This essay takes a different tack. The opposition is not between the real and the mediated but between different forms of mediated society. As the forms of mediation that constitute contemporary society change, so do the practices that constitute the political. In a society dominated by electronic networks of mediation, conflict is in large part waged by attempting to shape these mediations. What we know about Kosovo is what we learn from the news media. It then follows that to shape the news is to shape "the pictures in our heads."[3]

This essay examines how states seek to shape these pictures. In particular, it examines the way in which governmental press officers, colloquially "spin doctors," seek to mediate the mediation of the international that is provided by the news media. This provides us with an insight into the nature of power as well as into the constitution of the international. At times the international is produced in the spin doctor's statement rather than existing "out there." The problematic nature of the international and the importance of representations of the international are ideas that have driven the emergence of poststructural approaches.[4] However, a focus on spin treats representation as the consequence not of an agentless discourse but of a constant struggle to impose and construct meaning on a chaotic reality, one in conflict with others. Meaning and narrative are objects of a consciously waged daily battle fought by spin doctors and journalists, a battle fought out in briefing rooms and telephone calls.

Spin brings together the international and the cultural in a way that disrupts both international and cultural studies. For international studies there is the disturbing realization that the "international" is often constituted as spin-off from the pursuit of the next day's headline. Spin underlines the fact that the international is invariably cultural. Spin also brings agency back into the cultural picture, making us aware of how meaning is produced. Spin tells us that the challenge of meaning is not thinking the thought but organizing its communication. Spin is the process by which agents struggle to define the meaning of reality for others. Lest this seem overly abstract, let me introduce the views of a practitioner.

Writing about the aftermath of the American cruise-missile attack on the Al-Shifa chemical factory in August 1998, a senior State Department spin doctor wrote: "[s]uddenly and unexpectedly, the United States found itself competing with the dictatorship of Sudan in a global effort to interpret the meaning of the strikes. . . . Without winning the struggle to define the interpretation of state actions, the physical acts themselves become less effective."[5] Even for foreign ministries the struggle for meaning is a crucial part of their task. Underpinning Metzl's argument for the importance of this battle is the realization that spin is a weapon that can be wielded not just by the powerful, but also by the weak. In an age of global media, the Sudanese government as much as the United States can contest meaning. This is also something that campaigners have been quicker to learn than many governments. The image of Princess Diana in a minefield may have alerted millions to the problems of antipersonnel mines, but it also represented the deliberate manipulation of the system of mediation provided by the machinery of news.

Mediation, Politics, and Spin

Spin raises fundamental issues about the nature of modern life and I begin by locating the contemporary practice of spin in relation to two key ideas: first, any society can be thought of as a system of mediation; second, politics is inevitably a mediated and hence rhetorical activity. As the way in which mediation is organized in society changes, so must the nature of political practice.

The first point stems from the work of what are sometimes called the medium theorists. The central claim of medium theory is that the form of a society is shaped by its practices of mediation. Changes in the form of mediation—particularly, but not exclusively, associated with the technologies of communication—lead to changes in the form of the social. In this perspective, mediation does not only *stand between* or even *transform* but actually *constitutes* the social. Any society or system of social relationships is shaped by the nature of its mediative practices. What the medium theorists do not share is a consensus on the nature of the social. For Harold Innis, society was a nexus of power and culture thought of in terms of a spatialized political economy. Marshall McLuhan leaned toward a psychologistic version of the social world. Joshua Meyrowitz treats the social world in terms of microinteractionist sociology.[6] Nevertheless, we can follow Asa Briggs or John Thompson in the view that modernity is constituted around its systems of mediation.[7] Mediation here is both constitutive of the cultural possibilities that exist and a function of organizational forms. The telegraph and the telephone made possible the organizational forms that shaped modernity from the business corporation to the all-embracing state. If all societies are constituted by their practices of mediation then the issue is not between the real and the mediated but between the implications of different forms of mediation.

The second point can be captured in the tripartite relationship between Athenian democracy, rhetoric, and philosophy. If philosophy was about what was good and true, rhetoric sought the secrets of political effectiveness in the ability to shape representation. The politicians of the classical world sought to use mediation as a tool of political effectiveness. The listener is always alienated from the speaker and rhetoric seeks to bridge this gap by presenting a view of events, people, or the public sphere. Yet, this view is not "real" but imagined in the words of the speaker. In *The Republic,* Plato seeks to weld together the true and the political, but in the practice of politics the relationship between what is represented and what exists has always been problematic. To think in terms of rhetoric is to think in terms of a plurality of political possibilities. To engage in rhetoric is to recognize multiple versions of the world. The practitioner of rhetoric recognizes that to choose one argument and mode of presentation over another argument and mode is to choose between outcomes. One argument may alienate the audience, whereas another will win them over. For practitioners of politics this has rarely been a problem—politics is a matter of choice—but theorists have rarely engaged with this.[8] Politics has been treated as a matter of objective interest, truth, or right, not as a matter of practice. This has obscured the centrality of rhetoric to political life.

From the perspective of medium theory and political communication, spin can be seen as the way in which rhetoric is done in a world of television and the Internet. But what do we mean by "spin"? In English one "spins a story." But it seems that the origin of spin as a political phenomenon lies in the world of sport. In a ball game, spinning the ball affects how it bounces. A coach who works with players on how to put spin on the ball is a "spin doctor." In its sporting sense, spin implies taking an object and influencing how it travels. In politics, the original sense of spin was to take an event that had occurred and attempt to impose a favorable "spin" on the event by persuading the public, or, more usually, the media to report it in a way that suited the interests of the protagonist. For instance, in the wake of American presidential debates, spin doctors for the candidates explain to the journalists what they have just seen.[9] The spin doctors insert themselves between event and observer to provide their own version of the events. They compete in trying to persuade the reporters to interpret the event in one of the many possible ways. Of course, a multitude of interpretations can be sustained, but the demands of journalistic production demand a simple and easily understood story.[10] Frequently, the events that the spokespeople report on took place out of the view of the journalists. Spin is no longer an interpretation of a public event but becomes the event itself. In summary, spin can be thought of as efforts to influence the interpretation of political events. Yet, as we will see, the interpretation can come to replace the event itself.

Spin is not the same as lying, although it may involve an element of falsehood. Although sometimes spin is used to imply telling a lie, this interpretation narrows the meaning of spin too much. Practitioners are unanimous in rejecting the notion that spin can involve the conscious attempt to persuade the media to accept an untruth. Their reasoning is simple: if they are to attempt to persuade their audience to accept their version of the world every day, their audience must grant them a degree of credibility.[11] What spin often involves is statements that are literally true but lead the audience in entirely the wrong direction through emphasis or ambiguity.

To conflate spin and propaganda is also a way of narrowing the concept. Propaganda suggests a deliberate campaign of persuasion. Much of what constitutes spin is in the daily press releases, responses to questions and events. Although the impact of these responses is great, they are often given little thought. Spin is better thought of as being a continuum of persuasion that reaches from an off-the-cuff response to an unexpected question to a deliberate effort to persuade or reeducate.

Although the concern with politics as rhetorical practice is fundamental, the changing forms of mediation in modern society produce a distinct mode of rhetoric. The contemporary practice of spin originates from the inability of political actors to dictate the content of the media. Where there are multiple and competing sources of information and multiple and competing political agents, the news media can choose between them. In this sense the modern practice of spin grows out of the demands of pluralist and, in a weak sense, democratic politics. Writing of Edward Bernays, the American pioneer of public relations, Stuart Ewen traces the emergence of PR to

> that moment when aristocratic paradigms of deference could no longer hold up in the face of modern, democratic, public ideals that were boiling up among the "lower strata" of society. At that juncture, strategies of social rule began to change.[12]

These strategies were in part carried out via the mass media. Authoritarian governments can dictate the content of the media, but democratic governments can only attempt to influence it.

Spin implies at least a double mediation, and on occasion a triple mediation. The first mediation is in the way that the news media mediate the events. The news is not "what happened" but a product of a complex system of selection and shaping. The news media stand apparently between the consumer and the event. The spin doctor understands that the news media transform events and meaning rather than transmitting them. Thus, he or she provides a second level of mediation standing between the event that the news media seek to report and attempting to influence the way they report it. At times, though, the spin doctor may go beyond this. Rather than reporting on an event that happened in the absence of reports, the event is geared simply to the desire to produce coverage. A cynical view of the annual opening session of the United Nations is that it attracts so many heads of state and government simply because they can be photographed shaking hands with other heads of state and government and recorded addressing the General

Assembly. At this level of analysis, Baudrillard's theory of the media as simulated reality systems comes to mind.

The concept of spin has developed in domestic media spaces, yet these national media spaces are gradually and unevenly melding into something more unified. Over the past two decades, several developments have eroded this separation. New tools of news gathering and dissemination from satellites to the Internet allow a greater contestation of international issues. Where once international news was provided to a national audience by a national broadcaster shaped by national governments, the gradual emergence of a global media space is forcing spin doctors to struggle in the international arena just as in the realm of domestic politics.[13]

Why Does It Matter?

Spin becomes important precisely because experience of the international is mediated. Yet, this experience extends to the apparent center of the political sphere. How does an NGO or a government know what is going on in the world? Very often, the answer is by reading the newspaper or watching the news on TV. Of course, we are not solely dependent on the media for information. We can turn to friends or neighbors, we have contacts closer to the action, we rely on the Internet. Governments have access to diplomatic and intelligence reporting. But the role of the media should not be underestimated. Much diplomatic reporting is concerned with the content of the local press. Although agents have access to other sources of information, the general media supply a general picture of events. Bernard Cohen's study of the way foreign-policy makers use the press, though nearly forty years old, retains its plausibility. Citing a senior State Department official, Cohen concludes that

> [y]our vision of the world . . . comes at you from the paper, it hits you at breakfast. The press's definition of the structure of international affairs, or parts of that structure, may even become the prevailing definition among these top officials—indirectly, because it is the one so many other people accept; and by default, because these officials are physically unable to read everything that comes into the State Department through official channels.[14]

Drawing on interviews with an international group of diplomats, W. Philips Davison notes that the "mass media provide a set of facts and opinions available to both sides in a negotiation, since all governments monitor substantially the same news outlets." The sources he lists are newspapers and news magazines. The nearly three decades since his re-search was conducted has probably added only CNN to his list.[15] Even for the most senior policy makers, a good part of their view of the world comes from the news media.

Looking back on his experience as director of the Arms Control and Disarmament Agency, Kenneth Adelman lamented the attention that officials paid to the daily digest of the news media:

> The clips helped fashion the agency's agenda for at least every morning, if not the entire day. They prod otherwise groggy bureaucrats to scramble for explanations—how some fresh disaster could ever have happened.... just as damaging is their effect on their boss who comes to believe that his or her agency's service or problems are forefront on the minds of every American.[16]

If even perceptions within a government of its own doings are shaped by press reports of dubious provenance and accuracy, the impact among external parties will be even greater.

Public communication is how we evaluate private statements and public actions. Our understanding of what is actually going on emerged from an evaluation of all that we know. For instance, in his memoirs, former U.S. Secretary of State George Schultz notes how he evaluated promises that the Israeli government made to him in private against what he took to be signs of off-the-record briefings appearing in the Is-raeli press.[17]

Public reactions strengthen or support international negotiating po-sitions. Take the example of the Reykjavik summit in 1986. Ronald Rea-gan refused to accept a deal on nuclear forces in Europe that would have constrained his ability to deploy antimissile defenses. Given the degree of skepticism and political opposition to his Space Defense Ini-tiative (SDI), the U.S. government was faced with a perception both that it had failed to reach an agreement and that an unreasonable com-mitment to SDI had produced the failure. Broadcasting to the nation, an exhausted George Schultz described the "magnificent" achievement of the president at the summit. However, his body language belied this achievement. The journalists mediated Schultz's attempted "spin"—ABC's Sam Donaldson said that he looked as if "his dog had been run over by a truck."[18] The response to this perception had to involve an enormous effort to persuade the media, and through them, allies, other political actors, and the public that, if Reykjavik had not been a total success, this could not be attributed to the policies of the administration. It is the perception that follows from such an event that shapes its consequence, not the event itself.

Of course, if a government can control the media and isolate its constituency from other sorts of information, then spin control is easy to achieve. The more a polity is marked by multiple political actors and multiple sources of information, and the more autonomy media organizations have, the more spin becomes a battle that must be waged on a daily basis. The failure to wage it is to abdicate the battle for the definition of meaning.

Doing Spin

How that battle for meaning is waged offers an insight into the constitution of the international and the tools and tactics by which the political object is produced. It also shows that meaning is constantly contested. A leading British journalist recently made the observation that in "the spin doctor's ideal world, all is managed, smoothed and predictable." This is correct, but this statement needs to be balanced by a paraphrase of Clausewitz's observation that "[e]verything in war is very simple, but the simplest thing is difficult."[19] Producing a "managed, smoothed and predictable" reality is a continuous battle against the encroaching chaos.

The spin doctor provides an interface between three social fields: the "inside" of the government, the "outside" political world (or worlds), and the world of the media.[20] Placed in this position the press officer is not simply a frictionless conduit but an active mediator orchestrating events and describing scenes that are invisible to the observer.

When a spokesperson walks into a briefing room, he or she encounters representatives of the news media who are motivated less by a search for the truth than by their need to find something to fill up the bulletin or the paper. A good news story has exactly the same characteristics as any other story: it has drama, conflict, characters, a comprehensible plot, and a happy (or tragic) ending, all features not readily available in real life. As international events are often complex and unfamiliar, journalists will cheerfully convert them into something simpler and more understandable.[21] Journalists want the press officer to give them a story that they can use. The press officer can do this either by directly telling the journalists a story that fits with their definition of news or inadvertently through being caught out. Being caught out might involve demonstrating that the press officer does not know what is going on. A journalist might confront them with a statement from a critic or an adversary. They might look for an inconsistency with a previous statement or a statement from another member of the government. For the journalist, this is "a real story," not one that has been manufactured by the machinery of presentation—although most of the time the journalist will be happy to accept as such these "unreal" stories. Being caught out damages the credibility of the spin doctor. It may damage the person that the spin doctor speaks for and it may damage the government or state or country. It is this experience that led Larry Speakes to observe that "everybody wants to be the press secretary but nobody wants to go into the briefing room."[22]

What happens in the briefing room is affected by the broader political context. The questions that the press officer is asked and the response that they get are supposedly a product of events in the wider world. In practice, journalists' knowledge of the world is shaped by their own consumption of the media—whether it is the newspaper or report that they saw earlier or the cables and pictures from news agencies that provide the backbone of almost all newspapers and television news services. All governments seek to set the news agenda to select the issues of the day, but they only partially succeed. The ability to choose the story is not unlimited. Relations with the media become more strained when a policy is unpopular or controversial. The more the governmental mandate is called into question, the less willing the journalists are to accept at face value the story the press officer gives them. At the same time, the more insecure a government feels, the more its staff will try to exercise direct controls over the media. As Marlin Fitzwater puts it in discussing the relationship between Secret Service personnel and the press, "the more that power is challenged by sources outside the White House, the more it is exercised within the White House" through searches, identity checks, and lack of cooperation.[23]

Notionally the press officer is called upon to provide a line or a spin that will shape the way the media report events. This is only half the story. In many respects, the more interesting part of it is the mediation of what happens inside the government. The more closely we look at this, the more it appears that the press officer is less a channel of communication than a fabricator of news. As Fitzwater put it, "one wrong word and I make policy."[24]

The rhythm of the press officer's life is set by the demands of the journalists, who in turn are under the pressure of their deadlines. This forces the spin doctor to go searching for information, to try to find out what is going on. Particularly in the field of foreign affairs, policy makers may refuse to tell the press officer anything. Despite this, the press officer still has to face the press and tell them something. At many points in government there is no clear agreement about what policy is or what is really going on. Despite this, the press officer must convert confusion into a meaningful account of events. The conventions of political practice and media reporting mean that an honest expression of uncertainty or ignorance will be taken as a sign of weakness. The combination of uncertainty and desire to win, to shape the story in a way that helps, can turn the press officer from a reporter of events into a fabricator of information. Concerned that Reagan was losing the battle to define the meaning of the Geneva summit, Larry Speakes told the media that, as Reagan had stood with Gorbachev at the end of one session, he remarked that the "world breathes easier because we are talking together" and "our differences are serious, but so is our commitment to improving understanding." These comments were prominently reported but had never actually been uttered by Reagan. Instead, they came directly from the pen of the deputy press secretary.[25]

The other side of the story is that if the relationship between the spokesperson and the principal is close, then the press officer may enjoy almost unlimited access to the principal's meetings and activities. The spin doctor will sit in on the highest-level meetings as either participant or observer. Through a close relationship with the principal, the spin doctor gains the authority to interpret the doings and thoughts of the leader and to communicate them to the media. As the specialist in "presentation," the press officer will contribute to forming policy in such a way as to ensure that it can be presented in a favorable way. Here we run into the situation where the mediator of government policy is actually the producer of government policy. The communicator provides his or her own spin on the doings of the state. This may involve providing quotations from the leader to support this spin, even at the cost of putting words in the leader's mouth. Very often the bond between the leader and the mouthpiece is such that the spin doctor can enunciate what the leader would have said. Alastair Campbell, Tony Blair's press secretary, testifying before the Parliamentary Select Committee on Public

Administration, put it thus: the prime minister "has to have somebody who is doing . . . and who is organising . . . whom he can trust, who knows his mind, who knows what he thinks about the big issues of the day, and indeed about the small issues of the day, and who can brief at the drop of a hat so that if anybody asks me a question, I can answer it."[26]

The mutual dependence of policy makers and journalists on the news for knowledge of the world means that very often they take the spin for what policy is. The *public* statement becomes the *authoritative* statement of policy. Few people will bother to pore over what the leader actually said. Instead, their understanding of what occurred will come from the media accounts. Even those who do minutely scrutinize what was said will note the spin placed on the statement. In the daily play of politics, an authoritative statement stands for authority.

Effective spin requires the consistent presentation of a consistent line. If we say the same thing enough times, people will begin to believe us. If Machiavelli's prince was ultimately the plaything of *fortuna,* the modern prince is just as much at the mercy of shifting media agendas and internal disagreements. Getting consistency is hard and, in modern government, consistency is difficult to maintain. Even if a senior figure does not criticize a policy in public, he or she has the option of talking to the media indirectly via the medium of the leak.[27] The refusal to support the policy publicly and fully may be all that is required to signal disagreement and undermine the impact of the message. The rhythms of the news dictate the spin cycle. The emergence of twenty-four-hour news channels and the Internet only means a greater chance that the spin doctor can be caught out, that the narrative of policy will break down.[28]

Spin is not simply words or images. It lies in the performance of those words: finding the right words, at the right time, by the right people, using the right channels of communications. This is the most problematic element of spin. Getting the logistics and politics of the utterance right is central to its effectiveness. The spin doctor is not simply a communicator but also an orchestrator of communication. The ability to spin effectively becomes dependent on the power of the communicator within the organization. The perceived closeness to the boss and the hegemony of that boss over the organization become the source of power that allows the communicator to operate effectively. In itself, position in the internal policy field will not be sufficient. The technical skills of the spin doctor are necessary to communicate effectively. Failure will erode

the position not just of the press officer but also of those who are represented. As Philip Gould put it, referring to the revival of the Labour
Party under Tony Blair: "in a modern media environment, competence
and good communications are inseparable: you cannot have one without the other."[29] This simple statement is open to a variety of readings
that go to the heart of spin. At its most innocent level, it can be read as
saying that if you are not good at communicating, your competence
will not be noticed and you will be assumed to have failed. It may also
be that if you cannot organize your communications, you will not be
able to organize your policy effectively. However, if you can communicate so effectively, then does it matter how competent you really are?
The representation of competence stands for competence itself. We find
ourselves back with Machiavelli, who so well understood how reputation was power.

As I suggested earlier, the importance of spin grows out of the partial
autonomy of the media field from any particular political actor. Studies
of the media over many years suggest that national news outlets in most
countries tend to take a high proportion of their stories from those holding official positions.[30] Yet this is balanced by the finding that the media
also faithfully reflect splits within the governing elite. When an elite is
united around a policy, the critics will find it difficult to make their
voices heard. But as dissenting voices emerge within the elite, they open
a path for critics in the media.[31]

The need to spin emerges from the existence of multiple viewpoints,
whether those emerge from the professional norms of the media or from
political opposition. The transnationalization of mediation via satellite
television and the Internet reduces the degree of autonomy in national
media spaces and allows "foreign" actors to contribute to the debate. It
increases the visibility of foreign actors and, in doing so, takes spin into
the realm of foreign policy.

Mediating the Mediation: Spin and the International

Diplomacy involves maneuvering between different fields of action. The
nature of the mediation between the fields transforms the stakes and
the identity of the actor. Within this process of diplomatic mediation,
the representation of the process in the information media creates a
reflexivity that plays back into the diplomatic process. The diplomat
must know when to speak and when to remain silent. But in a world

where mediation takes place via the news media, not in the mediation of diplomats speaking across a table, how one speaks and remains silent changes.

For those conducting diplomacy in the glare of publicity, spin is the basic tool. Comments to the media are carefully weighed to impact on those within the home government, interlocutors, and multiple publics. The public statement is not simply a report of an event distant in time and space, but a move in the game in itself. For instance, in his memoir of his time as American mediator in Bosnia, Richard Holbrooke clearly demonstrates the significance of the media reports in shaping developments within the political game.[32] The importance is reflected not only by the pervasive presence of the media as Holbrooke makes his shuttle, but in his concerns to deny some information to the media while feeding them other information.[33] For players of the diplomatic game, the media are a field of contestation where each player seeks to define events and mobilize supporters. The global media field allows those who obey the logic of that field—by providing a good story—to reach out, mobilize friends, and demobilize opponents.

NATO's experience during the Kosovo crisis is suggestive of the way in which spin becomes integral to policy. From a media point of view, the Kosovo crisis, practically from the first day, was a story about a failed strategy and a fracturing alliance. That NATO had "no choice" in continuing the war until it achieved a semblance of victory because failure would have been too damaging to contemplate might have been true from the perspective of foreign ministries. However, for democratically elected political leaders, rising criticism and disenchantment with the conflict could easily have forced a defection from the agreed strategy and a movement to define whatever had been achieved as "success."[34] NATO's strategy was to convince Serbia of its resolve to continue the war. That resolve had to be achieved by a process of internal mobilization. The centerpiece of NATO's strategy was communication, both to persuade Milosevic and to persuade itself. In the absence of direct, that is to say, military, action against the alliance, the threat that NATO faced was political entropy, a loss of resolve in the face of factors ranging from lack of progress in the campaign to rising civilian casualties.

From this perspective, the key to understanding the conflict is less a focus on the bombings than an emphasis on the ability to sustain a particular framing of the conflict. For both journalists and briefers, the information environment was global and active twenty-four hours a day. This came as a surprise to NATO briefers. At some points, NATO's spokespersons at the main afternoon briefings would try to focus on the previous day's events while the journalists already knew about the morning's attacks and wanted more information about those.[35] Time differences meant that by the time the main American briefings took place, the journalists already had access to a full day of reports from Serbia and Kosovo. In order to avoid being caught out, briefers had to prepare to deal with questions about very recent events as well as the statements of other political leaders and spokespersons.

In the wake of the infamous bombing of a refugee convoy in Prizren and with the subsequent inability of NATO to create a persuasive narrative about this event or even to kill the story, Alastair Campbell was dispatched to NATO to review the media operation. The result was an effort to expand the media resources of NATO and to ensure that the operation could work better. NATO spokesman Jamie Shea was given more staff to monitor the media as well as better access to information from Supreme Headquarters Allied Powers Europe (SHAPE)—which allegedly was reluctant to share too much with civilians. A second part of the strategy was to extend the daily "quint" (United States, Great Britain, Germany, France, Italy) conference calls to include press spokespersons.[36] The importance of the Campbell initiative was acknowledged by NATO commander Gen. Wesley Clark. Clark declared that it "was completely crucial in getting ourselves organized at NATO. What we discovered with the modern media is that you cannot afford to wait around." Journalists also noted the improvements in the NATO operation. The aftermath was an appreciation of the need for NATO to develop its own Media Operations Center.[37]

There are signs of a growing appreciation of the value of spin in foreign policy. The State Department has been reorganized to bring together the U.S. Information Agency with the department proper, and to merge public diplomacy and public affairs in order that the "foreign policy of the United States, the advocacy of that foreign policy, the communication of that foreign policy to foreign audiences, is done in a more coherent and more effective way."[38] On April 30, 1999, President Clinton promulgated Presidential Decision Directive (PDD) 68 creating an International Public Information Coordinating Group, a step that attracted criticism because of its blurring of boundaries between foreign and domestic matters, political and nonpolitical, and objectivity and propaganda. Although PDD 68 is concerned with foreign audiences, a draft leaked to the media requires that information released to domestic audiences "be co-ordinated, integrated, deconflicted and synchronized to achieve a synergistic effect for strategic information activities."[39]

The conclusion that can be drawn from these cases is that the changing forms of mediation in contemporary society are encouraging actors to change their strategies and to evolve new structures to permit them to wage the information battle more effectively.

Conclusions

Spin is a neglected element of foreign policy, but it is a site of mediation that tells us much. To study spin is to focus on the practice of foreign policy. For many students of the international, spin will seem too ephemeral to be significant. Yet it is the ephemeral, the accidental, that often shapes the outcomes of international political events.

Spin also brings agency back into the cultural and media picture. Although we can study the texts of spin, what the spin doctor said or wrote, and, from this, try to understand the ideology, the motives, and the discourse that produce it, spin also has to be interpreted as part of interplay between multiple fields of power. Spin causes us to be aware of how meaning is produced. Spin tells us that the challenge of meaning is not thinking the thought but organizing its communication. The practice of spin takes as its starting point the need to conduct politics in the middle space provided by the news media. But in doing so, it also comes to constitute the political world. Mediation can always be contested and challenged. Spin is about the short term. But for the journalist and the spin doctor, what is the long term but a series of daily events and reports? As NGOs, for example, have rapidly learned in the field of spin, there is always space for a new actor with an interesting story to tell. And in a world where the networks of mediation are increasingly interconnected, there will always be someone who is willing to listen.

Notes

1. Michael Cockerell (dir.), *News from Number 10*, BBC 2, July 15, 2000.
2. Jean Baudrillard, *Simulations*, trans. Paul Foss, Paul Patton, and Philip Beitchman (New York: Semiotext[e], 1983).

3. Walter Lippmann, *Public Opinion* (New York: Macmillan, 1922), p. 3.

4. See, for instance, James Der Derian and Michael J. Shapiro, eds., *International/Intertextual Relations: Postmodern Readings of World Politics* (Lexington, Mass.: Lexington, 1989).

5. Jamie Frederic Metzl, "Popular Diplomacy," *Daedalus* 128.2 (spring 1999): 177.

6. Harold A. Innis, *Empire and Communications* (Oxford: Oxford University Press, 1950) and *The Bias of Communication* (Toronto: University of Toronto Press, 1951); Marshall McLuhan, *Understanding Media: The Extensions of Man* (New York: McGraw-Hill, 1964); Joshua Meyrowitz, *No Sense of Place: The Impact of Electronic Media on Social Behaviour* (New York: Oxford University Press, 1985). On medium theory as a theoretical approach, see Joshua Meyrowitz, "Medium Theory," in David Crowley and David Mitchell, eds., *Communication Theory Today* (Cambridge: Polity Press, 1994). Ronald Deibert has consistently argued for the application of a medium theory approach to international relations. See Ronald Deibert, "Typographica: The Medium and the Medieval to Modern Transformation," *Review of International Studies* 22.1 (January 1996): 28–56, and *Parchment, Printing and Hypermedia: Communication in World Order Transformation* (New York: Columbia University Press, 1997).

7. Asa Briggs, *The Communications Revolution* (Leeds: Leeds University Press, 1966); John B. Thompson, *The Media and Modernity: A Social Theory of the Media* (Cambridge: Polity Press, 1995).

8. Machiavelli's *The Prince* is an obvious exception.

9. For an observer's account of the 1996 version of this, see Philip Gould, *The Unfinished Revolution: How the Modernizers Saved the Labour Party* (London: Little, Brown, 1998), pp. 333–34.

10. The literature on the sociology of news production is extensive. Key contributions include Herbert Gans, *Deciding What's News* (New York: Pantheon, 1979); Michael Schudson, *Discovering the News* (New York: Basic Books, 1980); Philip Schlesinger, *Putting "Reality" Together: BBC News* (London: Methuen, 1987).

11. For practitioners' views on the relationship between credibility and lying, see Bernard Ingham, *Kill the Messenger* (London: Fontana, 1991), pp. 159–60; Larry Speakes, *Speaking Out: The Reagan Presidency from inside the White House* (New York: Avon, 1989), pp. 279–80; Marlin Fitzwater, *Call the Briefing!* (New York: Times Books, 1995), pp. 198–201.

12. Stuart Ewen, *PR!: A Social History of Spin* (New York: Basic Books, 1996), p. 13.

13. On these developments, see Robert M. Entman, "Declarations of Independence: The Growth of Media Power after the Cold War," in Brigitte Nacos, Robert V. Shapiro, and Pierangelo Isermin, *Decisionmaking in a Glass House: Mass Media, Public Opinion and American and European Foreign Policy in the 21st Century* (Landham, Md.: Rowman and Littlefield, 2000).

14. Bernard C. Cohen, *The Press and Foreign Policy* (Princeton, N.J.: Princeton University Press, 1963), p. 211.

15. W. Philips Davison, "News Media and International Negotiation," *Public Opinion Quarterly* 38.2 (summer 1974): 176–77. In assessing the impact of newer technologies such as the Internet and satellite television, it should be noted that, historically, foreign ministries and major embassies had "tickers": teletype machines that provided the news feed from news agencies; hence they had access to informa-

tion much more rapidly than did the general public. See Cohen, *The Press and Foreign Policy*, pp. 141–43, and Davison, "News Media," pp. 175–76.

16. Kenneth L. Adelman, "Woefully Inadequate: The Press's Handling of Arms Control," in Simon Serfaty, ed., *The Media and Foreign Policy* (New York: St Martin's Press, 1991), p. 152.

17. George P. Schultz, *Turmoil and Triumph: Diplomacy, Power and the Victory of the American Ideal* (New York: Simon and Schuster, 1993), pp. 69, 211.

18. Speakes, *Speaking Out*, p. 184; Schultz, *Turmoil and Triumph*, p. 774.

19. Jeremy Paxman, "All Is Not What It Seems," *Media Guardian*, May 8, 2000, p. 11; Carl von Clausewitz, *On War*, trans. Michael Howard and Peter Paret (Princeton, N.J.: Princeton University Press, 1976), p. 119.

20. The notion of fields is characteristic of the sociology of Pierre Bourdieu. See Pierre Bourdieu and Loïc J. D. Wacquant, "The Purpose of Reflexive Sociology (The Chicago Workshop)," in Bourdieu and Wacquant, *An Invitation to Reflexive Sociology* (Chicago: University of Chicago Press, 1992), pp. 94–115; Pierre Bourdieu, *On Television and Journalism*, trans. Priscilla Parkhurst Ferguson (London: Pluto, 1998), pp. 39–68.

21. Robert Darnton, "Writing News and Telling Stories," *Daedalus* 104 (spring 1975): 175–94.

22. Speakes, *Speaking Out*, p. 299.

23. Fitzwater, *Call the Briefing!*, pp. 80, 81.

24. Ibid., p. 93.

25. Speakes, *Speaking Out*, p. 170.

26. "Testimony of Alastair Campbell before House of Commons Select Committee on Public Administration," June 23, 1998, question 400, available online at http://www.publications.parliament.uk/pa/cm199798/cmselect/cmpubadm/770/8062301.htm; see also Stephen Hess, *The Government/Press Connection: Press Officers and Their Offices* (Washington, Brookings Institution, D.C.: 1984), pp. 26–27.

27. On leaks, see Leon V. Sigal, *Reporters and Officials: The Organization and Politics of Newsmaking* (Lexington, Mass.: D. C. Heath, 1973), pp. 143–48, and Robert J. McCloskey, "The Care and Handling of Leaks," in Serfaty, *The Media and Foreign Policy*, pp. 109–20.

28. "Testimony of Alastair Campbell," question 400; Howard Kurtz, *Spin Cycle* (London: Pan, 1998), pp. xxii–xxiii.

29. Gould, *The Unfinished Revolution*, p. 334.

30. See, for instance, Sigal, *Reporters and Officials*, chapter 6.

31. See, for instance, Daniel C. Hallin, *The "Uncensored War": The Media and Vietnam* (Berkeley: University of California Press, 1986), pp. 213–14.

32. Richard Holbrooke, *To End a War*, rev. ed. (New York: Modern Library, 1999). See also Carl Bildt, *Peace Journey: The Struggle for Peace in Bosnia* (London: Weidenfeld and Nicolson, 1998).

33. This is accomplished, for instance, by restricting the circulation of information via what Holbrooke regards as leaky State Department channels (Holbrooke, *To End a War*, p. 135).

34. The role of NATO concessions in producing an agreement is controversial. See Barry R. Posen, "The War for Kosovo: Serbia's Political-Military Strategy," *International Security*, 24.4 (spring 2000): 39–84, and Zbigniew Brzezinski, "Why Milosevic Cracked," *Prospect*, November 1999, pp. 10–11. For the official view on the importance

of media strategy to the campaign, see Alastair Campbell, "Communications Lessons for Nato, the Military and Media," *RUSI Journal* (August 1999): 31–36.

35. For instance, see the transcript of the May 21, 1999, briefing available online at www.nato.int/kosovo/press/p990521a.htm.

36. "NATO Calls for Spin Doctor," *The Times*, April 17, 1999, p. 5; Nicholas Watt, Stephen Bates, and Ian Black, "Nato Bids to Get Its Media Act Together," *Guardian*, April 19, 1999, p. 2; Jonathan Freedland, "No Way to Spin a War," *Guardian*, April 21, 1999, p. 17; George Jones and Tim King, "Blair Takes the PR War to NATO HQ," *Daily Telegraph*, April 21, 1999, p. 1; Alastair Campbell, "War of Words over Kosovo," *Guardian*, April 21, 1999, p. 21; Martin Walker, "Clinton's Prince of War," *Guardian*, April 26, 1999, p. 16; Peter Oborne, *Alastair Campbell* (London: Aurum, 1999), pp. 204–7.

37. Clark cited in Andy McSmith, "Kosovo Spin Attacked by Shea," *Observer*, July 25, 1999; see also Martin Walker, "The Spin Doctors Hit Back," *Guardian*, May 15, 1999.

38. Patrick Kennedy, assistant secretary for administration, cited in U.S. State Department briefing, "Final Status of the Reform and Restructuring of the Foreign Affairs Agencies" (Washington, D.C.: State Department, September 30, 1999), available online at www.state.gov/www/policy_remarks/1999/990930_ken_gnehm_reform.html.

39. Cited in Ben Barber, "Group Will Battle Propaganda Abroad; Intends to Gain Foreign Support for US," *Washington Times*, July 28, 1999, p. A1.

EPILOGUE

Romantic Mediations of September 11
Cynthia Weber

The United States has thrice suffered surprise aerial attacks on its soil.[1] The first was by Japanese bombers at Pearl Harbor on December 7, 1941, the second by al-Qaeda terrorists in New York City and Washington, D.C., on September 11, 2001, and the third by ninth-grade Palm Harbor resident Charles Bishop in Tampa, Florida, on January 5, 2002.

In the immediate aftermath of September 11, the attack on Pearl Harbor morphed into America's imaginary about September 11. Although the differences between the two attacks were duly noted—mainland attack versus offshore attack, targeting symbols and civilians versus targeting a military base and military personnel, terrorist attack versus state attack—these real differences did little to disrupt the symbolic circuits of exchange that governed the two events.

As the film *Pearl Harbor* (Touchstone, 2001) replayed in cinemas across the country, narratives about "the first great sneak attack on America" reemerged as a way of making historical, emotional, and moral sense of September 11.[2] The December 7, 1941, attack on Pearl Harbor and the terrorist attacks of September 11, 2001, were described as two dates that will live in infamy, two days on which American innocence was lost (again) thanks to surprise attacks at moments of American history when the rhetoric of isolationism was in place.[3] Because of these historical similarities, Pearl Harbor was conjured up in American discourse as a foreign-policy response model and as an emotionally parallel time that justified "rage and retribution," what one commentator called "a unified, unifying, Pearl Harbor sort of purple American fury."[4] September 11 and Pearl Harbor were also morally twinned. As one American commentator speaking about the United States' war on terror in early November 2001 put it, "Certainly in the States right now I don't think you have any sense of moral ambiguity about the rightness of this particular cause that America's engaged in. September 11 has an almost December 7 kind of clarifying impact for Americans. So I don't think that the war on terrorism is going to be fraught with ambivalence and ambiguity, at least in the American imagination."[5]

Given the dramatic recirculation of ideas, images, and emotions about Pearl Harbor, it is little surprise that Pearl Harbor itself became a material site of return for relatives and colleagues of the firefighters, police officers, and rescue workers killed or injured on September 11. Over Pearl Harbor remembrance week, they visited Hawaii at the invitation of the state's governor.[6] Following September 11, even World War II veterans of Pearl Harbor experienced a sudden surge of popularity. As they returned to Pearl Harbor on the sixtieth anniversary of the attack, "they have been applauded . . . in airport departure lounges, beautified by pilots in midflight monologues and pestered for autographs in Honolulu hotel lobbies." One veteran explained, "People are saying thanks for protecting us, and they never used to say that."[7]

Americans seem to be thanking Pearl Harbor vets now not only for their past protection of the nation's land and lives but also for their present protection of the nation's image; for Pearl Harbor functions in American discourse as the historic root of the country's contemporary self-image, that of the heroic yet benevolent leader of the "free world" loved and admired within and beyond its shores.[8] Yes, Pearl Harbor marks the moment when the modern United States first felt violated and vulnerable, and its memorials have become national sites of mourning. But Pearl Harbor also marks the moment when, in the United States' narration of its own history, its legacy of sustained heroic global engagement began. President George W. Bush made this explicit on December 7, 2001, stating that "[w]hat happened at Pearl Harbor was the start of a long and terrible war for America. Yet, out of that surprise attack grew a steadfast resolve that made America freedom's defender. And that mission—our great calling—continues to this hour, as the brave men and women of our military fight the forces of terror in Afghanistan and around the world."[9]

What Pearl Harbor also symbolized was one of the last moments in American history when victory seemed to be inevitable. America's victory was inevitable because, as Tom Engelhardt explains, "Triumphalism was in the American grain.... After all, hadn't American history [as Americans told it to themselves] been a processional of progress from the moment European explorers and settlers first set foot on the continent?"[10] Engelhardt terms America's triumphalist narrative its "victory culture," a culture that sees defeat as "only the springboard for victory" (p. 11). He argues that "As Pearl Harbor combined the sneak attack ('a stab-in-the-back on Sunday morning') and the last stand (where the racialized other's desire for the total annihilation of America merely foreshadows how 'each white death had to be repaid in advance by untold enemy ones'), it proved a singularly mobilizing event. It was the First Stand of a renewed cult of victory" (pp. 43, 39–40).

Engelhardt argues that the United States' belief in its inevitable triumph was finally frustrated in Vietnam, but that President Bush's appeal to Pearl Harbor in the wake of September 11 reactivates its "triumphal certainty of World War II" (p. 13), something the American mood longed for in the aftermath of its most recent tragedies. This is why President Bush could tell the nation: "We are fighting to protect ourselves and our children from violence and fear. We're fighting for the security of our people and the success of liberty. We're fighting against men without conscience, but full of ambition—to remake the world in their own brutal images. For all these reasons we're fighting to win— and win we will."[11]

In addition to seeing victory as inevitable, the United States' tradition of victory culture also sees its victory as fully justified. At Pearl Harbor, America as a force of pure good was morally warranted in defending itself against its evil enemy. Whereas Engelhardt argues that the country's own sense of unquestioned moral purity ended when it dropped the nuclear bomb on Hiroshima (p. 10), President Bush reinvested America with moral purity in its response to September 11 by reciting a World War II narrative that claimed "the terrorists are the heirs of fascism" *and* temporally linked that claim to Pearl Harbor, before the United States dropped the bomb.

Overall, then, it is a sense of untroubled heroism and moral responsibility born of necessity coupled with a unified sense of nation and national purpose opposed to an external enemy that the September 11 discourse on Pearl Harbor captures.

Cinematically, materially, and rhetorically, Pearl Harbor stands as among the most powerful sites of romantic mediation of the events of September 11. As François Debrix explains in his Introduction to this volume, in rituals of romantic mediation, "Mediation is a technique reserved to the self who takes a pause to contemplate the world, reflects on his or her place in accordance with nature, and then finds the proper aesthetic medium that can best express the grandeur of the entire edifice (world and man as one)" (p. xxi). Reading America's collective unconscious as the self and the world of international politics as the "natural world" into which the country projects itself, Pearl Harbor functions as the political, social, and aesthetic medium through which it affirms its wound in order to once again rise up and gloriously restore its sense of self.[12] Romantic rituals of engagement with Pearl Harbor become its "method of self-expression, a practice of *transformation* of the world" (p. xxxi). What these romantic mediations seem to achieve is the world's re-creation from chaotic to ordered and America's reimagination from victimized to valiant.[13] As such, it ceases to be a territory on which meanings are written by others (al-Qaeda terrorists) and is transfigured into a subject that "becomes the main (often heroic) source of meaning in [global] society." In so doing, its romantic mediations of Pearl Harbor reinstitutionalize the relations of power and domination it unquestioningly enjoyed between World War II and September 11.

But, as Debrix also points out, romantic mediations not only harmonize narratives of (collective) self and (constructed) nature. They may also challenge these narratives, rupture them, and attempt to alter them. Or, as he puts it, because "some selves are more heroic and meaningful (to modernity) than others... one man's self-affirmation is often another man's alienation.... As some critics of the romantic mind have noted, as much as mediation transforms (and creates subjectivity), it also alienates (and produces subjection)" (p. xxxii). America's romantic return to Pearl Harbor is no exception.

Less than four months after September 11, the country's recovery from that tragic day through multiple engagements with Pearl Harbor was violently and dramatically interrupted by events in Palm Harbor. On a Saturday evening in early January 2002, fifteen-year-old Charles Bishop stole a single-engine Cessna from his Florida flight school, flew it over

MacDill Air Force Base (headquarters of the U.S. Central Command, which directed combat in Afghanistan), ignored a Coast Guard helicopter sent to intercept him, and flew head-on into the twenty-eighth floor of the forty-two-story Bank of America building in downtown Tampa. That Bishop's was the only life lost in the crash and that the Bank of America building was left standing did little to lessen the immediate impact of this event on the American public; for by doubling the visual grammar of September 11 in miniature, Bishop's personal suicide mission activated the pictorial memory of hijacked commercial jet airliners crashing into and causing the collapse of the World Trade Center's Twin Towers, a memory that most Americans still experienced all too vividly.

Even though the Bush administration quickly assured the public that Bishop's act was not an instance of terrorism, this act returned homeland security from terrorist aerial attacks to the top of the policy agenda.[14] American soil once again felt strategically insecure, for even a "troubled young man" could crash a light aircraft into a skyscraper.[15] As if all this were not distressing enough, Americans received another rude shock when it was reported that Bishop was carrying a note expressing his sympathy for Osama bin Laden and the September 11 hijackers.

In the days following the discovery of Bishop's note, politicians, professionals, and parents struggled to make sense of what he did and why he did it. What, they wondered, could possibly drive a fifteen-year-old white American male who "earned straight A's, carried the flag at school assemblies, planned bake sales for his school, entered essay contests run by the Daughters of the American Revolution and wanted to join the Air Force" to commit suicide in solidarity with Osama bin Laden and the September 11 hijackers?[16] Social, medical, familial, and ethnic answers abounded. Maybe Bishop was a depressed loner who changed schools too often.[17] Or he could have been an acne-marked, Accutane-maddened adolescent made suicidal by prescription.[18] Or his parents' ineffectually executed suicide pact as teens who were denied a marriage license could have had lingering effects on their son.[19] Or maybe Charles Bishop—formerly Charles Bishara—acted as he did because of his Arab Syrian (albeit Christian) heritage.[20]

What interests me about Bishop's act is not his motives but the multiple ruptures his act performs to romantic mediations of September 11 through their engagements with Pearl Harbor, which are part of a more general narrative about the United States itself. Moving from Pearl Harbor to Palm

Harbor, the remainder of this essay explores what Bishop's other romantic mediations of September 11 do to America's self-understanding.[21]

From Pearl Harbor to Palm Harbor

If Pearl Harbor's romantic gesture is to provide America with a sense of
historic destiny, moral duty, and heroic agency by making the glorious
past present, then Palm Harbor's alternative romantic gesture is to disturb these American sensibilities by insisting that the present is not
yet—and will not soon be—past. It does so by transforming not only
the temporality in the September 11/Pearl Harbor narrative, but also its
morality, space, and characterization of U.S. subjectivity. In each case,
these disruptions are performed through the category of Charles Bishop's
youth.

Youth has long been a disruptive category. Writing about youth culture in America, Henry Giroux explains that youth is "a metaphor for
historical memory," "a symbol of how a society thinks about itself," and
"an indicator of changing cultural values, sexuality, the state of the
economy, and the spiritual life of a nation." In these ways, "youth haunts
adult society because it references our need to be attentive to a future
that others will inherit." But more than haunting, youth is also troubling. "Youth as a self and social construction has become indetermi-
nant, alien, and sometimes hazardous in the public eye. A source of repeated moral panics and the object of social regulation, youth cannot
be contained and controlled within a limited number of social spheres.
Youth cultures are often viewed in the popular press as aberrant, unpre-
dictable, and dangerous in terms of the investments they produce, social relations they affirm, and the anti-politics they sometimes legiti-
mate. Contemporary youth, especially from the inner city, increasingly
signify for the mainstream public an unwarranted rejection of an idealized past, a homogeneous culture, and an evangelical Christian future."[22]

Youth is what makes Bishop's act significant yet insignificant. By tap-
ping into some contemporary understandings of American youth, his
act violently unhinges America's romantic story of September 11/Pearl
Harbor. This makes it extremely significant. Yet, at the same time, Bishop's
youth allows his story to quickly fade from the headlines, as the insignificant act of a mere "troubled young man." In what follows, I explore
how troubled youth troubles America's romantic engagements with
Pearl Harbor. I do so by focusing primarily on temporal disruptions,

weaving disruptions to morality and space into my story, and finally concluding with an analysis of U.S. subjectivity post-September 11 and post-Bishop.

From Memorialization to Mimetic Identification

The temporality of Palm Harbor is a temporality of the present. Although, like Pearl Harbor, it evokes images from the past, this is a past not decades but months old, a past that was not buried in memory but lived daily. By playing on youth, Palm Harbor also conjures up a future in its present. But unlike Pearl Harbor's narrative, which predicts progress and triumph, Palm Harbor's narrative does not allow the country to move from this event into a better future. Rather, it predicts more of the same. It is a future frozen in the present. The temporal tropes that affect Palm Harbor's presentation of past and future are memorialization and repetition.

Flying his plane into Tampa's Bank of America Plaza, Bishop visually and symbolically re-presented the events in New York City on September 11. Unlike the September 11 hijackers who flew into the World Trade Center, he stole his plane, evaded interception by the U.S. armed forces, and intentionally collided with a towering symbol of U.S. capitalism. Bishop's act not only doubled the visual grammar of that fateful day. It also doubled its grammar of memorialization. Yet Bishop's grammar of memorialization was unlike that of the American mourners who, in memory of the tragedy of September 11 and the heroism of those who responded, placed tokens at the Twin Towers, the Pentagon, and the empty field in Pennsylvania where a fourth hijacked airliner crashed. Nor was it like that of the families of police and firefighters and the World War II veterans who traveled to Pearl Harbor, thereby mixing the memorialization of both events in contemporary memory. What Bishop's grammar of memorialization seemed to memorialize were the al-Qaeda terrorists rather than their victims. Bishop memorialized them by offering himself, his aircraft, and his intended collision as a tribute to them.[23] Bishop, it seemed, had (anti)heroically laid himself down in memory of those who planned and executed terrorist acts against his own country. As such, he literally and figuratively flew in the face of an America mourning its citizens, its symbols, and itself.

Bishop's dramatic suicide earned him the name "bin Laden's other American boy soldier," with American-born Taliban fighter John Walker

being bin Laden's original. But Bishop's act and the allegiances it suggested are far more damaging than those of Walker. For one thing,
whereas Bishop's act raises innumerable questions about why he did it
and what it meant, Walker's act does not. Walker's allegiances appear to
be straightforward. Rejecting nation in favor of religion, Walker seemed
to abandon his country, fight against it, and suffer what in America's
narrative were the inevitable consequences—defeat and capture. As a
captured "unlawful combatant," Walker could be interrogated.[24] And
even if these interrogations offer no definitive answers about Walker's
activities, at least in the immediate aftermath of September 11 he could
be contained and confined in an American narrative of treason and
treachery and in an American military prison.

In contrast, the allegiances and acts of "bin Laden's other American
boy soldier" are harder to understand. The motivation and meaning
behind Bishop's act are confounded rather than clarified by what has
been reported of his note expressing sympathy for Osama bin Laden
and the September 11 hijackers. Unlike Walker, whose opposition to the
state made him the subject of defeat, interrogation, and containment,
Bishop and his act cannot be defeated, interrogated, or contained. Unlike Walker's actions, which are made meaningful to America through a
tale of defection from its patriotic narrative of citizenship, Bishop's act
is not about a singular defection from America but a repeated infection
of America. The infectious aspect of Bishop's act is captured in another
name he was dubbed after his suicide, "Charles Bishara Bishop—Osama
bin Columbine."[25]

Calling Bishop "Charles Bishara Bishop—Osama bin Columbine"
captures the infectiousness of Bishop's act in two ways. By mentioning
Bishop's original surname, Bishara, Bishop's Arabness is evoked and
then linked to Osama bin Laden. The naming of Bishop's Syrian heritage and the linking of it to bin Laden recognizes that Bishop's personal history challenges America's official national history around race
and ethnicity, a narrative about non-African immigrants that has moved
over time from the assimilation of the melting pot to the incorporation
and respect of benign difference through multiculturalism. Substituted
in place of this particular national narrative is one that fails to safely incorporate personal histories or respect and celebrate their claims to
difference, be they Bishop's Syrian ancestry (however distant and partial) or Bishop's repeated claims to his teachers and friends that for all

he knows he might be part Arab.[26] Instead, Bishop's personal history becomes a conduit for other evil influences to infiltrate America—Osama bin Laden, Arabness, terrorism.

The movement in Bishop's name from Bishara to Osama bin also expresses his ambivalent link to paternity. Although both Bishara and Osama bin mark Arabness, they also denote a complex site of identifications, disidentifications, and misidentifications that Bishop may have made. As reported by the U.S. press, Bishop seems to have disidentified with his birth father Bishara, a man he had had no relationship with since his early childhood. This disidentification is voiced in statements he made to his grandmother as she was driving him to the flying lesson where he planned to steal a plane: "If something happens to me, don't let my father come to my funeral."[27] Misidentification seems to occur around Bishop's heritage. Although he rightly notes that he could be part Arab, his Arab heritage is not Muslim but Christian, thereby making any identification with Osama bin Laden and the September 11 hijackers harder to understand and indeed confused and incorrect.

Finally and most importantly, Bishop identified with bin Laden and the hijackers through his expression of sympathy for them and through his act of crashing his plane into the Bank of America building. This identification was not a straightforward disidentification with one father (Bishara) that enabled a misidentification of/with another symbolic father (bin Laden), although there may be some truth in this. The act itself is a mimetic identification—an identification performed through resemblance and repetition—with what the hijackers did.[28] It is an identification act for act rather than individual for individual. As such, it is the only identification of Bishop's that we can have any degree of certainty about, for it does not rely on understanding motives and causes but just recognizing and reading effects.

By mimetically identifying with the act of hijacking a plane and crashing it into an American skyscraper, Bishop's act stands as evidence for an America trying to protect itself against foreign terrorist forces of the infectiousness of Arabness and terrorism; for this is a case of a homegrown American boy who seemed to identify with Arab terrorism by violently reenacting a plot hatched by foreign terrorists. By reading Bishop's act as the infectious effect of Arab terrorism, the act at first seems to fit neatly within the clash-of-civilizations rhetoric popular in the West, especially in the early days of the war against terrorism.[29] And yet it isn't quite so simple, for Bishop's act makes a mockery of the U.S. foreign-policy position on the war on terror that "you are either with us or against us" by acknowledging that the "us" in the U.S. of A. marks a fractured, multiple subjectivity, some aspects of which may well defy safe assimilation, be they (in this case) ethnicity or youth.

Bishop's act also makes a farce of the U.S. government's discourse on "homeland security" by locating internal threats and fractures that may be dangerously exploited not only by foreigners but by Americans. By locating dangers not only within American territory but within American subjects through mimetic identification, Bishop's act raises the question of how it is possible to protect America and Americans when Americans themselves might act against their state, their citizenry, and themselves. Guarding the state and its citizens is not, this case suggests, a mere matter of increasing aviation security. Nor is it a matter of assuring the American public that Bishop is not a terrorist and dismissing his act as that of a "troubled young man," a move that, by locating trouble within his character, attempts to contain the troubling effects his act might have on America's understanding of its own character. Rather, protecting America additionally requires the policing of identifications, something Americans recognize cannot be properly policed.

This problem of policing identifications is highlighted by the remainder of Bishop's second post-suicide name—"Charles Bishop-Columbine." Charles Bishop is the ordinary name of an ordinary American teenager, whereas Columbine is the site of one of America's most violent school shootings. This part of Bishop's new nickname reminds us that ordinary American teens regularly commit dramatic acts of violence against their teachers, their peers, and themselves.

Bishop's act was, of course, not a school shooting. It in no way involved Bishop's East Lake High School. It did not take place on school property. It did not target teachers or fellow students. And Bishop did not choose his school as the target for his suicidal crash. To the extent that a school was involved, it was Bishop's flight school, from which he stole the single-engine Cessna. But again, Bishop targeted neither staff nor students nor school. Indeed, that his point of departure was a Florida flight school does more to connect his act with the September 11 hijackers—some of whom attended flight schools in Florida—than it does to connect it to school shootings.

Yet, in spite of these obvious differences, Bishop's act and school shootings in the United States share striking similarities, both in deed and in effect. As deeds, both are very public acts of violence carried out in and targeted against public spaces. In the planning and execution of these deeds, both involve (anti)heroic displays of masculinity, almost exclusively by white, middle-class boys (although this is beginning to change). Both are carried out by children, and these children are more often than not described by parents, teachers, and friends as "good kids," "model students," and, in Bishop's case, "patriotic." So described, these teens are not usually marked as future troublemakers. Rather, they appear to have been assimilated into social institutions such as their schools, communities, and nation. These kids, then, rarely exhibit signs of alienation. Instead, their alienation (if it is alienation that drives them to commit these violent acts) is unmarked. It is only retrospectively—after the violence—that these youths are characterized as "troubled young men."

Finally, school shootings and Bishop's act proceed according to logics of mimetic identification. Although of course there was an "original" school shooting and, in Bishop's case, an "original" episode of a teenager flying a stolen plane into a skyscraper, the original is less important than what the original copies (and subsequent "originals" copy too). School shootings often copy violence depicted in the media, be this on film, on television programs, or in newscasts and newspapers reporting school shootings. In the logic of school shootings, an identification is often made with an act of violence and copied, albeit in a slightly different form. The same can be said of Bishop's act. It is a copy of the September 11 hijacked jetliners crashing into New York City's Twin Towers. Bishop's act, like acts of school shootings, identifies through imitating prior acts of mediated violence.

Because they adhere to logics of mimetic identification, school shootings and Bishop's act unleash a similar dangerous effect—copycat violence. As themselves instances of copycat violence, these acts glorify copycat violence and seem to encourage further repetitions of it. This is the second way in which Bishop's act is an instance of infection. Like school shootings, it infects America with violence through the repetition of mimetic identifications—present and future. The temporal effect of this repetitive logic is not progressive. It offers no promise of moving on to a future free of acts of violence. Instead, it affirms that the violence of the present is likely to be repeated again and again and again.

Another danger of these sorts of violent mimetic identifications is that although they are repeated, they are always repeated with a difference. The so-called Trench coat Mafia killers at Columbine High School did not straightforwardly enact the dream sequence of the film *The Basketball Diaries* (1995) in which Leonardo DiCaprio's character shoots up his classroom with an automatic weapon. Rather, Eric Harris and Dylan Klebold teamed up, wired the school with bombs before they entered it, attacked students and teachers with an array of weapons, and died in a suicide pact. Whereas the Columbine shooters upped the actual violence from the mediatic display of violence that some say inspired them, Charles Bishop downscaled the violence in his terrifying tribute to September 11. Yet even these changes of scale can be read as mimetic identifications. For just as the consistent ratcheting up of violence in the media was captured in the Columbine "reenactment" of the violence of a technicolor, trench-coated teenager, so too is the September 11 hijackers' change of scale from guns and grenades to box cutters and a willingness to die repeated in Charles Bishop's fatal flight, which involved a single-engine plane rather than a commercial jet, killed no one but Bishop, left his target damaged but standing, and left his plane embedded in the side of the building like an eerie antimonument to September 11.

Bishop's mimicry of both an act and that act's reduction of scale is arguably more worrying than the presence of school shooter after school shooter upping the ante of violence in subsequent "repeat" performances. This is because scaling down what is needed to carry out a violent act means the act is less likely to be detected beforehand and is more likely to succeed. This is worrying not only in terms of Bishop's act but also in terms of the possible future "replays" of this act by teens who grasp the dual levels of imitation in such violent mimetic identifications. Parents, teachers, and peers know to be on the lookout for teens amassing arsenals in their bedrooms and their school lockers. But how does one detect and protect against an act on the scale of Bishop's by a "patriotic" individual like Bishop? Not only did the pending violence of his act go undetected before it occurred, it went undetected while it was occurring. Before his suicide note was found, the owner of his flight school described Bishop's act as "the aviation equivalent of someone stealing a car for a joy ride."[30] And the U.S. military spokesperson at MacDill Air Force Base explained that the military did not regard Bishop's illegal flyover as threatening, which is why the base merely alerted an unarmed, already airborne Coast Guard helicopter to intercept Bishop and did not send up intercepts of its own.[31]

That Bishop slipped under and over America's security detection systems is also a matter of scale, this time expressed through age. How would it look for the U.S. military to shoot down the plane of a fifteen-year-old boy who seemed to be out on a joyride? And how would it look for the U.S. government to later label this boy a terrorist? Not good. This is because a fifteen-year-old child—even in a stolen plane during a war on terror—is regarded in American discourse as a troubled youth and not as a terrorist. Youths are regarded as troubled rather than evil because youth as a category is often placed beyond morality and youths themselves are seen to be moving toward moral maturity. By labeling Bishop troubled, the Bush administration officially placed him (unlike the anthrax killer and the al-Qaeda terrorists) beyond good and evil. In so doing, Bishop and his act trouble the clear moral dichotomy America relies on in its war on terror.

Overall, the Palm Harbor "collision" of September 11 with Columbine accomplishes "the apparent cross-pollination of an angry extremist Islamic terrorist conspiracy with an emerging American archetype: the ravenously suicidal, male, loner, teenage killer."[32] In so doing, it stands in stark contrast to Pearl Harbor. Unlike America's romantic returns to Pearl Harbor, Palm Harbor does not romantically suture America into a heroic, moral, and progressive narrative. It does not offer a narrative that contains by externalizing violence and evil. Instead, as an alternative, interruptive romantic mediation of September 11/Pearl Harbor, Palm Harbor offers (anti)heroism, moral ambiguity, and the repetition of violence and terror without the promise that violence and terror can be contained or externalized. Like school shootings, it demonstrates that violence is not something that can be controlled and contained by a state or by a state's narrative about itself. Instead, contemporary violence sometimes functions through the exchange of mimetic identifications.

Conclusion

The move from Pearl Harbor to Palm Harbor has chilling effects on the collective American psyche. School shooters rupture local narratives of community and family, but Bishop's act ruptures national narratives of patriotism, unity, and homeland security. Who is for the state and who is against it? Who is fully incorporated within the state and who is not (yet)? And who or what might be risks to the state and who or what might not? These questions arise as a result of Bishop's act because the act discloses the risks to America of the unmarked alienation it contains within itself—its not-yet rational, not-yet moral, not-yet citizen youth. By insistently posing these questions, Bishop's act retemporalized America's national struggle for identity from its heroic Pearl Harbor past to its alternatively (anti)heroic Palm Harbor present, making America not seem like the envy of the world (as President Bush declared it) but a place in which violence has long circulated out of the control of the state.

Moving from the romantic mediations of Pearl Harbor to the alternative romantic mediations of Palm Harbor reminds us, to quote Debrix again, that "the critical work of romantic mediation cannot end as long as a large part of modernity remains in the shadows" (p. xxxiii). The difficult lesson of Palm Harbor is that these parts of "modernity" are not only foreign terrorists but America's own troubled teens.

Notes

1. This was the tally of attacks as of the time this book went to press.

2. For an in-depth analysis of the film *Pearl Harbor,* particularly how it expresses the United States' moral grammar of war through codes of sex, gender, and sexuality, see Cynthia Weber, "Flying Planes Can Be Dangerous," *Millennium* 31.1 (2002): 129–47. See also Blaine Harden, "Pearl Harbor's Old Men Find New Limelight since Sept. 11," *New York Times on the Web,* December 7, 2001. Although Pearl Harbor may now be commonly remembered as the first sneak attack against the United States, read against the country's racialized birth-of-the-nation narrative, "Pearl Harbor stood at the end of a long line of sneak attacks that helped explain any success a nonwhite enemy might have against American forces" (Tom Engelhardt, *The End of Victory Culture: Cold War America and the Disillusioning of a Generation* [New York: Basic Books, 1995], pp. 39, 16–36.

3. For a discussion of the United States' incessant loss and rediscovery of its innocence, see Dick Crepeau, "Lost and Found," available at http://www.poppolitics.com/articles/printerfriendly/2001-10-01-innocence.shtml.

4. Lance Morrow, "The Case for Rage and Retribution," *Time,* September 11, 2001, n. p. See also Fareed Zakaria, "The Real World of Foreign Policy," *Newsweek,* October 8, 2001, p. 15.

5. Thomas Doherty, professor of film studies, Brandeis University, speaking on "Four Corners," BBC Radio4, November 5, 2001.

6. "Grieving New Yorkers Are Guests of Hawaii," *New York Times on the Web*, December 6, 2001; "Officer Marries in Paradise after He Survives a Hell," *New York Times on the Web*, December 9, 2001.

7. Harden, "Pearl Harbor's Old Men."

8. The self-image is far more complex than I have put it here. And, of course, there is no one American imaginary that appeals to all people within or beyond the country's borders. Yet circulating in American popular and political discourse at least since World War II is an image of America as hegemonically masculine, heroic, and loved. For a discussion of these aspects of the country's self-image and their connections to codes of sex, gender, and sexuality, see Cynthia Weber, *Faking It: U.S. Hegemony in a "Post-Phallic" Era* (Minneapolis: University of Minnesota Press, 1999).

9. George W. Bush, "We're Fighting to Win—and Win We Will," remarks on the USS Enterprise on Pearl Harbor Day, December 7, 2001, available at http://www.whitehouse.gov/news/releases/2001/12/20011207.html.

10. Engelhardt, *The End of Victory Culture*, pp. 10–11. Subsequent references are given in the text.

11. Bush, "We're Fighting to Win—and Win We Will."

12. Debrix writes of how romantic "mediation is now deployed to transform, affirm, and glorify" (p. xxxi).

13. Debrix describes romantic mediations as "re-creative or re-imaginative rather than representational" (p. xxxi).

14. Matthew L. Wald, "Student Pilot, 15, Crashes Plane into Bank in Florida," *New York Times on the Web*, January 6, 2002.

15. This is how Tampa's Chief of Police Bennie R. Holder described Bishop. See David Firestone, "Teenage Pilot Left Note Praising September 11 Attacks," *New York Times on the Web*, January 7, 2002.

16. Scott Rosenberg, "Bin Laden's Other American Boy Soldier," Salon.com, January 9, 2002, available at http://www.salon.com/news/feature/2002/01/09/bishop/index-np.html.

17. Ronnie Blair, Beth Perretta, and Karen Haymon Long, "Teachers Did Not See Freshman as a Loner," *Tampa Tribune Online Edition*, January 8, 2002.

18. "Teen Pilot Might Have Taken Acne Drug," CNN.com, January 8, 2002, available at http://www.cnn.com/2002/US/01/08/plane.suicide.mother/index.html. The Accutane theory circulated widely in the media, even though no scientific data confirmed the relationship between Accutane and depression or suicide and it was not immediately known whether Bishop had actually taken this medication found in his home. Ten days after the crash, it was reported that Bishop had no drugs, alcohol, or Accutane in his bloodstream when he died. See "No Drugs Found in Florida Teen Pilot Body," January 16, 2002, *Reuters*, available at http://www.news.yahoo.com/020116/80/cphwg.html.

19. Associated Press, "Parents of Teen Pilot Tried Suicide," *New York Times on the Web*, January 10, 2002.

20. Jan Hollingsworth, "Flier Craved Limelight, Told Pal to Watch News," *Tampa Tribune Online Edition*, January 9, 2002; "Police: Tampa Pilot Voiced Support for bin Laden," CNN.com, January 6, 2002, available at http://www.cnn.com/2002/US/01/06/tampa.crash/index.html.

21. It is, of course, possible to read the acts of those who carried out the attacks on September 11 as themselves romantic mediations or, really, counterromantic

mediations of America's self-narrative. I find this a less interesting project because these mediations can so easily be characterized as counterromantic, whereas those carried out by Charles Bishop differently and, in some ways, with more complexity, disturb America's ideas of itself.

22. Henry A. Giroux, *Fugitive Cultures: Race, Violence, and Youth* (New York: Routledge, 1995), pp. 10–11.

23. Bishop's suicide note established that his collision was intentional.

24. The United States has refused to categorize its prisoners from the Afghanistan campaign against terrorism as prisoners of war, regarding them instead as illegal combatants and thereby refusing them the rights granted to POWs.

25. This is the name given to Charles Bishop by Rayelan on a Webcast News posting, January 8, 2002, available at http://www.indymedia.org/front.php3?article_id=116200&group=webcast.

26. "Police: Tampa Pilot voiced support for bin Laden."

27. Oliver Burkeman, "Death Wish," *Guardian* (G2), January 9, 2002, p. 3.

28. For a reading of mimetic identification in the film *Single White Female*, see Ellen Brinks, "Who's Been in My Closet? Mimetic Identification and the Psychosis of Class Transvestism in *Single White Female*," in Sue-Ellen Case, Philip Brett, and Susan Leigh Foster, eds., *Cruising the Performative: Interventions into the Representation of Ethnicity, Nationality, and Sexuality* (Bloomington: Indiana University Press, 1995), pp. 3–12.

29. For the origins of this discourse, see Samuel P. Huntington, "The Clash of Civilizations?" *Foreign Affairs* 72.3 (1993): 22–49.

30. Michael Fechter, eds., "Teen Planned Joy Ride, Owner Says," January 6, 2002, *Tampa Tribune Online Edition*.

31. Firestone, "Teenage Pilot."

32. Paul Vitello, "In Teenager, al-Qaida Meets Columbine," January 8, 2002, Newsday.com, available at http://www/newsday.com/news/local/logisland/columnists/ny-livito82541084jan08.column.

Contributors

Robin Brown is senior lecturer in international communications in the Institute of Communications Studies, University of Leeds.

David Campbell is professor of international politics at the University of Newcastle upon Tyne, United Kingdom. He is author of *National Deconstruction: Violence, Identity, and Justice in Bosnia* (Minnesota, 1998) and *Writing Security: United States Foreign Policy and the Politics of Identity* (Minnesota, 1992; revised 1998), and coeditor (with Michael J. Shapiro) of *Moral Spaces: Rethinking Ethics and World Politics* (Minnesota, 1999).

François Debrix is assistant professor of international relations at Florida International University. He is author of *Re-Envisioning Peacekeeping: The United Nations and the Mobilization of Ideology* (Minnesota, 1999).

Michael Dillon is professor of politics at the University of Lancaster. He is author of *Politics of Security* and has written a forthcoming book titled *Biopolitics, Security, and War;* he publishes in international politics and political and cultural theory. He is coeditor of the journal *Cultural Values: Journal of Cultural Research.*

Debbie Lisle is a lecturer in politics and director of cultural and media studies at Queen's University, Belfast. Her research explores the intersections between travel, tourism, cultural representations, and world politics.

Moya Lloyd is senior lecturer in political theory at Queen's University, Belfast. She is author of *A Feminist Politics of Difference* as well as numerous articles and chapters on feminist political theory.

Timothy W. Luke teaches international politics and political theory in Blacksburg, Virginia, where he is University Distinguished Professor of Political Science at Virginia Polytechnic Institute and State University. His most recent books are *Museum Politics: Power Plays at the Exhibition* (Minnesota, 2002); *Capitalism, Democracy, and Ecology: Departing from Marx;* and *Ecocritique: Contesting the Politics of Nature, Economy, and Culture* (Minnesota, 1997).

Patricia L. Price is assistant professor of geography in the Department of International Relations at Florida International University. Her work explores spatial theory, gender, political organization, and urban processes throughout the Americas. Most recently, she has examined the role of narrative in the construction of identity and place. Her book *Place Visions: Narratives of Belonging and Exclusion in a Dry Land,* is forthcoming.

Jayne Rodgers is a lecturer in international communications at the University of Leeds. Her research centers on global and local uses of the Internet as a tool of political activism, and she is author of *Spatializing International Politics: Analysing Activist Use of the Internet.* She is currently writing a book on activism and the U.S. Missile Defense project.

Cynthia Weber is professor of international studies and director of the Centre for International Studies at the University of Leeds. Her work, located at the intersections of international studies, gender and sexuality studies, and cultural studies, addresses such topics as sovereignty, intervention, hegemony, and U.S. foreign policy. She is author of *Faking It: U.S. Hegemony in a "Post-Phallic" Era* (Minnesota, 1999).

Marysia Zalewski is reader in the Centre for Women's Studies, Queen's University, Belfast. Her research interests include the relationship between traditional and contemporary forms of feminist theorizing, gender and international relations, and feminism's engagement with postfoundational thought. She is author of *Feminism after Postmodernism: Theorising through Practice.*

Index

Adelman, Kenneth, 161
Afghanistan, 177
Africa, 69–90; famine in, 69–90
Airport, 3–26; commercial imperative of, 20–22; functionalism of, 17–20; and passenger profiling, 23; and power, 7; and national identification, 12–17; and security 9–12; and sovereignty, 11–12; and subjectivity, 22–25
Airport, 25
Allen, Paula Gunn, 52
Al-Qaeda, 173–86
American collective unconscious, 176
Americanization, 126–28, 130
American morality, 174–75
American self-image, 173–86
American victory culture, 175
Anthrax killer, 185
Antiglobalization, 30, 38
Art, 97–110
Augé, Marc, 6, 9, 26
Avila Gress, Adriana, 55
Aztecs, 49; modern-day, 50
Aztlán, 49–63

Barthes, Roland, 83
Bataille, Georges, xxiv; accursed share, xxiv; sacrificial rites, xxiv
Baudelaire, xxxii, xxxiii–xxiv; primal scene, xxxiii–xxxiv

Baudrillard, Jean, 102, 115, 121, 126, 128, 155, 160
Beauty, 84–88
Bentham, Jeremy, 147
Berman, Marshall, xxxiii
Bernays, Edward, 159
Bin Laden, Osama, xvi, 177, 180–81
Biopolitics, 135–51
Bishop, Charles, xvi, 173–86
Blair, Tony, 154, 164, 166
Borders, 49–63
Bowden, Charles, 55
Brady, Ian, 108
Brenson, Michael, 80
Briggs, Asa, 157
Brown, Hannah, 106
Brown, Robin, xv, 154–72
B2C commerce, 115–31
Buber, Martin, 83
Buchanan, Pat, 51
Bulger video, 103
Bush, George W., president, 174, 175, 186

Campbell, Alastair, 154, 164, 168
Campbell, David, xii, xiv, 69–96
Carter, Kevin, 88–89
Cartier-Bresson, Henri, 80–82
Castells, Manuel, 149
Cataldi, Anna, 75
Chernobyl, 36

Chicano movement, 49
Children, 97–110
Clark, Wesley, general, 168
Clash of civilizations, 181
Clausewitz, Carl von, 162
Clinton, William, president, 168
CNN, 161
Cohen, Bernard, 160
Communication, xxiv; Internet, 30–45;
    political 30; and spin, 154–69
Connolly, William, 76
Conrad, Sir Terence, 21–22
Crain, Mary, xxiv
Crush, Jonathan, 144, 149
Cultural analysis, vii
Culture, 135–51
Cyberspace 32–45; social relations
    of, 32

Davison, W. Philips, 160
Debrix, François, viii–ix, xvi, xxi–xlii,
    72, 176, 186
Decartes, René, xxix, xxx, 120
Development, 136, 140–46; cultural
    policies for, 144–46; development-
    security complex, 137
Diana, Princess, 13, 156
Diego, Juan, 57, 58
Dillon, Michael, xv, 135–53
Donaldson, Sam, 161
Duffield, Mark, 137

e-activism, 39
Edwards, Susan, 80
Engelhardt, Tom, 175
Evans, Walker, 86

Femininity, 99–110
Fitzwater, Marlin, 163
Foucault, Michael, 4, 26, 135, 150;
    power/knowledge, 135–51
Frank, André Gunder, 73
Fukuyama, Francis, 122

Galeano, Eduardo, 75, 83, 84
Genetically modified foods, 30–45
GenetiX, 38, 43
Giuliani, Rudolph, xiii, 98, 101, 109

Globalization, 126–28, 130
Goethe, Johann, xxxi
Goodman, Nelson, 74
Gorbachev, Mikhail, 164
Gould, Philip, 166
Governance, 135–51
Gramsci, Antonio, 151
Grundberg, Andy, 87
Gulf War, 51

Haraway, Donna, 53
Harvey, Marcus, 98–107
Hindley, Myra, xiii, 98–110
Hiroshima, 175
Hodgson, Francis, 78
Holbrooke, Richard, 167
Homeland security, 177, 182, 186
Hughes-Freeland, Felicia, xxiv
Hulme, Keri, 76
Humanitarianism, 139
Hume, David, 120

IRA, 9
Innis, Harold, 157
International Coffee Organization, 73
International Monetary Fund (IMF),
    xv, 141
International studies, vii
Internet, 30–45, 160, 165; protests
    30–45
Iyer, Pico, 5, 7, 9, 13

Kant, Immanuel, 120, 147
Keane, Fergal, 70–71
Kirstein, Lincoln, 86
Kryst, Sandra, 57

Lafayette, Marquis de, xxxv
Lefebvre, Henri, x, 31, 39–44, 45;
    organization of space in society, 39;
    representations of space, 41–42;
    space practice, 40–41; spaces of
    representation, 42–43
Levinas, Emmanuel, 83
Lisle, Debbie, ix–x, 3–29
Lloyd, Moya, xiii, xiv, 97–114
Los Estados Unidos Mexicanos, 49
Luke, Timothy, xiv, 115–32

MacDill Air Force Base, 177, 185
Machiavelli, 165, 166
Márquez, Gabriel García, 75
Martin, Angela, 57
Marx, Karl, xxxiii
McLuhan, Marshall, xxxvi, 157
Médecins san Frontières, 78, 79, 89
Mediation: of B2C industrial democracy, 118–31; and Christianity, xxvii–xxx; definition, vii, xxi–xxii; of difference, 49; of disaster, 72; of immediacy, 102–4; and Internet, 30; method(s) of, xxi–xxvii; mobilization of, xxi–xxii; of morality, 97–110; as pluralization, xxvii, xxxiv–xxxix; of power, 7, 26; as representation, xxiv, xxvii–xxx; romantic mediation, xxx–xxxiv, 173–86; and ruptures, 176–86; of system of objects, 115–31; televisual, 154; as transformation, xxv, xxx–xxxiv; of transnationals, 115–31
Mediator, 154
Metzl, Jamie, 156
Meyrowitz, Marshall, 157
Mimetic identification, 179, 181–85
Mitchell, W. J. T., 74
Monroe, Marilyn, 106
Moral shock, 36–38
Morrison, Toni, 76
Mother Teresa, 106
Multinational corporations, 34, 35

NAFTA, 56, 167–69
Nasseri, Merhan Karimi, 8
Nathan, Debbie, 55, 56
National interest, 10
NATO, 167–69
Nelson, Horatio, admiral, 15
New social movement, 43
NGOs, 31, 33, 34, 36, 37, 39, 143, 160, 169

Ofili, Chris, xiii, 98–107
Okri, Ben, 75
Organization for Economic Cooperation and Development (OECD), 141

Palm Harbor, xvii, 176–86
Pearl Harbor, xvi, xvii, 173–86
Pearl Harbor, 173
Pentagon, 10, 12, 24, 179
Perlmutter, David, 88
Perot, Ross, 51
Photography, 69–70
Plato, 157
Political activism, 30–45
Political protest, 30–45
Price, Patricia, xi, 49–65

Rabinow, Paul, 144
Reagan, Ronald, 74, 161, 164
Realpolitik, 121–26
Reid, Bill, 14
Representation, vii, xxiv, 135
Ripper, the, 54–56, 59
Ritchin, Fred, 80
Rodgers, Jayne, x, 30–48
Rojas, Christine, 141
Rosales, Irma Angelica, 55
Rosler, Martha, 4, 24–25
Rowley, Jennifer, 21
Rushdie, Salman, 75

Sahel, 73–90
Saldívar, José, 51
Salgado, Sebastião Ribeiro, xii, 73–90
Schopenhauer, Arthur, xxxi
Schultz, George, 161
Sensation: Young British Artists from the Saatchi Collection, 97–110
September 11, 2001, 136, 173–86
Shapiro, Michael J., 75
Sharif, Sharif Adbel Latif, 56
Shawcross, William, 78
Shea, Jamie, 168
Sheth, D. L., 148
Short, Claire, 70–71, 89
Sischy, Ingrid, 85–87
Slack, Frances, 21
Slim, Hugo, 78
Smith, Adam, 151
Soguk, Nevzat, 8
Sovereign authority, 5
Speakes, Larry, 164
Spin and spin doctors, 154–69

Stallabrass, Julian, 79, 87
Steiner, George, 86
Stoddart, 89
Strauss, David Levi, 77, 83
Sudan, 70, 73–90
Sweeney, John, 89

Terrorism, 176, 177, 179, 181, 185
Thalheimer, Richard, 125
Thompson, John, 157
Torpey, John, 10–11
Transit area, 8
Trickster, 51–55
Twins, the, 54–55, 58–63
Twin Towers, 179, 183. *See also* World
    Trade Center

UNESCO, 144–46
United Farm Workers, 49
United Nations Development Program
    (UNDP), 141
United States, 173–86; hegemonic
    imaginary of 49; as hyperpower,
    116

Vietnam, 175
Virgin Mary, 76, 98, 100–110
Virgin of Guadalupe, 54–55, 56–58, 59
Virilio, Paul, 10–12, 17–20; and
    dictatorship of movement, 19

Walker, R. B. J., 33
War against terror, xvi
Washington, George, xxxv
Watts, Michael, 148
Weber, Cynthia, xvi–xvii, 173–88
Whitehall, 8
Wilson, Pete, 51
Wodiczko, Krzysztof, ix, xxvi, xxxiv–
    xxxix; *Alien Staff*, xxxvii–xxxix;
    Homeless Projection, xxxv–xxxvii
Woman/women, 97–110; (im)possibility
    of, 107–10
World Bank, 140, 141
World Trade Center, 10, 12, 24, 109, 130,
    179
World Trade Organization, xv, 35, 38

Zalewski, Marysia, xiii, xiv, 97–114
Žižek, Slavoj, 107